The Roots
of
Nazi Psychology

The Roots of
Nazi Psychology

Hitler's
Utopian
Barbarism

Jay Y. Gonen

THE UNIVERSITY PRESS OF KENTUCKY

Publication of this volume was made possible in part
by a grant from the National Endowment for the Humanities.

Scholarly publisher for the Commonwealth,
serving Bellarmine College, Berea College, Centre
College of Kentucky, Eastern Kentucky University,
The Filson Club Historical Society, Georgetown College,
Kentucky Historical Society, Kentucky State University,
Morehead State University, Murray State University,
Northern Kentucky University, Transylvania University,
University of Kentucky, University of Louisville,
and Western Kentucky University.

Editorial and Sales Offices: The University Press of Kentucky
663 South Limestone Street, Lexington, Kentucky 40508–4008

04 03 02 01 00   5 4 3 2 1

Library of Congress Cataloging-in-Publication Data

Gonen, Jay Y., 1934–
      The roots of Nazi psychology : Hitler's utopian barbarism / Jay Y. Gonen.
            p. cm.
      Includes bibliographical references and index.
      ISBN 0-8131-2154-X (alk. paper)
      1. National socialism—Psychological aspects. 2. Hitler, Adolf, 1889–1945—
Psychology. 3. Ideology—Germany—History—20th century. 4. Jews—
Persecutions—Germany. 5. Germany—Politics and government—1933–1945.
6. Racism—Germany. 7. Germany—Territorial expansion. I. Title.
DD256.5 .G595   2000
943.086'092—dc21   99–047300

This book is printed on acid-free recycled paper meeting the requirements
of the American National Standard for Permanence of Paper for Printed Library
Materials.

Manufactured in the United States of America

To my loving wife,
Mary Coleman,
who enriched my thoughts

Contents

Acknowledgments

I thank Noel Kinnamon, who provided excellent copy editing to the book. I am also deeply indebted to very special persons who are all both colleagues and friends. David Beisel gave the manuscript a thorough editing and greatly enriched it with his psychohistorical acumen. During various stages of the work Bernhard Blom strengthened my hands with insightful suggestions, editorial help, and moral support. David Ihilevich reviewed the manuscript and reinforced my attempts to present psychoanalytic theory in terms that the sophisticated layman could understand. Last, but not least, I am most grateful to Rudolph Binion whose groundbreaking work on Hitler and the Germans has been a source of inspiration for me. He made invaluable contributions to the final shape of the work through many editorial comments, historical suggestions, questions, and challenges. I thank them all.

1

The Role of Ideologies

Political discussion is, from the very first, more than
theoretical argumentation; it is the tearing off of disguises—the unmasking of those unconscious motives
which bind the group existence to its cultural aspirations
and its theoretical arguments.

Ideas, forms of thought, and psychic energies persist and
are transformed in close conjunction with social forces. It
is never by accident that they appear at given moments in
the social process.
                    —Karl Mannheim, *Ideology and Utopia*

The resonance which Hitler's words evoked among many Germans in
the period between the two world wars has been of great interest to
Germans and non-Germans alike. The basic premise of this study is that
the Nazi success in mobilizing the masses was not due merely to the
deliberate use of fear and terror but primarily to the Nazi ideological
messages that fell right on target.

Any progress in fathoming the underlying causes of this responsiveness, which characterized the interaction between the leader and the
masses during the Nazi era, could advance our understanding of the
fateful course of events in the first half of the twentieth century. And in
this respect it is of paramount importance to try and shed as much light
as possible on the underlying dynamics of the German response to the

humiliation and defeat of World War I, which escalated into unleashing a new world war and perpetrating a holocaust. An analysis of Hitler's ideology, its manifest content as well as its underlying psychology, is therefore indispensable for gaining a better understanding of why so many horrible and seemingly incomprehensible things could have happened. The application of psychoanalytic models in this study relies on Freudian rather than Jungian postulates. It should be borne in mind, however, that essentially what psychoanalytic concepts provide is a metaphorical language.

At the point of contact between leaders and followers reside ideologies. The term "ideology" is used here in quite a loose sense. It refers to any idea or set of ideas that provides a prescriptive view of life. The term is therefore not confined to lengthy doctrines that are systematized in the form of a tract or a dissertation, since ideologies may also be expressed by short slogans. Moreover, they can be loaded with different layers of meaning. They can consist of a formalized and presumably conscious worldview that includes many parts. But they can equally well be comprised of unconscious shared group fantasies, which have the power to charge up the entire group with sufficient energy to trigger unified mass action. Consequently they frequently include myths while their promoters engage in the selling of those myths. Moreover, slogans, catch phrases, enticing ideas, poignant jokes, stirring songs but also a variety of visual images that appear on posters, placards, and walls as well as in illustrations and cartoons published by newspapers and magazines may all represent small bits or chunks of ideologies. Whatever form they take, whether it is one picture that is worth more than a thousand words or an uplifting short slogan, these bits and chunks of ideology encapsulate succinct and rather unidimensional views of the world or of national life. What is more, they may be widely dispersed and "float in the air." When that happens, the ideological prescriptions frequently express themselves through aphorisms. A current American example would be the saying "winning isn't everything, it's the only thing." An earlier German example which is taken from a Nazi marching song would be the lines "For today Germany belongs to us and tomorrow the whole world." As can be seen, such small ideological segments, which prescribe what to expect from life, ride on a variety of "carriers." That is why they may frequently be lifted from songs, plays, jokes, drawings or paintings, political speeches and similar layers of the cultural repository. They are embedded in the culture but their drawing power fluctuates according to the position they happen to occupy in the particular zeitgeist, or spirit of the time. The zeitgeist is a concept that denotes the ripening of a cultural image or idea to the point where its time has arrived. It also connotes a notion of movement where ideas float to the foreground when their time comes or sink to the background when their time is gone. The issue of when an ideology's time for action has arrived is largely determined by changes within the zeitgeist that reflect an altered emotional climate and the shifting winds of public mood.

Sometimes, when a very forceful theme or even a whole constellation of highly energized themes emerges in the life of the collective to dominate the zeitgeist, one encounters the phenomenon of shared group fantasies. These are the shared psychological basic assumptions that dictate the group identity. Not only do they determine for the members who they are by virtue of their group identity, they also instill expectations concerning what future life would be like, for good or bad, because of this group belonging. These fantasies are therefore dynamically charged, include large unconscious elements, and also function as psychological defenses. Consequently the images they present of both self and world tend to be distorted because they filter reality through an intricate grid of defense mechanisms. Thus, failures become rationalized, blame projected, self-fulfilling prophecies adopted, affect reversed, and contradictions maintained by separating them into walled-off mental compartments (the mechanism of isolation). Then expectations are tailored to fit the preexisting basic assumptions concerning the life of the group. All this means that nothing less than reality itself is being distorted. Yet reality stands in the way between wish and wish fulfillment. And a cardinal wish of individuals and groups is to preserve their distinct continuity and to maintain a gratifying self-image devoid of narcissistic wounds, i.e., emotional injuries that are destructive of self-esteem. This is why shared group fantasies modify, distort, and even fabricate reality in a highly defensive fashion.

It is important to emphasize that the occurrence of group fantasies is not confined to any particular national group although different groups can have specific fantasies. In earlier works concerning Jewish psychohistory, I have illustrated the operation of shared group fantasies such as the Israeli illusion of omnipotence following the Six Day War (Gonen 1978) and the suicidal Masada Complex (Gonen 1975, 213–36). After the 1967 lightening Israeli victory over three Arab states, there was a collective Israeli illusion that mideastern regional conflicts could be solved by massive military power. But soon afterward the Israelis also experienced renewed fears that they were on the verge of reenacting the old Masada scenario: in 73 A.D., the Jewish defenders of Masada committed mass suicide rather than surrender to the Romans. These two fantasies became part of an interrelated network of shared group fantasies, which, on the one hand, were based on the legacy of Jewish history but, on the other hand, distorted it. Some of these fantasies had even included reactions to the Holocaust in which the victims themselves were blamed. This inappropriate condemning attitude was an outcome of the desperate need to draw a sharp distinction between the nonfighting Jews of yesteryear and the fighting Israelis of today. So horrendous was the reality of the Holocaust that it became deeply ingrained in the Jewish psyche as a prototype for what Jews should expect and what could always happen. Hitler has now joined the other biblical and timeless enemies of Israel such as Amalek or Haman while Jews continued to torment themselves with the question of why they allowed themselves to be led like sheep to the slaughter. Thus at this shared fantasy level the Six Day War, in which victorious Israelis wished that the murdered European Jews could see them now, clearly was a response to the Holocaust demonstrating that Jews can fight and are not predestined to passively accept extermination. Yet because of such a long history of victimization, this switch from holocaustal impotence to victorious omnipotence triggered a new obsession with the Masada Complex, reevoking fears that even fighting Jews can meet their death either on the battlefield or by their own hand, in order to avoid being captured alive. It can be seen from even these brief illustrations that group fantasies can be psychodynamically interconnected and collectively shared.

This last point can be confusing. In what exact sense could group fantasies be collectively shared? The concept may evoke images of a group mind or a collective mind, which can easily be misunderstood. The concept of a collective mind is not meant to deny the obvious fact that only individuals have brains. Nor is it meant to imply extrasensory processes or parapsychological methods of communication connecting individual brains. What it does imply is the easy availability and reach of a variety of prototypical or dominant themes within a given group. These themes are able to evoke similar reactions in most group members who embrace them because of their common history and shared cultural background. Moreover, these themes are inculcated by the culture as the particular sacred lore is fed into individuals since early childhood. The sacred lore includes not just religious texts, but all art or literature that traditionally denotes what it is like to be a member of the group. This shared cultural repository makes it possible for group members to experience common themes whenever they rise to dominance. But even when a group fantasy is being activated, not every person down to the last group member has perforce adopted it. The implication of a group mind as reflected in shared fantasies was never meant to be that literal and all inclusive. There is no one "group brain" that commands, so to speak, all the individual brains. This was not true even with a select group and on very special occasions such as the annual Nazi party rallies, although it almost seemed to be the case.

The emergence of shared group fantasies, out of current interplays of themes competing for zeitgeist dominance, is a highly dynamic process. The concept of a zeitgeist implies a public recognition of and a readiness to accept certain ideas as both valid and timely. In the case of the highly emotionally charged group fantasies, this timeliness, which surfaces out of the interaction of competing ideas, feelings, and the unfolding of current events, can even generate public pressure and a clamoring to transform the fantasy into reality. This is why the zeitgeist is frequently the outcome of the interactions of psychological forces with historical developments that are very subtly "negotiated" between followers and leaders. And this elusive gamesmanship is being conducted under a psychohistorical law of supply and demand, which on the surface mandates that the leaders do the selling while the masses do the buying. Yet just under the surface it is the masses who signal, both knowingly and unknowingly, which ideas now have a magic impact on them and can therefore mobilize them. It is the charismatic leader—the expert scanner of the zeitgeist—who for some reason has an uncanny ability to read the masses correctly; he guides them with his illuminating "new" ideas that, in truth, are borrowed from the ones he leads.

All this points to a fascinating meeting between psychobiography and group psychohistory. The point of intersection is where a significant individual (be it a political leader or an artist or a man of ideas) and the group at large interact. This interaction is likely to create a joint reinforcement of underlying psychological drives and motives. Erik Erikson (1962, 254) once described that point of intersection as the interdependence of individual aspiration and societal strivings for optimal psychological states. The interdependence that Erikson alluded to can assume an even more crucial importance when both the individual's and the society's psychological state is pathological. In such instances the interdependence can be expected to result in mutual reinforcement of pathologies. And if the individual happens to be a supreme political leader who controls the state's power, then the reinforced pathologies are likely to be acted out en masse.

A major stride in this line of enquiry was made by the psychohistorian Rudolph Binion (1979). As we shall see further along in this work, Binion explicated a double-track theory of Hitler's aims consisting of solving the imaginary Jewish problem as well as the imaginary problem of inadequate living space. In this connection he demonstrated how the interdependence of the two tracks as well as the interaction between the leader and the led was mutually reinforcing with catastrophic results. Yet while it lasted, this interaction provided the leader with ongoing opportunities to repeat earlier personal traumas. One was the trauma of his mother's death from a cancer, which in Hitler's fantasy was seemingly inflicted by her Jewish physician; the other trauma was a war injury, which reinforced the earlier one. At the very same time, however, the interaction between leader and led also provided the masses with similar opportunities to replay the national trauma of defeat and territorial loss in World War I at the hand of the allies. Through the wide embrace of a shared group fantasy, this stunning defeat was "explained" as due to Jewish machinations and treachery. Binion consequently subscribed to the basic notion that beneath the historical plays of current events unfolded a drama of psychohistorical replays of the group. And as the basic ingredient of the drama happened to be trauma, the replays and their variations were bound to produce replicas in their compulsive repetition of the central emotions and impulses. Because of the remarkable accuracy of the repetitions, the results were also doomed to be once again a total failure in mastering the trauma. Therefore, the new defeat that results from each current reliving of the unresolved trauma keeps the shock as alive and as intense as ever and sets the stage up for the inevitable next replay, which would be equally doomed to failure.

The psychohistorian Helm Stierlin has, quite justifiably, emphasized Hitler's ability to weld together the art of power politics or political stagecrafting with the art of mythmaking or, better, myth selling. Therefore, Hitler in the political field came to resemble Richard Wagner, who in the artistic field created the *Gesamtkunstwerk* or total art work (Stierlin 1976, 74). It is well established indeed that Hitler, who prided himself on being an artist, elevated politicking into a new art form in which he controlled and enchanted his national audience as if in a theater. But even more than his theatrical skill, the key for his success was the selling of the right myths. If we are to combine Stierlin's underscoring of myth selling with Binion's emphasis on repetition of traumas, then our conclusion would be that Hitler's highly successful myth selling was due to the peddling of those psychological goods that happened to be in highest demand—repetitions of traumas. If unconscious repetitions of traumas have indeed been the German psychological malaise, then what Hitler offered was a perfect solution to the German problem—a solution that consciously promised redemption but actually courted disaster. In other words, it seemingly offered a new utopia but inevitably led to the new catastrophe. In accordance with this emphasis, the aim of our present enquiry would therefore be to explain as well as possible the psychological significance of that which Hitler sold. The psychological loadings which permeate various components of his ideology will be identified and related to each other. Possible implications of these psychological factors for German history will sometimes be suggested. But the immediate focus of this study will remain the uncovering of the underlying psychology of Hitler's ideology. To what degree the results accord with Hitler's life and with the German heritage is a judgment that this author primarily leaves to other scholars.

Identifying the major psychological ingredients of Hitler's ideology and exploring their full meaning is of vast importance because they struck such a responsive chord among many Germans. This responsiveness alone suggests not only the likely involvement of unconscious motivation, but also that an older history may have created a receptivity and even cravings and yearnings for certain myths and mottoes. This can be well illustrated by "the stab in the back" theory as an explanation for the defeat in the First World War. Germans were led to believe almost until the end that they were winning the war and were therefore stunned by the apparently sudden and seemingly treacherous surrender. Ernst Nolte (1969, 388–89) averred that, in the propagation of this lie, Germany's very downfall has been used as a proof in an argument to turn a lie into a so-called truth. And this truth was useful in blaming anything that looked like a weakness, especially remnants of the tradition of civil liberty. And it was in its most primitive form that this legend had the greatest appeal to the masses. Nolte was right, but there was even more to it than the clever turning of the reality of defeat into a myth of betrayal for use against political opponents. The fact that there was a need for such a myth to begin with (for without a myth the defeat could remain inexplicable) in itself suggests that the defeat was unacceptable and simply could not be swallowed. It represented not a shock, which was somehow coped with, but rather a trauma which was not assimilated and which became an object of obsession that could lead to compulsive repetition. But a symbol for an unassimilated traumatic defeat does not necessarily have to be "a stab in the back." That this particular symbol was adopted by many Germans and exploited by Hitler probably was due to an already existing cultural heritage that included the *Nibelungenlied* and Richard Wagner's operas, and which played on the theme that the unconquerable Siegfried could only be killed by a stab in the back. In like fashion, it was imagined that German soldiers during the First World War had been courageous and invincible, so that nothing but a stab in the back could possibly explain their subsequent defeat.

The choice of the imagery of a stab in the back to "explain" the indigestible defeat suggests that this imagery had, in the past, already stood for unassimilated psychic elements. It could have even represented a traumatic verdict concerning a fatal flaw in the German character and notion of peoplehood. It may have been the notion that the Achilles heel of the German folk, or people, which accounted for their geographic divisions and political retardation, was the failure to watch themselves against surprise blows by undetected external as well as internal enemies, and that this failure could spell their undoing. If it were an external enemy, then the fatal flaw might have been inadequate borders. If it were an internal enemy then the fatal flaw could be either the existence of a fifth column, comprised of a foreign element, or a dreadful defect in the German character itself, which made each German his own worst enemy. And if it were all of the above, then the implications were that new ways should be found to reverse the present unacceptable outcome in such a fashion as to supposedly guarantee that the new, yet old, trauma will never again repeat itself. In sum, in the German heritage of both history and myths, an emotional disposition or psychological expectation has already been built up for despicable treachery as the explanation for the defeat of unblemished German heroes.

Another example of such a psychological expectation was the grim warning to be forever on the alert against evildoers who cleverly disguise themselves. The prototype for this image can be found in medieval notions concerning the cleverly disguised devil who does his harm by fooling the people. But this theme of ominous disguisability received an added reinforcement in the nineteenth century in the famous collection of fairy tales by the brothers Grimm. Ranke (1966, xviii–xix) emphasized that the tales of the brothers Grimm included vilifications of Jews, and he underscored the fact that the Nazis reintroduced the *original* version of the tales which included bloodletting and violence. Waite (1977, 262–63) provided a few telling examples of bizarre physical and psychic cruelty in the tales. Yet the tales were extremely popular. Consequently almost every German child came to know, for instance, that in "The Wolf and the Seven Kids" the mother goat's warning to her seven children not to open the door of their house to the wolf was to no avail. The children were fooled just the same because the scoundrel wolf cleverly disguised himself as their own mother. With this preexisting prototype already embedded in German culture, Hitler's labeling the Jews as masters of disguise was bound to be an effective ploy.

As mentioned earlier such national myths as the stab in the back or the disguised Jews are referred to in the field of psychohistory as shared group fantasies. These shared fantasies are capable of setting the stage to new psychohistorical replays of old historical issues and foster great receptivity to new ideologies so long as the latter tap into the existing public pool of emotional dispositions and psychological expectations. Whenever that happens, the new ideologies are capable of reactivating the old myths so as to channel their energy potential into the mobilization of the masses. Those particular ideological themes that promise newness while connecting to powerful old stuff are the very ones that prove to be effective energizers of the masses. The promised newness can be offered under the banners of change, revolution, messianism and utopia, but in all its attires the newness remains essentially a promised reversal of the status of any of a number of old psychocultural prototypes or myths, such as a stab in the back, that stand for an unacceptable psychological condition.

By the same token, ideological themes such as respect for authority that promise a future that would be the same as an idealized past are also most powerful. In this case, the potent current mottoes, which evoke highly charged psychocultural prototypes of the past, play to conservatism, fear of change, and even ruthlessness in preserving the status quo against unacceptable and traumatizing threats. The common denominator of these mottoes is the ultimate protection of all that is precious in the past and present from destructive changes that seem to emanate from the present and future.

It matters not, however, whether the available mottoes promise a future that reinstates the past or a future that breaks with the past, although the latter carries a greater revolutionary aura. Either way the consequences are the same. Powerful ideological themes that hover within the zeitgeist now need only mounting public pressure to achieve dominance and exert the power of myths. It is therefore a good psychohistorical bet that whenever a leader's ideological mythmaking and myth selling resonate among the followers, it is likely that he is selling something old yet new or vice versa. If that which is old can be packaged as new, while that which is new can be clothed with past tradition, the success of the myth-selling job will be phenomenal—so long as the ideological mottoes represent highly charged themes that already exist in the cultural repository. Indeed, Hitler's great success in his selling job suggests that the psychological factors with which his ideology was loaded represented the kind of timeless mythic elements whose recurrent visibility and cultural prominence is timed by the elusive zeitgeist. As a side note, it is interesting to observe that when Hitler entered the German Workers' Party in September 1919 as an Army spy, he gave his profession as "salesman." (Here was a disguise that suited him!)

Hitler expounded his ideology in the two volumes of his famous book *Mein Kampf,* which were published in 1925 and 1926 (Hitler 1943).

He also preached his ideas in his speeches (de Roussy de Sales 1941; Baynes 1942; Domarus 1990 and 1992). The basic tenets of his ideology are interrelated and form a fairly consistent set of messages. The interconnectedness of the basic notions could be sensed intuitively by Hitler's followers and added to the psychological appeal of the separate elements. The drawing power of the ideology was enhanced by the tacit perception that it added up to a coherent totality that presumably made sense. And since the appeal that the central ideological motives held for the masses was largely of an emotional nature, it did not require any elaborate formal systematization of the ideological body. Actually, when a more systematized version of Hitler's ideology with an accent on foreign policy was prepared in the form of Hitler's so-called second book— *Hitler's Secret Book* (T. Taylor 1983), it was shelved by Hitler probably because it would have not had much of an impact. Eberhard Jäckel (1981), who was interested in the issue of how comprehensive Hitler's weltanschauung, or worldview, was, traced its development from a more rudimentary world picture to a more systematized worldview. This development corresponded to the progress he made in formulating his ideas during his Vienna years from 1907–1913 to post–World War I years which produced *Mein Kampf* and later the second book. True enough, the second book was more specific and detailed on certain foreign policy guidelines. It was also more systematic in tying the principle of inherent merit among individuals and peoples to its foreign policy derivatives. Nevertheless, a formal systematization of a weltanschauung is not necessarily the secret of its power. The truly effective and shared group "secrets" were neither highly systematized nor locked in Hitler's desk drawer. Jäckel himself cautioned that he did not contend that Hitler's later and more systematized weltanschauung was the cause of his political impact. It therefore seems that the added systematization of the second book is not going to provide us with the key that unlocks the hidden source of Hitler's effectiveness.

Indeed, Hitler himself was a nonbeliever in the effectiveness of complicated discourse that would prove too cerebral for the masses. Moreover, the second book does not seem to contain anything new in principle. The underlying notion about the interrelatedness of such key ideas as race, the Jewish threat, world domination, the folkish state, living space, the femininity of the masses, and the leadership principle was already present in *Mein Kampf.* Jäckel correctly pointed out that not only were the chapters of *Mein Kampf* complete in themselves but they also related meaningfully to each other. Hitler's ideology was consistent and fairly integrated while the interrelatedness of its repetitive themes was easy to grasp. Moreover, if one cares also to identify the psychological loadings that underlie each dominant theme, it becomes evident that they do not add up at random but form a well-recognized psychological pattern. As we shall have occasion to see later on, this pattern refers to primitive stages in ego development, which are characterized by infantile terrors that stem from archaic issues of power and boundaries. At any rate, all the important information was already available prior to Hitler's second book, which does not add much to the understanding of the basic assumptions that he was selling to the German people. What is more, unlike the speeches and *Mein Kampf,* the second book was written too much like a dissertation that was to be read by an "intellectual" eye rather than like a speech to be absorbed by an "emotional" ear. It may therefore be the case that Hitler decided to forego publication not so much because the foreign policy issue of South Tyrol became outdated due to the cultivation of Italian friendship but rather because as a myth seller the book was not written well. And although it was subsequently translated into English under the title *Hitler's Secret Book,* it contained no new secrets.

Regardless of how well systematized or how clearly organized Hitler's ideology was, it is evident from the very start of his political activity that he had a set of unshakable principles concerning German life and history. These principles, which also reverberated with underlying psychological basic assumptions, were definitely linked to each other and were not subject to opportunistic revisions in spite of Hitler's well-earned reputation for demagoguery. Much as he has been a manipulative actor each time in which he publicly lent his voice to the masses in order to express on their behalf the newly unified national will, he also was an ideological fanatic who could alter only the variations on the central themes but could not change the basic messages.

These unalterable messages in his ideology will be explored in this study, which is neither a psychobiography of Hitler nor a group psychohistory of the Germans. The spotlight will consistently remain on the ideology and its underlying psychological loadings. In a certain sense Hitler's ideology has been treated here as literary works are some-times treated. It is a common practice to treat a literary or artistic cre-ation as if it has a life of its own. It assumes its own fate and is allowed to stand on its own regardless of the personal fate of its author. Like some artistic creations, an ideology too is a literary creation that can achieve independence from its creator and outlast him, or her, however unfortunate the results. The impact of an ideology keeps changing, of course, in line with changes in the zeitgeist. And different elements of a single ideology may evoke a wide range of changing emotions, being felt as inspiring or repugnant by different sets of people. By and large it has been accepted that Hitler's speeches inspired German listeners much more than non-German readers. It stands to reason, therefore, that there just might have been an underlying psychology there specific to the Germans. For this reason, themes that Hitler repeated to the point of apparent boredom to non-Germans have been considered in this study as very significant. This is so because the repetition served as a clue that these specific themes were the very ones that were interconnected with the underlying psychology. In this connection, it is interesting to take note of Freud's contention in his essay "Beyond the Pleasure Principle" that what would be an exhausting and boring repetition for adults re-mains fresh and interesting for children who need the repetition in order to gain mastery (S. Freud 1955b, 35). This could suggest that Hitler intuitively treated his crowds like children in the Freudian sense. But he acquired this sense not from Freud but via Freud. It is ironic that Hitler probably picked up the technique of repetition from secondhand sources which were likely derived from Freud's summation of Gustave Le Bon's suggestions concerning how to handle the crowds.

Hitler was a constant borrower of themes that floated into promi-nence in the zeitgeist. In his youth he was an avid collector of bits of thinking and scraps of information from manuals, pamphlets, brochures, leaflets, street conversations, café arguments, and a variety of whatever other secondary sources he stumbled upon. It was therefore fairly easy for him to go fishing regularly for prominent themes and to come up with the catch of the day in a manner of speaking. On some of these central mottoes—as for instance the power of the will—he imposed his distinct personal imprint. Consequently his doctrine of the will became thoroughly magical and did not much resemble its antecedents. But some other mottoes he borrowed and utilized without major distortions because he found them to be very dear to his heart in their original form. This was the case with the central theme of conspiracy for world domination, which was lifted from the notorious forgery known as *The Protocols of the Elders of Zion* (Cohn 1970). The significance of this theme will be elaborated with reliance on the valuable contributions that Konrad Heiden (1944) made on this topic. The theme of world domination was tied to Gustave Le Bon's (1897) notions concerning the psychology of crowds, especially the qualities of femininity and suggestibility that left crowds wide open to mass manipulation. Furthermore, both the ideas of the infamous *Protocols* and the ideas of Le Bon were linked by Hitler to Otto Weininger's (1906) notions concerning sex and character. Especially attractive to Hitler were the notions of the fatal flaws of Jewishness, the fundamental defects of femininity, and the singularity of the genius, or the timeless man, who is able to impart meaning to events by virtue of his significant memories. Le Bon's and Weininger's works created a sensation in Europe at the turn of the twentieth century and easily attracted Hitler's attention. He then incorporated much of these timely elements into his ideology providing his own explicit or implied connections between them. The main thrusts of Weininger's and Le Bon's assertions are described in the chapters on the Jewish danger and on the leadership principle respectively.

Hitler's public pronouncements through speeches and writings accomplished the direct communication of a worldview from leader to followers through conscious as well as unconscious channels. The explicit ideology with its psychological undertones remained both consistent and interconnected. Though it is paranoid, murderous, racist, mystical, magical, Manichean, messianic, utopian, grandiose, counterphobic, and suicidal, it is not incomprehensible. There is meaning and "logic" in this horrendous ideology, which at bottom is actually an ontogenetically primitive worldview. This can be illustrated if one is willing to engage in a gathering of ideas and judge their coherence from a psychological standpoint that takes account of the peculiar "logic" of emotions.

But in so exploring the meaning of a body of ideas that had such a proven genocidal impact, it will be necessary for readers to allow themselves to be taken for an ideological ride making an effort not to apply personal brakes. In exploring any ideology, especially a revolting one, a person has to respect the ideological confines and check the basic meaning of each motto from within this thematic edifice. The material must be allowed to speak for itself, and the reader should try to imagine how the various messages were absorbed by Hitler's ideological cohorts at the time of delivery. At the end of this journey, after completing the exploration of the major dominant themes and their underlying psychological reverberations, an overall examination will attempt to check whether these themes do indeed coalesce into a coherent whole and an identifiable psychological pattern.

A word of caution is necessary concerning that final analysis. It will be based on a list of central ideological principles that interweave and crossconnect. These central principles, however, will not all represent overt statements by Hitler. Quite a few of them will not be so readily recognizable because they will consist of extracted principles that the present study will attempt to demonstrate are derived from the ideology. Without exception, however, all of the central principles will represent a set of the underlying and highly emotionally charged basic assumptions concerning German national life that are imbedded in Hitler's ideology. Bearing this in mind, the reader should not expect a standard summary of Hitler's ideology. It is hoped that the novelty of this approach will be justified by the results.

2

The Jewish Danger

Today it is not the princes and princes' mistresses who
haggle and bargain over state borders; it is the inexorable
Jew who struggles for his domination over the nations. No
nation can remove this hand from its throat except by the
sword.

—Adolf Hitler, *Mein Kampf*

The discovery of the Jewish virus is one of the greatest
revolutions that have taken place in the world. The battle in
which we are engaged to-day is of the same sort as the
battle waged, during the last century, by Pasteur and Koch.
How many diseases have their origin in the Jewish virus! . . .
We shall regain our health only by eliminating the Jew.

—Adolf Hitler, *Hitler's Secret Conversations*

In 1919, when Hitler was thirty years old and still in the army, one of his
superiors, Staff-Captain Karl Meyer, passed on to him a letter by Adolf
Gemlich, the former liaison man of Munich District Headquarters.
Gemlich's letter was a request for a position paper on the danger posed
by Jewry. Hitler dutifully and gladly complied and wrote his first political
statement (Maser 1976, 209–13). It included some telling pronouncements:

To begin with, the Jews are unquestionably a race, not a
religious community. . . . Everything that makes the people
strive for greater things, be it religion, socialism or democracy, merely serves the Jew as a means to the satisfaction of
his greed and thirst for power.

> The result of his works is racial tuberculosis of the
> nation . . . purely emotional antisemitism finds its final
> expression in the form of pogroms. Rational antisemitism,
> by contrast, must lead to a systematic and legal struggle. . . .
> Its final objective, however, must be the total removal of all
> Jews from our midst.

Hitler never wavered in these convictions, which only grew more virulent and more lethal with the passage of time. In his political testament of 1945, which he dictated at his chancellery bunker in Berlin prior to committing suicide, he stated with hatred and fury: "Centuries will go by, but from the ruins of our towns and monuments the hatred of those ultimately responsible will always grow anew against the people whom we have to thank for all this: international Jewry and its henchmen" (Maser 1976, 345). For Hitler and his followers what happened at the end of World War II seemed like the fulfillment of the apocalyptic dread of a final Jewish victory and Aryan defeat—a nightmare come true. Nazi ideology had predicted a different outcome and was being refuted by the reality of an Allied victory, but only after it succeeded in causing untold misery.

We shall now explore this ideology focusing first on the obsession with the Jewish danger. Some of the basic elements of Hitler's ideology can be found in his speech in Munich on April 12, 1922 (de Roussy de Sales 1941, 14–27). In this speech Hitler attributed to the Jews the national collapse of Germany after World War I, which resulted in the Treaty of Versailles and territorial losses as well as reparation payments to its former enemies by Germany. He accused the Jews of profiting from the collapse. He had been saying this ever since he entered politics; it was a routine allusion to the Jews as a people who live off other peoples' misfortune. But this time Hitler went further. Accusing the Jews of being creditors and seducers, he also characterized them as people who appear to be supranational while actually being intensely nationalistic. Thus he cast the Jews in the role of sly masqueraders who cleverly disguise their true nature. As we shall see later on, Hitler's belief that the masses could be easily fooled by the disguised Jews reinforced his conviction that a safeguard against this duping of the masses was necessary. This was one of the sources of his persistent belief in the national need for a single, nongullible supreme leader.

In the 1922 speech Hitler also condemned the Jews for trying to perpetuate disunity and weakness by keeping the people's hand and brain apart. This is a reference to a social split between the working class and the other classes. In alerting the people to this danger of an internal split, Hitler declared that the form of a state results from the essential character of a people. Obviously Hitler did not regard the current form of the state (the Weimar Republic) as a faithful representative of the people's true national spirit. In this connection he even stated flatly that democracy is not German but Jewish. This contention served as a call to the people to reshape their state according to their folkish character. It was also a call to the people to stay united by remaining loyal to their true racial character and by avoiding the confusion, division, and even corruption that can be caused by Jewish seduction, which always creates disunity. Relying on his favorite but distorted quotation from the noted historian of Rome Theodor Mommsen, which Hitler would use on future occasions, he reiterated the notion that the Jew is the ferment of decomposition in peoples. He interpreted this to mean that the Jew is compelled to destroy because of an inherent lack of true conception concerning the building of life in a community. In short, by his inherent racial nature the Jew is a destroyer, not a builder, of people's communal life. J.P. Stern set the record straight on Hitler's tendentious misquotation of Mommsen. Actually Mommsen complimented the Jews for being the ferment of the nations of Europe and expressed appreciation for Jewish learning and thought (J.P. Stern, 1975, 131, 205).

Hitler's concept of race rested on the mythical assumption of biologically distinct peoples with wide discrepancies in mental, cultural, and state-building capacities. What we have here is a fantasy that revolved around the mystical notion of a people with "good biology," a meritorious folk actualizing its great promise—its folkish spirit. But what we also have here is a paranoid fantasy that revolves around the lethal notion of a people with "bad biology" who epitomize all the malevolent and negative aspects of human, or even subhuman, nature.

No wonder therefore that the Jewish issue escalated in Hitler's early speech to the point where Aryan victory could be secured only by Jewish defeat. We shall encounter on future occasions this symmetrical conception of universal justice: victory on one side of the scale of justice can come about only through defeat on the other side. Thus in Hitler's eyes, in the aftermath of World War I, a German collapse had yielded a Jewish profit. The basic principle was the same: to get something extra here you must take something away there. It betrays an archaic conception of justice, which was reincarnated in nineteenth-century notions of social Darwinism, which Hitler espoused with great relish. (The psychological implications of the concept of justice that underlie Nazi ideology will be discussed in chapter 4 in the context of the living space issue.)

Having alerted the people to the Jewish danger, Hitler further reminded them that such "truth" remains valueless without an indomitable will that turns it into real action. It is worth noting that these ideological themes were interrelated with other favorite themes of his. On other occasions the necessity for an indomitable will was connected by Hitler to his leadership principle. The insult of Versailles with its painful territorial losses would also serve later on as a confirmation of the importance of another ideological theme—securing an adequate living space for the German race. Thus, the rudimentary ingredients of his interconnected ideology were already present in his early speeches. Throughout his lifetime he would reiterate the interconnectedness of these ideological ingredients. The leadership principle was the most crucial element in securing this interrelatedness, since without its implementation nothing else could be implemented either.

Hitler concluded his speech of April 12, 1922, by denouncing the peace treaty of Versailles as a crime and warning against the Jewish danger: "And finally we were also the first to point the people on any large scale to a danger which insinuated itself into our midst—a danger which millions failed to realize and which will nonetheless lead us all into ruin—the Jewish danger. And today people are saying yet again that we were 'agitators'" (de Roussy de Sales 1941, 25–26).

It should be noted that the present and pressing Jewish danger was regarded by Hitler as an ancient one. Already the Christian Lord had to shed his blood on the cross in fighting for the world against the Jewish poison. And now Hitler claimed that as a man he had the duty to protect human society from suffering the same catastrophic collapse as the one that ruined the civilization of the ancient world two thousand years before. Although it was highly unlikely that he was in the least religious, he was enough of a demagogue to claim the mantle of Christ, the Fighter, doing battle with the still unvanquished enemy, the Jew. More important, his speech carried the obvious message that he is the one who understands fully not only how national collapses come about, but also how shattered nations can come out from under them. Thus, an expert on racial destiny and on the ways in which history works has offered his people a blueprint for healing a national trauma through his indomitable will.

It is instructive, but not surprising, to detect so many of Hitler's ideological foundations so early in his career. His interrelated key concepts were emotionally laden with fanaticism and were destined to reverberate in his speeches and writings throughout his life. The speech asserted that the collapse, the crime, and insult of the *Diktat* of Versailles, was the work of Jews who profited from it. It was therefore a reiteration of the old concept of Jewish parasites who live off others. No less important was the theme of "the supra-national, because intensely national, Jews" (de Roussy de Sales 1941, 17). This was a malicious allusion to a presumed quality of deceitfulness on the part of alien people who are truly one thing (intensely nationalistic) but who intentionally present themselves in a different guise (internationalistic). This theme was developed further by Hitler more than once in relation to lebensraum, or living space. The Jews, who are actually a separate race and nation, only appear to represent a religion and presumably therefore seem not to be interested in other peoples' living spaces. But despite this misleading appearance, they constantly scheme and plot to subjugate all other peoples in all other lands. This disguise notion was subsequently related by Hitler even to dreams of world domination. Hitler was convinced that Zionists only appeared to be interested in building a country in Palestine and that what they actually wanted was to form a headquarters from which to subvert and then dominate the whole world. Moreover, the perception of Jews as seducers would eventually carry connotations of corrupting (both physically and spiritually) the racial development of the Germans through pollution. The latter danger had the potential of turning Germans to be more like the racially inferior Jews, who lack the capacity to build up true folkish communities and authentic cultures. The notion of Aryan victory versus Jewish defeat, which has already been mentioned in relation to the symmetrical conception of justice, bears also that quality that Eberhard Jäckel termed "a universalist-missionary touch" (Jäckel

1981, 54). He was referring to passages in *Mein Kampf* that suggested a holy mission: fighting for the Lord's work to save the planet from becoming empty of mankind in the aftermath of a Jewish conquest. Jäckel pointed out that this universalist-missionary touch, which appears in anti-Semitic passages of *Mein Kampf*, is absent from all other parts of Hitler's weltanschauung. He therefore concluded that these aspects of Hitler's ideology might not merit attention if Hitler had not said something similar two decades later when he faced military defeat.

It nevertheless does not seem correct that a universalist-missionary touch, i.e., a messianic touch, is really absent from other parts of Hitler's worldview. His expansionist dreams for Germany, his concern with the fate of Europe as well as issues of world domination, and his advocacy of a single leader principle all involved a global messianic touch. What is more, this universalist-missionary touch appeared not only two decades later but also before *Mein Kampf* was written, in the April 12, 1922, speech. It was part and parcel of a persistent ideological stance in which, with great grandiosity, Hitler placed himself in charge of the global battle that carried with it ultimate stakes. This had been the focus of his anti-Semitic worldview. The universalist-missionary touch was essentially "redemptive anti-Semitism" (Friedländer 1997), which promised redemption for the Aryans through victory over the Jews. Presumably only the Jews represented a global threat and dreamt of world domination. By contrast Hitler would have argued that his dreams for an adequate German living space were of a more limited nature. But the accusations against the Jews represented a classical case of projection; hidden dreams of German world domination endowed his expansionist drive with universal dimensions as well as with messianic and redemptive characteristics.

Other important themes in Hitler's early speech included the poison image and the decomposition notion. The equation of Jews with poison was a favorite of Hitler's, and its psychological meaning will be explored later in relation to the concept of blood. Suffice it to say here that undetected poison kills insidiously just as disguised Jews pollute unsuspecting victims. As for the decomposition notion, Hitler used it as a metaphor for the supposed Jewish racial predilection, even compulsion, to destroy thriving folkish communities which Jews themselves are incapable of building. This notion of destruction would easily tie itself in the future to the notion of internal splits and divisions within the German community that foster enfeeblement and impotence. Indeed, Hitler typically declared on September 18, 1922: "No salvation is possible until the bearer of disunion, the Jew, has been rendered powerless to harm" (de Roussy de Sales 1941, 45). The bearer of disunion is of course none other than the agent of decomposition. Decomposition via internal splits is a sure formula for impotence and is, as we shall see, the opposite of the magic power formula whereby internal unity under one leader and one will yields omnipotence. This brings us to the added theme of the requirement of an indomitable will as a necessary condition to translate knowledge of truth into real action. This principle became part and parcel of the leadership principle (chapter 3).

The only truly major ideological ingredient that is not directly alluded to in the April 12, 1922, speech is the importance of living space. But the emphasis on national collapse and on the crime of the Versailles peace treaty in which Germany lost territories leaves the door open to later introducing proper national remedies, including adequate territorial size.

What clearly comes across in Hitler's early speeches is how intricately the Jewish issue is connected by one means or another with everything else. The national collapse is because of Jews. The setbacks in racial progress and in building up the model national community or *Volksgemeinschaft* are because of Jews. Somehow Jews seem always to go out of their way, by virtue of their racial compulsion, to induce impotence by creating internal divisions. In the case of the April 12, 1922, speech, the division, as we may recall, is between the national brain and hand, meaning between owners or managers and workers. The remedy is to reunite the "national" and the "social" aspects of community life, which should really be identical but which were seen as contradictory because of the Jews who falsified the social idea by turning it into the class struggle of Marxism (de Roussy de Sales 1941, 22). Eventually the various divisive, antinational, antihierarchical enemies were combined by Hitler into a Jewish Marxism. And the ideological antidote to all these split creators remained the ideal of national-socialist unity and the practice of one will through the leadership principle.

It is of interest to observe that the images used to describe the splitting impact of the internationalist enemies are taken from the human body. The particular split between brain and brawn could also connote a breech between leadership and followership. But the entire evocation of the human body as a possible symbol of the larger national body carries with it an underlying suggestion that the nation is a living organism. Consequently there are hints here that the Jews interfere with the successful implementation of the "organic" approach within the life of the national body. Thus, the work of the Jews seems to be diametrically opposed to that of the leader, who with indomitable will works toward construction of a true folkish community and culture. Folk and folkish, incidentally, are German concepts that convey a somewhat different meaning from the English terms. They denote a notion of peoplehood with a national, cultural, and sometimes also racial imprint. It was exactly because the Jews and the single leader were perceived to work at cross purposes that the Jewish issue became closely connected in Hitler's mind to issues of leadership. It was a connection that would in time prove fateful for the Jews.

The close link of the issue of the correct attitude toward Jews, namely racially informed anti-Semitism, to the issue of leadership appears twice in the April 12, 1922, speech. After identifying the link we shall pick up its further development in *Mein Kampf*. In essence Hitler foresaw the end of the old and failed German leadership when the masses would come to recognize that the old-time leaders were seduced by Jews. The growing anti-Semitic wave would signal the end of these leaders and the rise of a new and worthier breed of leaders who truly merit their leadership position. Their main asset is proper, updated, scientific knowledge of anti-Semitism. Hitler took issue in his speech with Count Lerchenfeld, who declared that his feelings as a man and a Christian prevented him from being an anti-Semite. Hitler felt that those who recognized Jews for what they are became anti-Jewish fighters like the fighting Christ. Correct knowledge of facts and truth, which Count Lerchenfeld lacked, compels an unyielding fight against the Jews, which is the business of leadership. If one is to use terms that Hitler was going to use a bit later in *Mein Kampf,* Count Lerchenfeld was accused of letting "sentiments" rather than "reason" dictate his stance toward the Jews. Indeed, the crucial link between unsentimental anti-Semitism and leadership was to receive an even greater emphasis in *Mein Kampf.*

It was the importance of a more ideologically minded anti-Semitism based on racial knowledge, as compared to traditional religious anti-Semitism, that Hitler underscored in *Mein Kampf* (Hitler 1943, 119–21). This time there was no demagoguery or pretense, as there was in the April 12, 1922, speech, about his being incensed as a Christian: *"I say: my feeling as a Christian points me to my Lord and Saviour as a fighter"* (de Roussy de Sales 1941, 26). In *Mein Kampf,* Hitler both praised and criticized the Austrian Christian Social Party. He praised it for recognizing the value of large-scale propaganda in influencing the broad masses. However, he also maintained that, by its flawed struggle against Jewry, the party missed its chance to achieve the goal of saving Austria. The reason for this failure was the reliance on religious notions rather than on a scientific approach based on racial knowledge. This was no mere quibbling with words on Hitler's part. To the ideologically minded Hitler, the real choice was between the new racially grounded anti-Semitism and the old religious one. He regarded the latter as a sham anti-Semitism that was worse than none at all. The choice involved the crucial matter of having proper understanding of how history really works in the life of peoples. Merely shooting from the hip with traditional religious sentiments was worse than useless in view of what was actually going on in history. Religious anti-Semites were lulled into a false sense of security by failing to recognize the racial nature of the Jews. In other words, never underestimate Jewish cunningness or people's stupidity.

And lastly, there was an additional fatal flaw in the old religious anti-Semitism: it left an escape clause for the Jews in the form of "a splash of baptismal water" with which to save themselves and their businesses when all else failed. Baptism, of course, does not alter Jewish blood and leaves the specific racial characteristics intact. Even after baptism, Jews remain agents of racial decay because it is in their blood. Ignorance of the nature of race and history insured the practical failure of the struggle against the Jews when done in the old-fashioned way. It was also responsible for the dismal failure to realize that the Jewish problem concerned all humanity; the fate of not only Germans but all non-Jewish peoples depended on its solution. The Jews were thus perceived as a threat not only inside Germany but also outside, for the entire world.

From Hitler's own standpoint, his was not a capricious personal hate for Jews that gave rise to a flimsy ideology that merely rationalized the initial hatred. Rather, it was the hard lesson drawn from a scientific, i.e., racial, approach to history, which by the force of reason compelled him to change his initial sentiments of tolerance into justifiable hate. Hate was fully justified because these destructive people posed the greatest danger to everything dear and important. For Hitler, the Jew presented a danger to the fate and purity of the German race, the indivisibility of the land, the social unity of the people, and the political integrity of the folkish state. Last, but not least, the Jew also presented a danger to the availability of an extended, territorially connected, and uncrowded German living space that would include all the members of the German race within its borders and secure the flourishing of an uncorrupted culture as the highest expression of the German folk. All of these things were at stake, and the threat was not confined only to the German people because the cosmopolitan Jew was a universal parasite.

According to Hitler's criticism in *Mein Kampf* of the Austrian Christian Social Party, even such well-intentioned people lacked a racial understanding of Jewry and clung instead to a naïve, old-fashioned religious anti-Semitism. Surely, with proper leadership, such fateful points would not have been missed by party members while the ideological awareness of the broad masses could have also been raised. All in all, from his beginning days as a budding agitator and for the rest of his life, the proper understanding of the Jewish menace was a fundamental ingredient in Hitler's ideology. Moreover, this concept was inextricably interwoven into other major concepts.

From a psychological standpoint, Hitler's image of the Jews was a key concept in his ideology. The perception of a hovering and immediate mortal danger is the kind of preoccupation that constantly requires and gets attention. In this regard Nolte (1969, 524) has asserted that in the most general feature of Hitler's ideology, the global struggle for recovery, "the negative emerges more strongly than the positive, disease more strongly than health." Indeed, that is why Hitler gave his racial anti-Jewish stance ideological primacy. The full psychological significance of this new racial conception of the Jewish danger needs to be deciphered. It included such a horrendous sense of an impending lethal threat that it covered the psychological field of vision. Religiously hated Jews of the past were never able to strike such a cosmic fear in the hearts of Christians as the racially perceived modern Jews. Moreover, this scientific anti-Semitism suffused the rest of Hitler's ideology. With its omnipresence and persistence, it betrayed an obsessive preoccupation with the question of national health vs. sickness and national life vs. death. It touched upon archaic terrors that historically and epigenetically may belong to early stages of infantile development in persons' lives. Such terrors are not the uniform lot of all infants. But adults can get a glimpse of them whenever an infant shouts and yelps with such ferocity and rage that its voice seems to outmatch its small and limited bodily equipment. Chances are that this takes place when the infant's illusion of omnipotence has been temporarily demolished; a wish fulfillment has been blocked and a cruel frustration has given rise to an impotent rage. Yet infantile rage can be cosmic in its dimensions, and so is the infantile terror that underlies it. A punctured sense of omnipotence is not only a cause of rage but also a throwback to impotence with its concomitant total helplessness and overwhelming terror. Sometimes these moments of terror occur when the early interactions of power and boundaries between infants and their surroundings go awry. At other times, under the impact of chronic stress or traumatic experiences, adults are thrown back into infantile terrors as they either regress to earlier historical stages of their personal lives or adopt a more primitive mode of mentation that has existed all along in their behavioral repertoire. It is a potential option even though hitherto unused. In the case of Hitler's ideology, it was these archaic modes, primitive potentials and psychological remnants of a dark infantile past that now were coming to life through the trigger mechanism of an obsessive preoccupation with the Jewish danger. Such fears can become a national obsession if the particular history of the whole group happens to reinforce these concerns. The German history of prolonged worries over the issues of power and boundaries did just that.

On the surface it might seem that the ideal of a folkish state and its culture-producing potential was the cornerstone of Hitler's ideology while the treatment of Jews was a subordinate idea promoted for the sake of that primary ideal of folkish blossoming. But if we translate the polarity of true folkish versus corrupt Jewish into psychologically more loaded terms and substitute danger, sickness, and death for the word "Jews" and safety, health, and long life for the notion of "folkish state," then there is no doubt which polarity assumes psychological primacy. Even

though the two sets of notions are definitely linked, they do not constitute "the chicken and the egg" type of riddle. Here it is possible to tell
which came first. Concerns with lofty states of health in which people
thrive are, in spite of their importance, secondary. Immediate threats to
survival are primordial.

The lapse into or retriggering of such primordial concerns is a
mystery that has been only partly solved. These are the kinds of concerns that an infant may have as he attempts to differentiate himself
from the environment in very primitive and rudimentary ways. When
things go wrong while being a captive of such a process, it is more than
enough to strike hearts with terror at this preverbal stage. But this
preverbal legacy of or inherent potential for infantile terrors can later
receive verbal and symbolic expression, either individual or collective,
on the part of adult persons or of a group of people linked together in a
so-called "national organism," as was the case in Nazi Germany. This
organism handled its geopolitical environment with constant dread and
with urges to lash out violently with political threats and military violence analogous to the way an excited infant flails its limbs. Yet this
lashing out aimed to annihilate an existing trauma/threat. And this trauma
seemed to stretch without limits from the past to the future. All this
made the German national organism look very much as if it were still
trying to collectively cope with primordial dreads such as usually accompany early and rudimentary infantile dealings with the enveloping
environment. Obviously when such archaic frights persist within a whole
group, something must have gone wrong once upon a time. Sometimes
traumas, rather than being resolved, are compulsively repeated.

For now, however, it should be reiterated that in an ideology that
deals with what is dangerous (Jews), what is safe (folkish state in an
extended living space) and what should be done to fend off the former
and secure the latter (implementation of the leadership principle), the
psychological starting point is an acute sense of an imminent danger,
i.e., the diabolical Jews. They are the focal symbol of both an external
and an internal danger. They are the menace occasionally recognized
but only too frequently hidden and well masked. They are the threat to
healthy psychophysical integrity since they corrupt not only the body
but also the spirit. They represent the mortal threat that, should it remain
unrecognized, could visit upon the race a historical verdict of termina-

tion. This is the real Hitlerian bottom line: should the fatal danger not be dealt with immediately and effectively, then it is curtain time for everything valuable ranging from lofty spirituality to sheer bodily existence. This was a typical eleventh-hour psychology. The dangerous disease has already spread both inside and outside Germany, both within the precious Aryan race and among other peoples. Should it spread even further, then one's own separate and healthy existence might be gobbled up and destroyed. Thus, Hitler's ideology does have its motivational starting point. An immediate global danger (the Jew) is the primary sighting on the psychological horizon.

Consequently, Hitler made it clear in *Mein Kampf* that he considered the Jew to be "the mightiest counterpart to the Aryan" (Hitler 1943, 300). This is indeed the primal psychological fact in his ideology. From his vantage point it was simply an overwhelming fact that we live in a polarized and most dangerous world in which nothing is safe. It is a historical irony that this is how many Nazi sympathizers felt, not only Hitler. One could think that such a sense of precariousness should belong to the exiled, dispersed, and persecuted Jews rather than to the Germans. But Jews do not have a corner on cosmic fright, impotent rage, or compensatory dreams of omnipotence. Even a big nation can feel that it lives in a too dangerous world. And in Hitler's weltanschauung, it was a world characterized by an archaic split between racial forces of destruction and of construction. On one side there was a cosmic force of decomposition, degeneration, and poisoning that was seeping through everything to inflict fatal sickness everywhere. On the other side were those menaced—but not yet fully destroyed—who still retained a potential for future strength that endowed them with an eleventh-hour chance for deliverance. These were, of course, the decent folk with the racial disposition toward building, rather than destroying, communities: the state builders and culture producers who, when their health is intact, would be able to give noble expression to their inherent folkish spirit. Then, their culture could stand as a testimony to a successful, genuine expression of their innermost being—their folkish soul. This was the shiny promise of how wondrous things could be once the Jew is defeated and safety is restored. It sounded good, but there was a catch. The masses with a racially endowed spirit of construction were gullible and repeatedly duped by the cleverer Jews. The primary psychological sighting always reverted to the Jews as the deadly adversaries in the struggle for existence.

So things were not safe for the folkish spirit. A pervasive danger floated over the polarized world. In such a paranoid outlook, vigilance and suspicion defined reality and lent it coherence by providing an explanation, as well as an alibi, for why things have gone so badly. Everything now seemed exposed to an insidious and corrupting agent of sickness. Life is dominated by the need to protect against the killing disease. Important as are the high ideals of a culture-producing folk and state, they must take second seat to the most urgent and immediate eleventh-hour task of combating the fatal sickness successfully.

Hitler's perception was clear and ominous. An ill-understood evil is on the verge of triumph in this world. Nevertheless, it can still be successfully fought. Total education could produce understanding of the disease while only total fanaticism could sustain the all-out combat necessary to stem its course and even to eradicate it once and for all. Hitler passionately felt that people had to understand what kind of world they were living in. It was a world that hosted an enemy who cunningly infiltrated authority everywhere so as to undermine the racial health of good and unsuspecting folkish peoples. It was therefore high time to educate the duped masses about the true nature of the Jew—what he is and what he does.

What is it that the universal corrupting agent, the duplicitous Jew, actually does? For one thing, Jews sneak their way into different countries under a variety of pretexts and make other men work for them. It is a clever form of exploitation based on lying hypocrisy and malignant cruelty, which the hostile parasite accomplishes by means of lies and trickery (Hitler 1943, 150–51). The Jew robs and dominates a whole nation; he controls the national production through Jewish finance and sucks the blood out of the peoples' pores like a spider (Hitler 1943, 193). Hitler maintained that in effect the Jews strive for nothing less than world domination, as attested by the *Protocols of the Elders of Zion.* This book supposedly exposes the "inner contexts" (i.e., alien race) as well as "ultimate final aims" (i.e., world domination) of the Jewish people. The dissemination of this revealing document is therefore imperative: "For once this book has become the common property of a people, the Jewish menace may be considered as broken" (Hitler 1943, 307–8). The

Jews are out to corrupt the folk in both body and soul, which means both the political and moral well-being of the nation. As Hitler stated, the sickening of the body is only the consequence of the sickening of the moral, social, and racial instincts. The corruption is both material and spiritual. This point is important because of its connection to the ideology of totalism on the one hand and the psychology of magic on the other as discussed later.

One of the worst things that the Jew (he is by now a truly mythical entity) does is damage both the bodily and the spiritual health of the nation by corrupting moral and sexual standards. Hitler's favorite example for illustrating this was the political, ethical, and moral contamination of the people through syphilis (Hitler 1943, 246–57), with the Jew as its hidden agent: "The cause lies, primarily, in our prostitution of love. Even if its results were not this frightful plague, it would nevertheless be profoundly injurious to man, since the moral devastations which accompany this degeneracy suffice to destroy a people slowly but surely. This Jewification of our spiritual life and mammonization of our mating instinct will sooner or later destroy our entire offspring, for the powerful children of natural emotion will be replaced by the miserable creatures of financial expediency which is becoming more and more the basis and sole prerequisite of our marriages. Love finds its outlet elsewhere" (Hitler 1943, 247).

Very significantly so, the prostitution of love represents both the Jewification of spiritual life and the mammonization of the mating instinct. Thus, in this dual cause we encounter once again the interconnected duality of spiritual life and bodily conduct. There is really no true separation of the two. Body and spirit are perceived as two aspects of a monistic entity. They can both enjoy good health or both suffer from a killing disease. But they cannot go on separate ways. Their fate, whether slated for health or for illness, goes together. And this linkage had totalitarian potential because it could imply that the remedies would require complete control of both thinking and behavior.

Hitler reiterated these ideas in discussing educational practices in prewar Germany as afflicted by the Jewish disease of sinning against the body by a one-sided training of the mind. He concluded that in times when the fist decides instead of the mind (i.e., war), the physical weakness that is produced by this one-sided education will result in inability to defend oneself, let alone enforce one's will: "Not infrequently the first reason for personal cowardice lies in physical weakness." In other words, the consequences of sinning against the body are both physical and mental. Hitler drew the additional conclusion that lack of physical training encourages the emergence of sexual desires too early (which might lead to poor mating choices and to weakened offsprings). By contrast, the youth who "achieves the hardness of iron by sports and gymnastics" succumbs less to sexual needs and expects more from a woman than the youth who is "a prematurely corrupted weakling" (Hitler 1943, 253–54). This could be interpreted as a variant of a Freudian process of sublimation where through sports the sexual "hardness of iron" might be diverted into the battlefield's "hardness of iron." Moreover, the "hardness of iron" theme also evokes earlier historical associations of Bismarck's notorious declaration that the great questions of the day will be settled not by resolutions and majorities but by "iron and blood." It thus seems that in Hitler's statement, including its likely associations, base sexuality has been transformed into a seemingly nobler calling: the art of warfare, which traditionally came into play "when not the mind but the fist decides." The whole discussion is fascistic par excellence and reveals the roots of the fascist love affair with physical education. Sexuality should be used for the new production of future healthy soldiers. Beyond that, it should be mostly diverted to physical exercises that serve to train hardy warriors. When this is done in mass exercises, there is the added bonus of the merging of the crowd into a unified collective of one will. The whole conception is thoroughly monistic. Body and spirit, individual and group, all become alternative reflections of the same underlying entity. This brings us back to Hitler's monistic conception of the impact of syphilis.

Syphilis was a prime example for Hitler of how a loosening of moral standards that leads to promiscuous sexual behavior ends up in physical and mental decay and eventual destruction of the nation's offspring. And since Hitler believed that syphilization was primarily a Jewish activity that victimized Gentiles, its outcome was a tragic blood mixture with a resultant drop in the racial level, which was the sole cause of the dying out of old cultures. Thus, a racial disaster was in the offing as the old culture of the German folk needed to be saved, not a moment too soon, from dying out because of racial corruption. In sum, the dual corruption of body and spirit leads to the dual destruction of both. No wonder, therefore, that Hitler foresaw a terrible justice in which the sins of the profanation of the blood and the race by the fathers are avenged down to the tenth generation as the race's value declines and it simply dies out. Consequently he roared with prophetic fury: *"Blood sin and desecration of the race are the original sin in this world and the end of humanity which surrenders to it"* (Hitler 1943, 249). He repeated the notion of *"racial pollution as the original sin of humanity"* when castigating "Jewish-led" France and its desire for domination (Hitler 1943, 624–25).

Hitler, the ideological craftsman, has once again focused on a prime zeitgeist issue and milked it for all it was worth in drawing far-flung conclusions concerning the process of syphilization. In post–World War I Germany, there was a tremendous public concern about venereal disease that reflected a general anxiety about an alleged upsurge in immoral behavior. Fears about the collapse of the moral order were tied to demobilization of the army recruits, to demographic changes that created a shortage of eligible men for many women as well as to the actual specter of sex-starved servicemen visiting prostitutes in hospitals where the women were undergoing treatment for venereal diseases (Bessel 1993, 233–34). By and large, the whole postwar transition was characterized by fears of moral degeneration. In his excellent description of this development Bessel (1993, 220–53) suggested that the process involved deep-seated fears of women, who were seen as frivolous and inclined toward prostitution. What is more, this whole issue was seen as tied to the prevalent condemnation of the "licentiousness of the revolution," which referred to the abdication by the Kaiser and the establishment of a republic in 1918. Thus, issues of moral degradation in general and of venereal disease in particular visibly reverberated in the zeitgeist. Hitler decided to capitalize on it by zooming in on syphilization.

Hitler's notorious obsession with syphilization was motivated not only by racial anxiety but also by a totalistic impulse that was reinforced by the underlying monistic conception of the manifest duality of body and spirit. For him syphilization was a prime illustration of how the moral conduct of individuals affected the well-being of the national body. It was the living proof of the validity of the totalistic viewpoint that there are no such things as private affairs and that private conduct is the public's and state's business. What better illustration was there of the need for totalistic behavioral control than the gruesome fact that moral conduct has far-reaching political and physical consequences as the nation's offspring go down the drain because of the loosening of moral and sexual standards? It is sad to note that the Jewish angle in Hitler's outlook concerning racial pollution was influenced by a neurotic young Austrian Jew, Otto Weininger, who converted to Protestantism at age twenty-two and who committed suicide a year later in 1903. Hitler regarded Weininger with high esteem. He revealed this in his private conversations: "Dietrich Eckart once told me that in all his life he had known just one good Jew: Otto Weininger, who killed himself on the day when he realised that the Jew lives upon the decay of peoples" (Trevor-Roper 1953, 116). One could not come more highly recommended. It was from the admired Eckart and his ultrapatriotic German mysticism that Hitler borrowed the phrase *"Deutschland erwache!"* (Germany, awake!) and adopted it as the Nazi party slogan (Schuman 1935, 18). Weininger's influence on Eckart was especially noticeable in his essay "Jewishness in and around Us" where Eckart made the following statements: "To the Jew Weininger, his own nation appears to be an invisibly connected web of slimy fungus (plasmodium), always existing and spread over the wide earth. . . . Jewishness belongs to the organism of mankind as, let us say, certain bacteria belong to the human body. . . . The secret of Jewishness could not have been revealed more plainly. It wants the *despiritualization of the world* and nothing else; but this would be the same as its *annihilation*" (Eckart 1978, 24–25).

Weininger's stunning concepts created quite a sensation in Vienna at the turn of the century. They became an important part of the zeitgeist and were still around at the time that Hitler was formulating his ideology. Because of the strong influence of Weininger's ideas on Hitler, it is important to review a few of these concepts.

Weininger believed that human mating should follow the guidelines of his heterostylistic theory, which stipulated that the more masculine and less feminine a man is the more feminine and less masculine his ideal sexual partner would be. Deviations from this recommended heterostylism result in "illegitimate fertilization," which produces less healthy offspring who evolve into less fertile and less vigorous human beings (Weininger 1906, 43). This conviction was congruent with

Weininger's other deeply held belief that there is a universally acquired correspondence between mind and body (Weininger 1906, 60). This implied that the offspring of illegitimate fertilization were bound to suffer not only from a less vigorous body but also from a weaker mind. There are some similarities here between these ideas and Hitler's concern with the racial degradation that comes from the Jewification of spiritual life and the mammonization of the mating instinct even though Hitler was not specifically concerned with the male-female relationship per se.

Weininger also believed that masculinity represents a higher order of intellectual functioning while femininity represents a lower-level response to incoming information, which is limited to nonconceptual thinking and which is therefore incapable of rendering judgment because the latter is a masculine trait (Weininger 1906, 194–95). He further concluded that the female, who lacks soul, ego, individuality, personality, freedom, character, and will is more hypnotizable than the male (Weininger 1906, 207). It is well worth noting that, in his theory, this handicap of limited understanding coupled with exaggerated emotional reactivity is an outcome of the feminine component in every human being. It suggests that this crucial handicap is prevalent not only among women but also among a large number of men who are relatively low on masculinity and high on femininity. But a more lethal conclusion, which was related to the theory of heterostylism, was reserved by Weininger for the Jews. The essence of Weininger's verdict concerning the Jews was that they suffer from "a psychical peculiarity of the Jewish race" that boils down to the fact that "Judaism is saturated with femininity." This is why "so many points that become obvious in dissecting woman reappear in the Jew" (Weininger 1906, 303–8). At this point Weininger inserted a safety clause for Aryans: "It would not be difficult to make a case for the view that the Jew is more saturated with femininity than the Aryan, to such an extent that the most manly Jew is more feminine than the least manly Aryan" (Weininger 1906, 306). In later discussions of Hitler's attitude toward the German masses, it will become clear that their femininity was a great source of both concern and contempt by him in spite of Weininger's reassurance. In this respect Weininger's assertion that "Judaism is the extreme of cowardliness" (1906, 325) could only reinforce Hitler's suspicion of anything feminine including even the femininity of the German masses. At any rate Weininger emphasized that the overfeminized Jew lacks a proper sense of self, individuality, and personal attachment to landed property. This latter disposition is also what created in the unattached Jew a ready disposition toward communism. Such notions could only reinforce Hitler's tendency to merge all enemies into a single concept of Jewish Marxism. An added insult by Weininger in this list of negative characteristics is the assertion that because the Jewish family is maternal and feminine, it fails to instill among its members a meaningful relation to the state and society. Hitler, too, believed that the business of state belongs to the larger world of man, as we shall have occasion to see in chapter 5.

As Weininger added all of these deficiencies together, he reached the conclusion that Judaism has ceased to be national (healthy) and has become a spreading parasite (an affliction). Like the parasite, the Jew adapts himself to every circumstance and race and becomes a new creature in every different host although remaining essentially the same. He assimilates to everything and assimilates everything. This vicious judgment was, of course, adopted by Hitler lock, stock, and barrel. Lifting the wool from people's eyes so that they may see at last who the Jew really is without being fooled by his appearance was, he believed, one of his central educational tasks as the leader. As for Weininger, he went on to assert that, like women, Jews are without any trace of genius, but, unlike women, they have special gifts such as jurisprudence. Moreover, they are unable to believe in other masculine men (this latter characteristic would certainly have been sufficient in Hitler's eyes to write Jews off from ever being capable of reform). With even greater virulence Weininger considered the Jewish submission to God as an expression of the desire to be rewarded by "earthly well-being and the conquest of the world" (Weininger 1906, 313). This appears to be a lethal variant of the milder theme of a Christian making a pact with Lucifer. This time the allusion is to the Jew making an implicit pact with no less than God himself for the most ambitious of evil purposes: world domination. For Hitler Weininger's depiction of the Jews added oil to fire. As if the already existing femininity of the Aryan masses is not enough in itself, there is an additional danger of further degeneration of these masses through illegitimate fertilization by the overfeminized Jews.

Weininger's entire chapter on Judaism (1906, 301–30) is a classic example not only of Jewish self-hatred but also of the enormous impact that a "timely" work can have when it draws upon ideological ideas, images, and symbols that were building up and being reinforced in the collective cultural arena. Hitler picked up on these ideas from the same public pool. The theme of world domination struck a chord in his heart. On the one hand it betrayed his secret ambitions for himself and Germany, but on the other hand it represented overt fears of the designs of others. This theme originated from the infamous *Protocols,* was associated with Le Bon's ideas concerning the manipulation of the masses, and was reinforced by the prejudiced racial notions of the self-hating Weininger.

So far we have concentrated on Hitler's view of the spiritual as well as physical harm that Jews were supposedly out to inflict on the unsuspecting good peoples of this world. But we have not covered in great detail the alleged malevolent designs that Jews had regarding other peoples' states and countries. Here the cunning duplicity of the world-dominating mythical Jew reaches the height of diabolic cleverness. So good is he in disguising his activities and in duping people concerning his real nature and true aims that they fail to recognize the central fact that he represents a competitive alien race. Neither do they realize that his true goal is to become the greatest lebensraum infiltrator of all times. His business, on his road toward world domination, is nothing less than living off all other peoples' living spaces.

Lebensraum is a key ingredient in Hitler's ideology. It will therefore receive a detailed discussion in chapter 4. Hitler flatly stated in *Mein Kampf* that "only an adequately large space on this earth assures a nation of freedom of existence" (Hitler 1943, 643). It is advisable at this point to keep in mind that the dominant themes in Hitler's ideology were conceptually related to each other. And here we are approaching the all-important intersection of his three core ideological issues. These are the connected issues of the Jewish danger, the problem of an inadequate living space, and finally the implementation of the leadership principle as the only workable answer to the other two issues. Judging by the repeated harangues in which he reiterated these themes, Hitler must have felt them to the marrow of his bones. He was too consistent about these issues throughout his political lifetime for them to be dismissed as mere rhetoric. It could therefore be instructive to try, if possible, to get under

Hitler's skin, so to speak, and feel what it was that he was so passionately and fanatically trying to tell his people. The bottom line of his missive was that when it comes to these sneaky Jews all people must understand, even if it has to be drummed into their heads, that the question is never merely what the Jews are trying to do but also, and of equal importance, how they slyly and ingeniously go about doing it.

Hitler, after all, subscribed to a Darwinian *Realpolitik* of survival of the national fittest. But with regard to the Jews this gross and racially colored social Darwinian perspective presented him with a dilemma. To accuse one group of people of trying to rob the living space of another would be tantamount to no more than accusing it of normalcy, including effective coping and good health. Hurling this accusation at Jews without any added qualifications would have therefore fallen short of pinpointing the Jewish racial and historical uniqueness. He therefore had to add suppositions that would still retain the Jew in his role as the most formidable opponent but would clearly stipulate that he is not at all a normal kind of adversary. In addition to that he had to fit it all into his own broad outlook of history. What he saw generally in history was a continuous development that was created by the mighty forces of nature. In the process of this development stronger nations overcome weaker nations and consequently boundaries of living spaces change. He therefore concluded that state boundaries are made by man and are changed by man. But a careful reading of Hitler's ideology suggests that this process applied to decent and even heroic peoples of worthy races who, one might say, were capable of fighting manfully because they were brave and had a sense of honor. One would not expect such people to stab anybody in the back because honorable people are heroes—not sneaky yellow cowards. Naturally it all stems from racial merit, which structures the rules of honorable national struggles. But the Jews come from an altogether different racial stock. They are racial agents of decomposition, who parasitically sustain themselves out of the destruction of all other races. They therefore fight differently and they do not fight fairly. It is a psychological curiosity that Hitler, who prided himself for not being halfhearted but rather a steely decision maker, who unsentimentally subscribed to a ruthless political Darwinism in relation to the game of nations, was in essence whining hysterically about the Jews fighting deviously. This psychology is reminiscent of toddlers complaining vociferously about being unfairly hurt. At any rate, the origin of the unfair Jewish treatment of others is the Jewish core itself. How the Jews strive to achieve their aims stems from who they are. It is in the "how" aspects that the diabolical cleverness shows itself and the underlying alien racial nature reveals itself to discerning observers in spite of the ingenious Jewish attempts to disguise the real nature of their doings.

So greedy and ambitious are the despicable Jews that they desire to control everything on this earth. They are not like other people; it is not in their nature to aspire for their own patch of land that would be suited for their local national purpose. They want the whole world. The Jewish state is therefore territorially unlimited (Hitler 1943, 302). The Jews are out to destroy one state after another, turn each state into a heap of rubble and then establish the sovereignty of the eternal Jewish empire. These aims of Jewish world domination, which are supported by a "negrified" France, endanger the existence of the white race in Europe. What the Jewish-dominated France carried out in Europe was a sin against humanity. But the day of retribution was coming, as the white race in Europe recognized racial pollution as the original sin of humanity and turned on the Jews with avenging spirits (Hitler 1943, 624). But in the meantime the Jews wanted it all. They wanted nothing less than world domination and a global state without boundaries. Their insidious method to accomplish this was racial pollution. Racial pollution is of course the tainting of the blood so as to lower and eventually destroy the racial merit of another people. Yet this destructive assault on the racial value of the folk was carried out not by an open war but by seemingly harmless daily interactions, which included social and sexual intercourse. People cannot protect themselves from such attacks by going to the trenches to fight. Initially the combat can be carried out only in the form of education so as to preempt harmful contacts. At a later stage, the problem can be dealt with at the source by removal of the malicious initiators of the infecting contacts. At this point the fighting can be carried out by the sword so as to expel or even exterminate them, depending on how final a solution is desired. Either way it was incumbent upon non-Jews to resist this creeping pollution since ultimate stakes were involved. With a bit of paraphrasing it could be stated that when it comes to "the original sin of humanity," to sin or not to sin was equal to "to be or not to be" in the fateful battle for existence that was shaping up. One can detect the messianic end-of-days and timeless quality of this shaping battle that Hitler prophesied in *Mein Kampf.* Soon the battle will pit one side against the other: the eternal Jewish empire, which is already in the process of formation, facing the future German empire—the thousand (meaning eternal) year *Reich.* The outcome hinges on the focal question: Is the magical leadership principle going to be fully implemented or not? Left leaderless to fend for themselves, the gullible masses are no match for the Jews. In no time they will be fooled galore by the Jews as they have always been. Such an outcome is inevitable not only because of the stupidity of the masses but also because the Jews are master dupers by virtue of their alien racial nature. Duping is at the essence of how they do everything. It is in their blood.

At the heart of the Jewish strategic goal of world domination lie the tactics of incessant lies. It is no coincidence that many of the lies are directed at the one leader who could stem the Jewish tide: "While from innate cowardice the upper classes turn away from a man whom the Jew attacks with lies and slander, the broad masses from stupidity or simplicity believe everything" (Hitler 1943, 324). What Hitler was saying was that the Jew, i.e., the mythical Jew, was targeting many of his lies at the truth-telling Hitler, who was constantly exposing him. The lying Jew was clever enough to understand that his only deadly danger and mortal enemy who could possibly defeat him was the folkish single leader and not the cowardly upper classes, the old-style leadership, or the stupid masses. The barrage of Jewish lies serves the purpose of disguise. With proper disguise of who the Jews are, what they do, and what they want, other races will be completely fooled and lulled into sleep. They will continue foolishly to tolerate seemingly harmless activities by harmless Jews until it is too late. By then knowledge will come too late to reverse course. Knowledge or racial consciousness is needed now: "For a racially pure people which is conscious of its blood can never be enslaved by the Jew. In this world he will forever be master over bastards and bastards alone" (Hitler 1943, 325). Bastards, of course, are the progeny of polluted blood due to mammonization of the mating instinct. Yet it is hard to understand the truth in the face of constant Jewish lies: "Existence impels the Jew to lie, and to lie perpetually, just as it compels the inhabitants of the northern countries to wear warm clothing" (Hitler

1943, 305). It was therefore the current holy task of the single leader and prophet of truth to expose all the Jewish lies systematically.

The big Jewish lie concerning what Jews want involved the issues of living space and world domination. Zionism was the newest gimmick invented for masking the true Jewish goals. It was the latest lie concerning what the Jews really want as well as what they actually do. It was a sly Jewish device to dupe the *Goyim* (non-Jews). The Jews do not really intend to build a state in Palestine for the purpose of living there (a clear reference to the Zionist dream of normalization and "becoming like all the other nations"). What the Jews are truly trying to do in Palestine is to form there a central organization for their international world swindle. For Hitler, Zionism was a monumental fraud. Not even in their wildest dreams could the Jews actually opt for a small ancestral living space where they could revive their mystical links to the local landscape as all good folkish people do. Such normalcy could convert the Jew into a racial entity that is akin to the Aryan. Providence forbid! But of course Hitler, the infallible truth detector, was not about to fall for this bit of Jewish lies and trickery. Hence Zionism had to represent not genuine Jewish aspirations but new heights in the Jewish art of disguise and craft of duplicity. In essence, therefore, Zionism was a truly ingenious big lie of seemingly standard folkish practices on the part of the Jewish race, which was, nevertheless, by its inherent racial deviancy and limitations totally incapable of engaging in such practices. In the meantime, however, under the shelter of the big lie, world Jewry continues its relentless progress toward world domination by forming states within states and by being a parasite in the body of other nations (Hitler 1943, 150, 305). In sum, the hidden and hideous aim is Jewish and global rather than Zionist and local. Ultimately the Jews who are so good at disguising their real aims and true activities will drop the trickery after they no longer need it. By that time, though, it would of course be too late.

Perhaps the biggest Jewish lie of all concerns not what the Jews really do but who they truly are. As Hitler put it, "after all, their whole existence is based on one single great lie, to wit, that they are a religious community while actually they are a race—and what a race! One of the greatest minds of humanity has nailed them forever as such in an eternally correct phrase of fundamental truth: he called them 'the great masters of the lie'" (Hitler 1943, 232). It is worth noting here how Hitler traffics with absolutes. He was not carried away out of control but rather followed his intuitive sense, which told him that German audiences love absolutes. In this particular passage he spoke of such absolutes as a whole existence, one single great lie, greatest minds, nailed forever, eternally correct, and fundamental truth. These are meant to be the words of a genius who according to Weininger was the only timeless man. Following Weininger's model, Hitler attaches absolute meanings to events and also renders historical judgments that will remain valid for all time. And now he was uncovering for all eternity the absolute truth about the most convenient Jewish lie that so admirably suited Jewish purposes. So long as Jews are perceived as members of another religion only, they can still be perceived also as members of the same race or at least as members of the local nation. This is why the Jews cling to this first and greatest lie that they are a religion and not a race. Moreover, additional lies are being drummed up to support the original lie. The additional lies involve language games by means of which the Jews disguise their underlying racial and national difference to make it appear that they share in the local nationality and that their group distinction is merely a matter of religious difference. In order to provide a full sense of Hitler's fanaticism and venom, a typical expression on the subject is herewith quoted in full:

> On this first and greatest lie, that the Jews are not a race but a religion, more and more lies are based in necessary consequence. Among them is the lie with regard to the language of the Jew. For him it is not a means for expressing his thoughts, but a means for concealing them. When he speaks French, he thinks Jewish, and while he turns out German verses, in his life he only expresses the nature of his nationality. As long as the Jew has not become the master of the other peoples, he must speak their languages whether he likes it or not, but as soon as they became his slaves, they would all have to learn a universal language (Esperanto, for instance!), so that by this additional means the Jews could more easily dominate them! (Hitler 1943, 307)

So much for the presumed national loyalties on the part of Jews in their various local habitats. Everything Jewish is based on evil hidden intents that are masked by clever fake appearances. The Jew manifestly speaks in different languages but latently thinks in Yiddish. He overtly contributes to literature in many languages but covertly dreams of a universal language of enslavement. He seems accommodating as he aspires for domination. Everything Jewish appears different from what it really is; consequently, being fooled by the clever disguise and by the fake appearance is the easiest thing in the world. This fake appearance is always that of a loyal member of the local community that is native to the land. But the underlying reality, which is so successfully kept hidden by means of clever disguises, is nevertheless that of a universal alien race, and a dangerous one to boot.

Old echoes from medieval Europe seem to reverberate in Hitler's view of the essence of the Jew. What particularly comes to mind is the medieval notion of Satan as the master of disguise. The famous fifteenth-century tract *The Malleus Maleficarum* (The witches' hammer) of Heinrich Kramer and James Sprenger is replete with illustrations and warnings concerning the devil's ability to appear in many disguises so as to trap unsuspecting and therefore defenseless persons who are not on the alert to protect themselves from his approaches (Summers 1971). The devil is especially adept at disguising evil as something innocent. His is a brilliant strategy that stems from devilish cleverness. It is all done with God's permission. God allows the devil to carry on his temptations in order to provide man with valuable opportunities to be tested while he exercises free will. And man sometimes passes but some other times also fails the test, to his great peril. This is so because God provided eternal punishments for sin. As we turn to Hitler's ideology, God becomes the goddess of fate, or Providence, or what these metaphors really meant for him: nature. And nature has allowed the Jews to roam the universe under various disguises and tempt other people to stray away from the path of racial righteousness. It is the devil's work that the Jew carries out, and he therefore cuts a devilish figure: "With Satanic joy in his face, the black-haired Jewish youth lurks in wait for the unsuspecting girl whom he defiles with his blood, thus stealing her from her people" (Hitler 1943, 325). It is important to note here that the Jewish disguise is not perfect since being black-haired is a giveaway. (The significance of this will be discussed shortly.) At any rate, when the naïve people fall for Jewish sexual ambushes they commit nothing less than "original sin," which is Hitler's own term for racial pollution. But nature punishes the original sin of mating with Jews no less than God punishes the sin of cavorting with the devil. Indeed a terrible punishment is in the offing. The social Darwinian extinction of the racially unfit is just around the corner. It is a punishment that fits the crime. Hitler was well aware that he was conjuring up ancient religious images from the Europe of olden days and olden ways. It is just too transparent in such a statement as the following one: "Here he stops at nothing, and in his vileness he becomes so gigantic that no one need be surprised if among our people the personification of the devil as the symbol of all evil assumes the living shape of the Jew" (Hitler 1943, 324).

In the meantime the danger was escalating as the devil's work was spreading. The Jew continued to be "the typical parasite, a sponger who like a noxious bacillus keeps spreading as soon as a favorable medium invites him" (Hitler 1943, 305). Thus, from Hitler's point of view the Jews posed a mortal danger by virtue of both fatal goals and lethal means. Their sheer existence was the danger because they were an alien and evil racial being. Their evilness was sensed even in olden times although the tools of racial conceptualization were not available then. But at present, as the Jewish menace was better understood, something needed to be done for the sake of self-defense and self-preservation. Somebody had to do it, and Hitler knew who that somebody was.

But in order to support his claim to being that chosen person, he had to establish that he had the required personality to qualify for leadership. As noted before, his conceptualization of the Jews was ideologically tied to his two other major ideas: adequate living space and the need for proper leadership. In shaping his views concerning what a new noncowardly leadership ought to be, Hitler was influenced by popular zeitgeist notions that were circulating in various European countries, such as Italy, France, Austria, and Germany. One such idea, which was to prove very influential, was the dichotomy between sentiment and reason.

In his book on the ideology of Fascism, A. James Gregor dealt extensively with the impact on Italian Fascism of the ideas of the Italian Scipio Sighele and the Frenchman Gustave Le Bon (Gregor 1969, 51, 67, 79–80, 324). The young Benito Mussolini was among those who were deeply influenced by their works (Gregor 1969, 112–13). Mussolini and probably the younger Hitler were impressed by Le Bon's ideas, especially with the idea of the substitution of the unconscious actions of the crowd for the conscious activities of individuals (Mosse 1977, 12). Another central and very influential idea was the contrast between the crowd's emotive behavior based on sentiment and the more individualistic executive principle of reason that characterized the behavior of the leadership or political elite (Gregor 1969, 118–20). For members of the elite, reason became the adaptive instrument for changing the world and the major tool to insure survival (Gregor 1969, 122, 200). Hitler was influenced by the example and ideas of Italian Fascism. Chances are, however, that he had an additional exposure to the ideas of Le Bon because of the notoriety and popularity that Sigmund Freud gave to the ideas of Le Bon in his book on group psychology (S. Freud 1955c, 72–81).

Gustave Le Bon had indeed placed a major emphasis on the dichotomy of sentiment and reason. He averred that the masses are habitually driven by sentiment, i.e., by strong emotions that are evoked by simple ideas and images and whose motivation is largely unconscious. In contrast, leaders, heroes, or the small governing elite are motivated by reason. Reason, therefore, comes to have a bearing on historical events. The direction and meaning that those who govern impose through reason on the initially disorganized emotions of the masses serve not only as a safeguard for survival of the collective but also give the nation its cultural shape and moral justification. It was therefore possible to conclude from Le Bon's assertions that followers would be as blind without leaders as sentiment is without reason. The clear implication of Le Bon's discussions is that it is a sacred duty for leaders to lead, lest the masses would remain not merely disorganized but even without a coherent cultural and national identity. It is of interest to note in this connection that Freud was critical of Le Bon for neglecting the issue of the specific means through which leaders influence the crowd. But his criticism might have been a bit too harsh. After all, the focus of Le Bon's book was the regressive tendencies of the crowd. Yet his treatment of this subject left no room for doubt that, given the psychology of the crowd, things are destined to become a total mess unless the leadership picks up the slack.

As we have noted before, Le Bon's ideas left an impact not only on Italian Fascism but also on German Nazism. It should be borne in mind that in many respects Nazism, which underscored racism and accentuated totalitarianism, was in a separate category all to itself. Le Bon's book on the psychology of the crowd heralded the dawning of the age of mass man who could be easily manipulated. It is therefore no wonder that this notion was later embraced wholeheartedly by fascistic movements. At this point, however, our concern is with the particular way in which Hitler embraced the specific idea of the dichotomy of sentiment and reason by tying it to the Jewish question. We can see the direct or, more likely, indirect influence of Le Bon in revealing passages from *Mein Kampf* concerning Hitler's early days in Vienna when he "encountered the Jewish Question":

> I cannot maintain that the way in which I became acquainted with them struck me as particularly pleasant. For the Jew was still characterized for me by nothing but his religion, and therefore, on grounds of human tolerance, I maintained my rejection of religious attacks in this case as in others. Consequently, the tone, particularly that of the Viennese anti-Semitic press, seemed to me unworthy of the cultural tradition of a great nation. I was oppressed by the memory of certain occurrences in the Middle Ages, which I should not have liked to see repeated. (Hitler 1943, 52)

> My views with regard to anti-Semitism thus succumbed to the passage of time, and this was my greatest transformation of all. It cost me the greatest inner soul struggles, and only after months of battle between my reason and my sentiments did my reason begin to emerge victorious. Two years later, my sentiment had followed my reason, and from then on became its most loyal guardian and sentinel. (Hitler 1943, 55)

> When I recognized the Jew as the leader of Social Democracy, the scales dropped from my eyes. A long soul struggle had reached its conclusion. (Hitler 1943, 60)

This was Hitler's description of an intrapsychic struggle that resulted in a personality transformation. The battle between his "reason" and his "sentiments" raged for at least two years. In this quirk of logic it was sentiment or emotion that initially prompted tolerance toward Jews, but it was an unyielding intellect or reason that did not waver in viewing anti-Semitism as a moral necessity. It was therefore "reason" that emerged victorious within Hitler's soul. What he meant by "reason"—cold-hearted and unyielding calculations based on the logic of a correct racial ideology—was different from the standard use. Hitler has just made here one of his most poignant ideological statements. This fact was recognized by psychohistorian Rudolph Binion, who first maintained that apparently Hitler was not an anti-Semite until the end of World War I despite his claim in *Mein Kampf* for an earlier conversion. However, Binion also maintained that "the change in Hitler had an ideological aspect that seemed to govern the rest" (Binion 1979, 2). He thus recognized the key role that ideology and ideological statements play. But sometimes this important fact has been overlooked because of a lingering tendency to treat Hitler's expressions as merely overblown propaganda.

For instance, in Joachim Fest's well-known book on Hitler, the importance of this inner struggle lasting for two years is minimized. Fest regarded the so-called "greatest spiritual upheaval" as merely a development from an illusive dislike to fixed hostility or from mere mood to ideology (Fest 1974, 39). But this type of development is significant. A person who merely possesses a mood has only a budding political awareness, while a person who is equipped with an ideology is a person whose self-definition is now that of a confirmed political being. This can hardly be characterized as a minor development. What is more, Hitler's entire ideology is anchored on the centrality of the force of personality as opposed to the defunct democratic principle of a majority of numbers. This democratic principle of quantity represented to Hitler a sacrifice of quality. And indeed he testified in the above quotations that his vision cleared up once he recognized the Jew as the leader of social democracy. Thus, since the qualitative principle of the merit of personality was so crucial to his ideology, it behooves us to pay proper attention to a statement that describes a personality transformation, whether real or alleged. What we most likely have here is an autobiographical invention by Hitler in an attempt to provide retroactive validation to his leadership claim.

To recapitulate, the emotional use of emphatic terms such as "greatest transformation of all," "inner soul struggles," and "bitter struggle" might indeed represent a belated dramatization that is being applied retroactively to the years of adolescence. From the vantage point of ideology, though, the important thing is not the autobiographical accuracy of such statements but their current function, which was to underscore the importance of certain principles. The political scientist James Rhodes, who emphasized the millenarian aspects of Nazism, concluded that it is not possible to confirm the historical accuracy of Hitler's "greatest inner soul struggles" or to date it. It was therefore necessary to evaluate Hitler's narrative on its internal structure. Looked at in this way, the account seemed trustworthy not as literal truth but as an accurate record of the self-construction of an apocalyptic mentality (Rhodes 1980, 52–53). This conclusion appears generally true but may not be specific enough. Surely Hitler's anti-Semitism and mythical view of the Jewish danger were apocalyptic. But what he reconstructed in his narrative was his specific conversion path into an apocalyptic leader. The focal points here are reason and sentiments and their battle for ascendancy. In effect Hitler chose the prevalent terms that were used by Le Bon to describe his transformation from follower to leader. Since reason is the domain of leadership while sentiment characterizes followers or the crowd, the subjugation of sentiment to reason becomes an indispensable qualification for leadership. Yet Hitler imposed his own personal stamp on the conceptual dichotomy of Le Bon. He asserted, and this is of crucial importance, that the testing ground for the subjugation of sentiment to reason was the successful crystallization of the proper stance concerning anti-Semitism. By so linking Le Bon's leadership criterion to the correct form of anti-Semitism, Hitler took an irreversible step. The scales dropped from his eyes, and henceforward Jewish duping was never going to fool him. This meant, however, that from now on becoming soft-hearted toward the Jews would be tantamount to renouncing his claim to leadership.

With proper understanding of Hitler's specific use of the notions of Le Bon to describe his personal transformation, one may also grasp its dire implication for the Jews. It is highly likely that as Hitler claimed to have traversed the route from sentiment to reason in relation to the Jews, he politically transformed himself from a follower into a leader. One can therefore speculate that once the conversion to anti-Semitism (even if it were a rewriting of history) was identical in his own mind to the acquisition of the envied leadership quality of "reason," the Jews were doomed. How could he henceforth even contemplate tolerance toward Jews if such an occasional tolerance signifies a leader's fall to the emotive "sentiment" level of the masses. It can be seen in these quotations that such a misguided tolerance would have represented the erroneous conception of the Jew as someone of a different religion rather than a different race. And upholding such a misconception would have placed Hitler by his own reckoning within the ranks of the traditionally duped masses.

So it is clear that taking such a course would have been unthinkable for Hitler. Yet oddly enough this was considered quite thinkable in the fake diaries of Hitler, which created such an enormous sensation in Germany in 1983. There Hitler was sometimes portrayed either as being out of the loop and oblivious to the extermination that was going on or as having a more tolerant view of the Jews (Hamilton 1991, 64–65). The fake diaries suggested that Hitler may have had second thoughts over the fact that things may have gone too far with regard to the Jews. What a regression to sentiment this would have been for the master of cold reason. And what a forfeiture of all claims to being Providence's choice for the role of führer. Besides personal disgrace, it would have signaled a weakness of leadership at the very top and constituted the kind of fatal flaw that enfeebles the whole nation, as was the case with the duly castigated old leadership. Such a change of heart was never a realistic prospect for Hitler. It could only be imagined by someone who either did not fully understand his ideology or wished to soften his image. It thus seems that, with a better understanding of Hitler's ideology, it should not be overly difficult to detect fake diaries when they violate hitherto inviolable ideological credos.

At the end of the second chapter of the first volume of *Mein Kampf*, in which he described his personality transformation, Hitler also in effect equated Judaism with Marxism. He stated: "The Jewish doctrine of Marxism rejects the aristocratic principle of Nature and replaces the eternal privilege of power and strength by the mass of numbers and their dead weight" (Hitler 1943, 65). Jewish and Marxist have now become interchangeable. J.P. Stern noted the "peculiar logic" of this equation in which right-wing international financial interests—which Hitler claimed to be dominated by Jews—are not seen at odds with left-wing bolshevization but identical with it. Although this assertion was made without a word of explanation, it was nevertheless frequently repeated and dramatized. Stern saw the unique political advantage of this double-pronged attack in its ability to unite the political programs of the moderate left, the center and the nationalist right by creating a single common enemy. He also pointed out that this amounted to a major act of the political imagination on Hitler's part since nobody had thought of it before (J.P. Stern 1975, 80–81). By cleverly equating Bolshevism with Jewishness, Hitler was able to draw under one political tent all political camps that were anti-Bolshevik, including some that were not anti-Semitic.

The "peculiar logic" that Stern was talking about is the special logic of emotions, which does not conform to the rules of formal logic. It is more palatable emotionally to merge all enemies into one rather than to keep them apart. Once such an equation is established, collusion and conspiracy become an article of faith. It is, after all, easier to "explain" a complicated world as an outcome of conspiracy just as it is simpler to have one rather than many enemies. Simplicity always facilitates the focusing and mobilization of emotions in individuals but even more so in groups. Hitler sensed this, and therefore in a bold stroke and without explanation he identified the Jewish enemy and the Marxist enemy as one.

Consequently Russia acquired new characteristics that distinguished it from a normal state. Hitler explained this in a letter he wrote on December 4, 1932, to Col. Walther von Reichenau: "Russia is not a state but an ideology which at the moment is restricted to this territory, or rather dominates it, but which maintains sections in all other countries which not only pursue the same revolutionary goal, but are also organisationally subordinate to the Moscow headquarters" (Noakes and Pridham 1990, 2:620). In sum, both Jewry and Russia represented variants of the same abnormal entity that craves expansion (omnipresence) and world domination (omnipotence). The various enemies were thus fused into a single enemy in a classic maneuver of keeping images simple, as recommended by Le Bon. The Marxist enemy could be either Russia representing the outside enemy or German Marxists representing the enemy within. In a similar fashion, the Jews could be the secret controllers of the Bolshevist headquarters in Moscow and represent the external enemy. But they could also be the treacherous Jews in Germany, who attempt to pass themselves off as German nationalists but who actually constitute the inside enemy. It was therefore one global enemy who from now on posed a threat from both within and without. Hitler remained steadfast in this conceptualization. For instance, by October 9, 1938, he stated, "Further, we know that the international Jewish fiend looms threateningly behind the scenes on stage and it does so today just as it did yesterday. It has found its most succinct expression in those foundations upon which rests the Bolshevist state" (Domarus 1992, 1223). In the fused image of an omnipresent danger, the diffused Jews were now the behind-the-scenes manipulators of a specific state, which was the Russian living space, while the Marxists who ruled the Russian state were now spreading power and influence in a Jewish fashion under the guise of internationalism. Diffused but centralized (stateless Jewishness, which nevertheless has a secret global headquarters) or centralized but diffused (a meddling Marxist state, which is nevertheless based on an ideology of internationalism)—they all represented merely different facets of the same ubiquitous threat. At some future point a bold German strike against the deadly enemy was inevitable. It was to be that point at which dimensions become absolute and where the totality of the solution matches that of the original challenge.

By early 1939 Hitler was intent on taking the beginning steps to realize the long-held dream of a drive toward the east so as to expand the German living space at Slavic expense. On January 30, 1939, on the sixth anniversary of his taking power, feeling heady in the face of National Socialist accomplishments, he delivered an ominous speech to the Reichstag that provided broad hints concerning how he planned to deal with the common enemy (de Roussy de Sales 1941, 559–94). In that speech Hitler spoke emphatically about principles of leadership and about the necessity of an adequate living space. He signaled an unyielding national resolve by stating that "we have completely hardened to all attacks of sentiment" (de Roussy de Sales 1941, 583). He also reiterated that German culture is German, not Jewish, and that Europe will not settle down until the Jewish question is cleared up. Characterizing the Jewish race as "a parasite living on the body and the productive work of other nations," he issued the following warning: *"The Jewish race will have to adapt to sound constructive activity as other nations do, or sooner or later it will succumb to a crisis of an inconceivable magnitude"* (de Roussy de Sales 1941, 584). The choice he offered was no choice at all. From his standpoint the Jews had an inherent deficiency that made them incapable of constructive activity, i.e., building up an authentic culture in a piece of land to which they are attached. It was simply their inescapable racial characteristic to remain parasites and never be productive workers. And it was this very racial fact of life that left only one other choice available: "to succumb to a crisis of inconceivable magnitude." This latter threat served as a hint at or a euphemism for the Nazi final solution. Hitler made deliberate efforts to insure that he would be taken seriously. He therefore referred to his being ridiculed by Jews in the past for prophesying that he will one day take over the leadership of the state and settle the Jewish problem. Then he declared: *"Today I will once more be a prophet. If the international Jewish financiers in and outside Europe should succeed in plunging the nations once more into a world war, then the result will not be the bolshevization of the earth, and thus the victory of Jewry, but the annihilation of the Jewish race in Europe!"* (de Roussy de Sales 1941, 585).

Hitler was a messianic paranoid. To the Germans he offered salvation while suffering from extreme delusional fears concerning Jewish conspiracies. Finding himself dealing with ultimate stakes, he felt that Germany was left with no choice. Life free of the Jewish disease (bolshevization) was the only viable option. And in that kind of new and healthy life, in order to prevent a bolshevization of the self it was necessary to engage in the annihilation of the Jewish other. Two years to the day later, during a January 30, 1941, speech at the Berlin Sportpalast, he repeated his prophecy in a more succinct version. After extolling the ideal of a national community in body and spirit and after pointing to the greatest spiritual struggle that German history has ever known, he ended his speech by referring to a world that has been delivered from Jews and a Europe in which Judaism no longer plays a part. Once again he acknowledged being laughed at for his prophecies in the past but reaffirmed that the coming years would prove him right (de Roussy de Sales 1941, 911, 924). He was already gearing up for the invasion of Russia in an attempt to kill the Jewish-Marxist enemy within and without in one bold stroke. In the process, he was going to create a greatly extended and newly purged German living space. He intended to eliminate all Jews everywhere while enslaving the Slavs and killing their Marxist leadership. He was ready for the task as he was "completely hardened to all attacks of sentiment." Because of his geopolitical ambitions, he knew that the global settling of accounts was coming. The extensive reeducation of the folk in scientific anti-Semitism was largely completed, and consequently the nation stood in total unity behind its supreme leader. Things were coming to a head with the lebensraum to be at long last enlarged and the Jews finally destroyed. He felt secure in making his ultimate and lethal prophecy.

What sort of a psychological world underlies Hitler's portrayal of the Jews? A few important features come immediately to mind. First and foremost there is a basic assumption that an ideal state of health (utopia), which prevailed once upon a time, has been lost because of the introduction of a lethal intruder (a catastrophe). This basic assumption carried with it a certain mytho-historical outlook. In this outlook there was a period of history when the German tribes of yore could not match the Roman and Greek civilizations. However, it was the German tribes who retained a purer racial stock. And as their health was not yet infected, they were on the verge of creating magnificent cultural accomplishments in interaction with the older and more advanced Greek and Roman civilizations. The Germans were healthy barbarians who weakened and penetrated the Roman Empire but who also began to rejuvenate its civilization. The uncontaminated racial worth of their pure blood held the promise of a marvelous cultural potential. In short, once upon a time there was health.

And then there was sickness. An insidious agent of decay (Jews but also Christians, who were spiritually corrupted by Jewish influences) appeared on the scene. The almost utopian pure health of the race suffered a catastrophic loss due to the diabolic means of an agent of decomposition who perpetrated the original sin of racial pollution. Blood and its magic qualities is a central concept in this outlook. It is the stuff of life and death. Therefore, its pollution transforms a historical stage of near utopia into a post-catastrophic stage of disaster. Nothing is the same any more. Pure health has been lost, racial worth has been lowered, and sickness has now become hopelessly mingled with health in this disastrous post-utopian world. From now on the crucial question was whether a radical reversal of the course could combat the disease successfully and lead to a restoration of the original health once again. History was now viewed as posing the challenge of reparation in the current post-disaster but pre-utopian era. The potent psychological themes of a loss of ideal health and a slide into sickness and death combined to reinforce the third theme of overcoming the catastrophe by recreating the ancient utopia in an imminent and new utopia. Clearly this kind of a mythical outlook, which amounted to a shared German fantasy at that time, is a desperate resort to magic in order to overcome a trauma.

Another set of important psychological themes concerns the tricky nature of the multifaceted disease agent itself. On the one hand it is superorganized, highly centralized, and includes a global command center that reaches all parts of the world. It is almost as if even a Nazi state would not be ashamed of such a high-level systematization of its organizational structure. Psychologically speaking, this is a paranoid stance par excellence in relation to an outside danger or an outside enemy. Hitler's repeated endorsement of the *Protocols of the Elders of Zion* serves as a prime example of this paranoid stance. But the expected paranoid response of "kill before you get killed" was complicated by the fact that according to the *Protocols* the whole Jewish apparatus operates not like a visible state but rather like a secret organization, which remains well hidden in spite of its profuse activities. But this problem was nevertheless soluble by the sword. It was a matter of search and destroy activities where the alien racial others could be put to the sword once they were unmasked and properly identified. This is where the virulently anti-Semitic Gauleiter (regional leader) of Franconia, Julius Streicher, and his scandalously gross magazine *Der Stürmer* came in (Noakes and Pridham 1990, 1:541–47). The magazine reiterated the old medieval accusations against Jews for ritual murder of children and ceremonial use of their blood. Moreover, it published an educational book for children called *The Poisonous Mushroom,* which taught that there were good and bad people in the world just as there were good and poisonous mushrooms. Naturally, the latter were the Jews. The children were therefore taught "how to recognize a Jew." The clues included a nose that is crooked at the end like the figure 6 and was therefore called the "Jewish Six," thick lips with the lower lip hanging down and thicker, and more fleshy eyelids. The caricatured features of Jews in *Der Stürmer,* such as large crooked noses and magnified hairiness, were designed to amplify the otherness of the Jews. They were so gross that "even some of the senior members of the regime found his material hard to stomach, though Hitler protected him" (Noakes and Pridham 1990, vol. 1, 544). Hitler's stance was made quite clear in his secret conversations: "Streicher is reproached for his *Stürmer.* The truth is the opposite of what people say: he *idealised* the Jew. The Jew is baser, fiercer, more diabolical than Streicher depicted him" (Trevor-Roper 1953, 126). Hitler approved because he wanted *Der Stürmer* not only to emphasize the otherness of the Jew but also to signal that the task of identifying all hidden or disguised Jews is a feasible one. This aggressive paranoid stance represented an irrational fear of the conspiracy of and persecution by racially different others who cleverly masquerade as members of one's own race. But it was not the Jews who persecuted the Germans. It was all a projection and therefore signaled that, in actuality, persecution will be directed by the paranoid Germans at the Jews. To that end the exaggerated features of Jews in the anti-Semitic cartoons made them more recognizable inside the cartoons and consequently made the response by the sword to the Jewish danger look within reach.

How could Jews look ordinary and successfully pass themselves off as Germans but at the very same time have grossly exaggerated Jewish features? This riddle has something to do with the psychology of anti-Semitism in general as well as with the special impact of the Yiddish language in Germany (Gonen 1975, 237–57). Fenichel (1954a) emphasized the perception of Jews as "foreign," which he also connected to Freud's concept of the "uncanny" (S. Freud 1955, vol. 17). To summarize briefly, Fenichel pointed out that the original foreign element for all of us is our own unconscious. It is that part of all of us that cannot be acknowledged as "us" because this would cause unacceptable damage to our positive and integrated self-image. It is therefore repressed and banished from consciousness to reside somewhere else (where all foreigners who are not "us" reside). Therefore, the first and consequently also the original "foreign" territory where "foreigners" dwell is that unconscious territory that was carved out within the self. Fenichel's general identification of the original foreign element with the unconscious had a far-reaching significance with regard to anti-Semitism. This identification implied that the popular anti-Semitic perception of Jews as overwhelmingly foreign evoked an implicit equation of the foreign Jews with one's own foreign unconscious. What is more, Fenichel connected this phenomenon with what Freud called the "uncanny," thus adding psychodynamic richness to our understanding of such experiences.

Freud warned that early experiences, including older modes of thinking as well as infantile complexes, which were presumably "surmounted" long ago, can resurface at later times. Moreover, he maintained that the surprise encounters with these older modes create an uncanny dread. Freud (1955a, 220) defined the "uncanny" (*Das Unheimliche* in the original German) as "that class of the frightening which leads back to what is known of old and long familiar." This means that in order to qualify as "uncanny" it is not enough for an experience to be terrifying. The fright has to include a reestablished contact with long forgotten early infantile experiences. It thus constitutes a throwback to early infantile fears and infantile wishes. This was the age of the omnipotence of thoughts and also of animistic conceptions applied to inanimate objects. This can lead to the belief that the world was peopled with the spirits of human beings. These older thinking modes and complexes can subsequently give rise to uncanny experiences concerning the return of the dead and concerning spirits and ghosts. One may therefore say that the belated experience of infant narcissism revisited, which is at the heart of the uncanny experience, is bound to seem like a terrifying encounter with something foreign yet eerily familiar. Finally, it is worth noting for the sake of future reference that Freud postulated a principle of repetition compulsion in the unconscious mind and asserted that whatever reminds people of this inner repetition compulsion is perceived as uncanny. This issue will be picked up again in the discussion of the compulsion to repeat traumas in relation to the drive to expand the German living space.

Bearing in mind that in some uncanny fashion the foreign yet familiar Jew evoked ill-defined glimpses of one's own foreign but familiar primary narcissism of infancy, there were three additional and specifically German factors that tended to augment the uncanny quality of the perception of the Jew, making him even more surprising, terrifying, strange, utterly foreign but somehow eerily familiar. The first factor, which was pointed out by Leschnitzer (1969, 113–15), was that the German idiom for "The Wandering Jew" was *Der ewige Jude,* which meant

"The Eternal (=Everlasting) Jew." This conception made it easy to look at the Jewish group as a kind of "living corpse." Leschnitzer's assertion has far-reaching implications. The connection of such an uncanny perception to vampirism and to the fantasy of living corpses securing eternal life through the magic of drinking of their victims' blood can be seen. And the adverse reaction of the victimized group from whose members the blood has been drained could also be foreseen. As Leschnitzer hypothesized, out of their paranoid fears of destruction by eternal Jewry, the Nazis developed the wish to destroy the eternal enemy and in the process gain eternity for themselves. Leschnitzer's ideas make one wonder whether the Jews would have not fared somewhat better if they were seen by Germans as the cursed wandering Jews rather than as the Manichean eternal Jews who cheated death successfully at the expense of Gentile blood.

Yiddish was the second factor that contributed to turning the German encounter with Jews into an uncanny experience. "It was particularly in Germany that Jews seemed like an uncanny blend of the foreign with the familiar because of their use of the Yiddish language. Yiddish is mostly a blend of old Hebrew and Germanic dialects from around 1000 A.D. To Germans it sounded both comical and archaic (Leschnitzer) and made its speakers seem like ghosts from another era who speak a language which in some ways is homely and familiar to listeners but in others is foreign and strange. It was therefore easier for Germans than for other people to perceive Jews as eternal ghosts of the past" (Gonen 1975, 245–46).

The disdain for Yiddish on the part of Germans was even exploited in the theater for the purpose of reinforcing anti-Semitism. A theatrical performance in the Nazi era could include dragging to the stage of a Jew "whining in his jargon" and having him shot by an S.A. man for having bribed a communist to shoot and kill another S.A. man. Anti-Semitic writings and plays deliberately included Jews talking "jargon," which consisted of a mixture of Yiddish and German (Mosse 1999, 159, 168). Although many German Jews abandoned the use of Yiddish in the eighteenth century in an effort to complete the process of assimilation into the larger German society, it had never been forgotten by Germans that the Jews were foreign and that their global language was that strange Yiddish.

This brings us to the third factor. In no other European country did the Jews assimilate so completely that they came to regard themselves as more of that nation than Jewish. In no other country therefore, where Jews were also seen as foreigners, was it easier to ask the question of "how is it that this foreign people seem so much like us." In discussing the German-Jewish coexistence and symbiosis Leschnitzer maintained: "For a considerable time, the German Jews were closely and intimately related to their surroundings. They became assimilated to their environment, then rose in it and even began to be absorbed by it, when suddenly there came an end to the development" (Leschnitzer 1969, 24). Leschnitzer also suggested the reason for this course: "A striking feature of the German development is the circumstance that, though the rise of the middle class was remarkable in the economic and cultural spheres, its share in political power came too late and was incomplete. It can be shown that this characteristic largely determined the German-Jewish symbiosis" (Leschnitzer 1969, 40). Thus, in contrast to their French neighbors, the German middle class, which was unschooled in democratic traditions and riddled with tensions for lack of political empowerment, became less tolerant of the assimilation of the Jews and wished to roll it back. All in all, it seems that German Jews, the most assimilated Jews in the whole of Europe, were fated on the one hand to remain "foreign" but on the other hand to look like Germans. It was an uncanny fate.

We are well positioned now to provide an answer to the riddle of how the Jews could look like ordinary Germans while at the very same time they could be portrayed with grossly exaggerated "Jewish" features. An inherent contradiction is, after all, structured into the very nature of uncanny experiences. The uncanny experience is built on that which was once familiar but must be concealed, that which a person once explicitly was and still latently is. Because of this inherent contradiction, both fear and attraction form parts of the reaction to the encounter. In the final analysis the contradiction in the uncanny experience is between the wild fantasies of the old primary narcissism, which were presumably surmounted and "forgotten" long ago, and the present reality principle, which, contrary to its standard logic, has just ratified the long forgotten fantasies as currently valid perceptions. This is why the whole thing is terrifying and why the uncanny experience involves an encounter with something that is both recognizable and not recognizable, namely the old self. Similarly, the uncanny Jew is recognizable and not recognizable. His nondescript appearance stands for recognizable Germanism. But his deformed caricature appearance stands for the not-to-be-recognized older and more primitive German core.

In Hitler's ideology, the Jews were portrayed not only as disguised and racially inferior humans (or subhumans) but also as invisible carriers of infection. In this capacity, they can no more be seen by the naked eye than the causes of an abscess can be seen. This time the major hurdle is not the disguisability of degenerate humans but the invisibility of germlike or of viruslike creatures. This is an altogether different psychological factor. We are still dealing with fear, but in this case the fear is an outcome not of paranoia but of a phobia. When the disease agents are at times less humanlike and more viruslike, it becomes extremely difficult to guard oneself from contamination by invisible carriers. There may still be some shades here of the paranoid stance. Invisible inflicters of infectious disease lurk behind every corner, so to speak. But basically it is a phobia that shows itself through a delusional fear of infection with the contaminating agents being spread everywhere. What makes the situation particularly dreadful is that one can never be certain that all the disease agents have been properly spotted. Sometimes the infecting creatures can be observed, as is the case with maggots, while some other times they cannot be seen, as is the case with bacilli. In essence, however, agents of infection are invisible. They cannot possibly be put to the sword but they can definitely be removed by disinfection. The question here, though, is what does the infection phobia represent in the context of Hitler's ideology as it is being intertwined with paranoia.

From a psychoanalytic viewpoint, an infection phobia is likely to represent a morbid fear of being consumed from the inside. Its starting point is an obsession with the danger of contamination. Its midpoint is represented by compulsive avoidance behaviors as well as repetitious cleansing acts and rituals that may symbolize a mixture of a defensive avoidance of dangerous exposure with counterphobic attacks on the infecting agents. But its end point, as compulsive defenses fail to provide full protection, is living under the tyranny of the frightening perception that the treacherous body is consumed, or is about to be consumed and destroyed, from within. Using Hitler's pet phrases, it is possible to describe this process as the body being eaten up from inside by a parasitic agent of decomposition. The archaic psychological etiology of such phobias can sometimes be unconscious fears of retaliation by an introjected bad image that has been gobbled up and internalized long ago but is still capable of retaliation from the inside. At this point a cautionary word is in order. In clinical practice the same phobia can represent different things to different individuals. What is more, frequently the underlying psychological causation of the phobia cannot be discovered but the symptoms can nevertheless be treated successfully by desensitization techniques or by a combination of behavioral modification methods and hypnosis. But there is no "patient" as such in our present analysis of the possible psychological significance of the infection phobia. It is rather the ideology that is being treated here as an independent persona that came into being through numerous statements about self and world that amount to a prolonged declaration of who oneself really is. The ideology has been Hitler's construction of those elements of the German personality or soul that he thought he shared with the German collective as well as those elements that he criticized and wanted the people to discard. The overall ideological portrayal may have not been identical with either his own personality or with the German national character, but it is likely to have shared numerous elements with both and, at any rate, had acquired a life of its own. And it is within this context that the hypothesis of an introjected bad image makes sense. It focuses on a morbid process that infects the body from within. It suggests that within the larger national body, so to speak, a destructive development is making cruel progress. The clear implication is, therefore, that there is a hidden enemy within who works as relentlessly as the outside enemy. Thus, in the context of Hitler's ideology, phobia and paranoia represent the internal and external enemy respectively, even though they overlap. And it is only proper for them to be intertwined because the Jewish enemy is truly global to the point that his omnipresence encapsulates both inner space and outer space.

The fact that the widely disseminated yet invisible or unrecognized carriers of infection are so prevalent makes life murky, hazardous, and highly destabilized. It brings up the question of what is in and what is out, or when is the enemy confined to the exterior and when can he be expected to treacherously attack from the rear—from the inside. And this is the most ominous connotation of the "stab in the back" theme or the notion of being attacked from the rear. It is not so much a matter of homosexual assault as it is an existential dread about a perceived fatal flaw in one's self-structure. It is a frightening perception of one's collective being as defective and therefore incorporating in its inner workings a self-destruction program that guarantees final failure in the international game of jockeying for position. It is a terrible fear of a noncancelable inner mechanism, which keeps working to crank up the next surprise traumas. In this kind of perception, the "front" side is where the front or battle rages with the external enemy. The front is therefore the outside in general, which in its broadest sense could even include all exterior sides as is the case in encirclement. But the "rear" involves different kinds of encounter because it denotes the specific side that is opposite the front, but also connotes the side that is obscured from view. But that which is most effectively hidden from view is not so much that which resides in the back as that which resides inside. This is why being surprised by the internal enemy while fighting the external one represents a stab in the back. Actually at the last phase of World War I, the seemingly victorious German army with territorial gains found itself in an untenable position vis-a-vis the growing strength of the allied armies now reinforced by the Americans. The German high command therefore decided to sue for peace/surrender but let the civilian politicians carry out the unseemly task. It therefore seemed to the German public that all of a sudden the victorious Germany inexplicably capitulated. Hitler shared with many Germans a stab-in-the-back theory that the victorious front lines were undermined by defeatist propaganda to the rear. To recapitulate, the lethal aspect of the hidden side is not so much being posterior as being interior. It therefore represents an internal process that cannot be confronted in a straightforward fashion.

The all-pervasive enemy, however, continues to infiltrate and penetrate both inner space and outer space, doing well for himself by doing ill to others, and, in the process, saps the lifeblood of his helpless hosts. It is enough to make people both paranoid and phobic. Of great psychological significance is the fact that the universal afflicters inflict harm materially as well as spiritually, not only on the body but also on the soul. This touches upon the core concept of health, or perhaps we should say of lost utopian health. This is the most secure form of health people aspire to: collective immortality as well as individual longevity and security in all aspects of being. What is at stake here is psychophysical integrity as it came to be symbolized by pure and uncontaminated blood.

Blood is a central concept in National Socialist racial doctrine. For good or bad, everything is to be decided by the state of blood. If the blood remains pure, the folk can flourish in good health for eternity and give the most advanced cultural expressions to its inner character. The folk's activities are then regarded as truly representative of its soul. But if the blood becomes mixed, then the racial level of the folk no longer remains high. This lowering of the racial worth corresponds to a decline in health and raises a question mark concerning the survivability of the particular race. If the blood is too mixed, then sickness and mortality become inevitable for the group as a whole. Beyond a certain point, any further drop in the racial level of a people cannot be reversed. Should that happen, then the racially lowered stock of people loses its claim to eternity. Another way of putting it would be to say that if the drop in racial merit passes a certain critical point, then the fateful line that delineates Jewish victory and Aryan defeat has been crossed.

But the threat of a collective sickness and death is only half of the equation. The other half is the prospect of regaining the utopian, i.e., pre-disaster, purity level of blood, which holds a magical promise. This impending magic is, after all, the psychological function of ancient and lost utopias. As the status of the myths of past utopias is converted from legend to "history," the myths now affirm that what proved attainable in the remote past is also feasible in the imminent future. And it is through this utopian affirmation that magic seems to become once again an option in history. How else could it be? So magnificent, perfect, and ideal is the utopian state of being that its inclusion as a viable option perforce crosses over into the realm of magic. The dash toward utopia is a magical leap. And this is what the Nazi blood cult was. Stripped of its biological trappings and folkish mysticism, the blood cult remains in its bare essence a grab at magical, i.e., ultramanipulative, abilities.

Although Hitler had given the blood cult a certain bent, he was mostly using well-known and prevalent ideas that preceded him. The notion that blood is the stuff of life and stands for immortality or eternity is not new in western civilization. When the prophet Isaiah (63:1–6) wrote his poetic portrayal of the God of vengeance he used phrases such as "their lifeblood splattered on my garments" or "and I brought down their lifeblood to the earth." But it was well known by Christian biblical scholars and translators that the original term for lifeblood in the Hebrew text was "eternity" and that this term acquired the secondary meaning of blood. Thus, when the Lord splatters eternity on his garments or spills people's eternity to the ground, the reference is clearly to blood as the essence of both immortality and mortality. The English term "lifeblood" is therefore a fairly good translation. This biblical choice of the term "eternity" to designate blood alludes to hopes for immortality that were attached to the concept of blood. This particular naming of blood betrays human hopes that life, at least collective life, is eternal. But the eternity of the group serves also as a reminder of the mortality of individuals both by natural causes and by means of fatal bloodshed. Eternity may flow in blood vessels, but when it spills out of wounds it spells mortality. Thus, there is a duality even in the old biblical conception of blood that views it as the essence of life, i.e., as that precious substance that sustains life and grants eternity but also takes life away and enforces mortality.

The focus on the magical qualities of blood was later accentuated in Christianity. The Christian doctrine of the transubstantiation of the wine and wafer into the blood and body of Jesus betrays the residues of a pagan ritual in which the magical properties of the precious substance are acquired by means of an oral incorporation. The Jews were made to pay for this Christian fascination with blood through accusations of Host desecration as well as related accusations of ritual murder for the sake of the Passover ceremony. Presumably the Jews stole the Host and pierced it to make it bleed in a reenactment of the Crucifixion. And presumably the Jews also murdered Christian children in order to smear their blood over the Passover *matzos*. These accusations reflect a strong belief in the special powers of blood and an unshakable conviction that the wizardly Jews were somehow able to derive benefit from the blood of others. At any rate, Germany proved to be the most fertile soil for such accusations, as attested to by Max I. Dimont: "The Germans, perhaps because they were still closest to the barbaric strain which had nursed them, were the most barbaric in their persecutions. Most of the anti-Jewish measures one popularly attributes to the entire Middle Ages were of German-Austrian origin, and grew only on German soil. Here the ritual-murder charges, the Host-desecration libels, the Black Death accusations were used to whip the population into a frenzy by sadists and fetishists" (Dimont 1962, 243). What is of great interest in the above quotation is not the pathology of one group of fetishists but the fertile ground that Germany provided for blood accusations. The ground continued to remain fertile and to provide another string of blood notions that culminated in Richard Wagner, who was greatly admired by Hitler.

In composing the libretto for his opera *Parsifal,* Wagner resorted to older tales about the quest for the Holy Grail, which arose out of Celtic, Christian, and even Jewish origins (Anderson 1987, 13–33). In the Middle Ages there emerged from the old sources, especially Christian myths, Arthurian legends, and Celtic tales and fertility rites, a dominant theme that represented a blend of Christian and pagan notions. The theme was of the Holy Grail, which was the original chalice of the Last Supper, into which the blood of Jesus was dropped from the very lance that was used to pierce his side. This Holy Grail was a talisman with miraculous powers that made it very sought after. It could produce an inexhaustible supply of meat and, even more important, its potion could cure mortal wounds and illnesses. This set of dominant themes veered far off from the secret and ancient source of it all, which, according to Anderson (1987), was the creation of fire out of focused sunlight. These themes had captured the European popular imagination ever since the Middle Ages. The Grail Quest became an object of fantasy, but it represented an almost impossible task because the Grail could be visible only to a knight who is completely pure of heart. For generations European Christians continued to be inspired by this dominant theme of a heroic and arduous search for a bloody talisman. It should come as no surprise that eventually the notion of a quest for a container of sacred blood with healing powers lent itself to virulent racist interpretations. Richard Wagner was one of those who resorted to this kind of interpretation, and his case is important because of his great appeal to Hitler. Summing up Wagner's racist theorizing as explained in his article *The Wibelungs,* his essay *"Heldentum,"* and finally his opera *Parsifal,* Robert Gutman stated:

> *The Wibelungs* singled out the ancient line from which the Frankish-German and Hohenstaufen kaisers had sprung as that "one chosen race" rightfully claiming universal rule.

Indeed, Wagner said, such a tradition had persisted among the Folk even during its periods of degeneracy. . . . Picking up the thread of *the Wibelungs* in *"Heldentum"* and pursuing a piquant bit of Wagnerian ethnological-mythological anthropology, the composer described the Aryans, the great Teutonic world leaders, as sprung from the very gods, in contrast to the colored man, to whom he conceded the rather lowly Darwinian descent from the monkey. This was Wagner the scientist, evolutionary theory having arisen during the years between the two essays. As a devout anti-Semite he found unacceptable the Biblical explanation of mankind's origin in an act of the Jewish God. Sweepingly, he declared Aryan and human history to be one, for, without fortifying themselves with an admixture of godly white blood, the colored races could achieve nothing. In this way, Wagner believed, inferior peoples had through the ages drained Aryans of an indigenous purity, their distinguishing godly features being sucked out. It was his purpose in *"Heldentum"* and its artistic counterpart, *Parsifal,* to confront Germany with the seriousness of its racial crisis—to outline the perfection, decline, and hopes for regeneration of the debased Aryan. (Gutman 1968, 421–22)

Obviously Hitler did not need to reinvent racism, an old and well-established European tradition, one that reached explosive new heights in the nineteenth century under the impact of social Darwinism. It was during this century that the older Christian and pagan myths were given new life by the tendentious and distorted slant of evolutionary theory that applied the criterion of survival of the fittest to the social and political behaviors of various groups of human beings. By necessity this new application involved a shift of accent from the interspecies to the intraspecies arena and resulted in drawing wide distinctions between human groups as if they belonged to separate species. The unfortunate psychological need to create pseudospecies for the sake of projection and for the sake of feeling chosen, was an old, established trend, which has been described by Erikson (1968, 41, 240–41, 298–99). Now this trend was augmented by the new rush to separate the fit from the unfit. This is why social Darwinism is inherently racist and accentuates the primitive "us" versus "them" distinction. Hitler, the ideological sponger, soaked it all in from the zeitgeist, and then spewed it all out in a modified version as a new National Socialist revelation.

In a certain sense, Hitler had completed the Grail Quest and challenged the German collective with his findings. Searching for it far away was no longer necessary since it finally became visible to a modern "brave knight" of "pure heart" who has found its location. The precious blood, the divine stuff with a dual magic ability to grant immortality as well as to inflict mortality, was right here on earth and within the veins of the folk. As Vermeil (1956, 195) pointed out, "the Kingdom of the Grail was Germany, of course." Thus one possible interpretation is that the people as a whole became the long-sought-after container of magic. But in spite of the immediacy of the magic stuff, the old hurdle of its invisibility persisted for the plain people. For without proper racial awareness, people still remain oblivious to its existence and significance. Therefore, the old quest continues to take place in an ongoing struggle to make the invisible visible to the masses by means of a constant war against the Jews. Only by opening people's eyes to Jewish duping about race could the people really be made to see their own precious blood.

The central fact that the folk as a whole comprises the container of the magic stuff leads to tricky and dialectical implications. By itself the magical substance that is contained in the veins of the people does not guarantee omnipotence to the folk. Nature decrees that the precious substance is vulnerable to contamination and is itself therefore subject to the dual fate that it can dish out, i.e., immortality versus mortality. However, if the blood has proper guardians who protect its purity, then the decree of fate takes a decided turn for the better. If the magic substance of life-giving blood is protected by a race of people who know its value, then the intact blood invigorates the protectors. This is how the earthly guardians of the magical substance have a chance at exercising godly powers. This opportunity does occur whenever the correct relationship exists between folk and blood. This linked fate of the folk and its blood is both the Achilles heel and the magic wand of a race. And what activates the one or the other is the particular state of the folk's racial consciousness. A deficient awareness reduces the vigilance of protection from contamination and results in enfeeblement, while a high level of racial awareness preserves the purity and health of the all-empowering magic that flows in the folk's veins. One could say that the fate of the folk and its blood is linked because Providence willed it so. Either both decline toward an ignoble end or surge together toward a glorious omnipotence for all eternity, which in Nazi parlance received the operational definition of "a thousand years."

The dual godly aspects of blood—something like blood giveth and blood taketh away—were seized by Nazism as a mental adaptation to the modern shift of power from heaven to earth. Man could play God now by taking control over the manipulation of the magical substance of life and death. And since it goes without saying that men were not created equal, the most meritorious leader of the "chosen" people who were slated by fate to be the master race becomes a human god on earth. Another implication of the blood cult was that protection of the blood from Jews, Bolsheviks, and all other enemies within and without necessitates permanent war. It actually seemed proper that a grab for more power, which is what the safeguarding of the purity of blood represented, was to be accomplished by violence and war. After all, war and violence were spiritually ennobling. This basic sentiment, which penetrated many European radical movements, was given its most forceful early expression by the Frenchman Georges Sorel, who saw violence as beautiful and heroic and who regarded war as the source of morality par excellence (Sternhell 1994, 66–67). It was the increasing public fascination with Sorel's conviction of the absolute indispensability of war that reinforced Hitler's opinion that the world is not for cowardly people. Permanent war for the sake of safeguarding the blood was regarded by him and many others as a spiritual experience that befits a race of heroes. The quest for pure blood represented a quest for a spiritual substance and was therefore expected to evoke the kind of spiritual soul-searching that Hitler himself reportedly underwent during the inner battle between his sentiments and his reason. Such soul struggles over the protection of the blood were bound to be viewed as spiritual. Let us not forget that while the physical existence of the folk was perceived as a container of a divine essence, it was the blood itself that was seen as the true mystical reality within. Blood still remained a biological concept that represented the notion of the inheritance of both physical and mental characteristics.

But since this inheritance included not only visible physical characteristics but also mental dispositions and capacities, the concept of blood transcended biology and evolved into a mystical notion. Holding within it the physical as well as mental inheritance of future generations, it came to symbolize the mystical essence of the folk, its cultural potential and its soul.

With all this in mind, it now becomes easier to understand why for Hitler the Jewish danger constituted a threat to psychophysical integrity. The dual mystical and biological aspects of blood as such already suggest an underlying notion of psychophysical integrity. In addition to that, however, as the folk becomes body while its blood evolves into spirit, notions of sickness and health are bound to revolve around psychophysical integrity. The Jewish menace threatens both body and soul or both material and spiritual reality. As indicated before, the monistic approach to the psychophysical issue links the fate of both aspects of reality. Consequently, blood became a mystical biological concept that has psychophysical integrity as its core promise and psychophysical contamination as its core threat. A proper linking of the national body and soul gives the collective the kind of magical gifts that only the gods could grant: eternal youth in good health. This is why in the folkish state, which secures this proper linkage, the folk comrades will have power and feel rooted and connected by virtue of the shared racial consciousness of being blood brothers. By the way, this included Germans everywhere from the Volga to the Atlantic and the North Sea to the Adriatic. Unlike other states, the folkish state will be a living organism, which would leave no member disconnected. This is the magic of an organic national body in whose veins flows pure blood. It is the divine magic of a complete psychophysical integrity, which is granted only by pure blood.

This sounds almost like a simple stipulation, but its ramifications were horrendous indeed. To secure pure blood, one needs to wage a permanent war against the Jews, which means thoroughly regimenting the folkish state. Regimentation is necessary not only to maintain war vigilance but also in order to meet the enormous psychophysical threat with the kind of total psychophysical state control that would be equal to the task. Pure blood cannot be secured by one battle. It is a permanent war that serves as a continuous and relentless test of the national character. Its demands are so grueling as well as intricate that the people are likely to fail the test for lack of proper guidance unless the folkish state adopts the hierarchical leadership principle. And finally there is also one more catch in the treacherous road to acquire the magic of pure blood. It turns out that what needs to be secured is not just blood but "blood and soil." Hitler picked up this slogan from the folkish (*völkisch*) movement in Germany after World War I. This seemingly harmless slogan referring to the attachment of the farmer to the land was broadened to include the mystical link between members of a highly developed folk and the specific landscapes of their country. It was one more mystical notion referring to the powerful impact of the magical unity of a people and their land. As such it was still another variant of the magical expectations with regard to psychophysical integrity. Territorial expectations were also imbedded in the slogan. David Schoenbaum (1966, 50) viewed the "blood and soil" concept as a new folklore-type expression of antiurban tendencies: "The new folklore was a kind of ideology of the 'Wild East,' with the small homesteader as the cowboy and the Pole as the Indian." Sometimes concepts that float together in the zeitgeist acquire certain overlapping meanings: German attachment to soil in the "Wild East" denotes healthy farming life but also connotes an expanding lebensraum. Moreover, the deadly combination of "blood" with "soil" opened the door even further for the unleashing of an unprecedented racial mania and chauvinistic madness. Under the influence of Nazi ideology, the obsession with these twin concepts escalated into a new dual venture. One was the implementation of a final solution to the Jewish question by exterminating the blood polluters; the second was the safeguarding of the attachment of German colonists to their local soil outside Germany by expanding the German lebensraum through the great drive toward the east. This dual venture retained the underlying mystical link of a totalistic unity and integrity. The enchantment with the magic of blood was about to be converted into the kind of cataclysmic actions through which the messianic drive to secure utopia nets disaster.

3

The Leadership Principle

Heil Hitler!

Hitler's conception of leadership was a very important part of his ideology and served as the glue that tied everything into a unified whole. First and foremost his conception holds magical promises for the people. Its basic premise appears to be quite simple: if the right person becomes supreme leader or dictator, every problem will be solved. But the apparent simplicity of this sweeping promise masks a complexity of interconnected basic assumptions. These assumptions relate to the presumed lessons of German history as well as to the different natures of the German folk and of other races. Hitler took these assumptions very seriously. Although it is true that dictators traditionally seek elaborate excuses in order to justify and explain their power, this seems to have been different in Hitler's case. He was a true fanatic when it came to the racial ideology. The cumulative impression from his writings and speeches is not so much that he looked for excuses for being the absolute leader, but rather that he desperately sought to educate his followers as to the reasons why. In other words, he had a comprehensive weltanschauung that dictated the absolute necessity to implement the leadership principle. Consequently, the education of the masses could not focus solely on the leadership issue but had to include all the major factors of his comprehensive ideology. It had to include everything important ranging from Jews to living space or from racial health to the structure of a folkish state.

This education had to be tailored, of course, to the limited understanding of the masses. What this meant in practice was propaganda. But although it was propaganda, it was nevertheless a serious educational business. Propaganda is vital to a totalitarian system. While there is no free flow of ideas in such a system, those ideas are allowed to be voiced that are considered most important for the functioning of the state. It was the indispensable task of controlled education to convey a comprehensive worldview with such conviction that it would instill faith in the minds of the followers. Without such faith grounded in a proper understanding of Germany's past history and future course, the necessity for the implementation of the leadership principle might not be fully comprehended.

Hitler anchored his leadership theory in a basic tenet of the folkish state. The sacred task of the folkish state is to order life in an ideal fashion that allows the racial merit of the folk to manifest itself in tangible achievements and even to rise from generation to generation. The means toward this end is to provide all individuals with the proper chance to make maximum contributions to the national community according to their personality worth. The goal is to actualize the full expression of the inner racial spirit of the folk. It is all very mystical, of course, as has been noted before, but such notions were prevalent and did reverberate in the German marketplace of ideas. Thus it was clear to Hitler that the folkish state requires an "organic" community of interconnected, obedient individuals who place the collective interest above their own. This organic and very vitalistic conception was contrasted negatively with a mechanistic and rather deadening democratic form of government where disconnected people let the compilation of their combined idiocy and self-seeking become the voted-upon policy of the state.

It can already be seen that, for Hitler and a good deal of the German public, the idea of a folkish state was both a mystical notion and an organizational conception. On both counts it was different from democratic ideals of statehood. The mystical notion included biological as well as cultural aspects of the race. The organizational conception promised a natural ordering of roles in accordance with people's different inherent personalities but in actuality implied coercive aspects of totalitarian control. All of these notions concerning the folkish state revolved around the leadership principle and were markedly inconsonant with traditional democratic ideals and practices. Hitler was vehement in emphasizing the crucial differences between folkish and democratic ideals and practices. For him, democratic practice reinforced mediocre ideas because the small-minded masses enjoyed a majority of numbers and hence the deciding voice. In a way, it is possible to regard democratic rule in Hitler's frame of reference as the complete reverse of the leadership principle. Democratic rule put the limited masses at the helm of leadership while effectively barring the way of the select gifted ones. From Hitler's point of view, this was sacrilege. It worked by a Jewish principle of leveling and stupidity that incapacitated nations in the struggle for survival. In contrast, the folkish state is based on the ideas of racial distinction and personality worth. Consequently it insures that leadership and influence go to the most capable. In this connection, Hitler also wrote that unlike Marxism, which at least recognizes the value of race (while democracies do not) but not the importance of personality, the folkish philosophy is based not only on the notion of racial differences among groups but also of personality differences within a national community (Hitler 1943, 448). It was this latter difference that other systems of government could ignore only at their own peril.

In order to understand Hitler's concept of leadership, it is important to underscore the fact that his ideology emphasized the stratification of merit not only from race to race but also from person to person within the same folkish or racial community. This personal ranking could imply that the quality of a good deal of the human material even within the German community is below par. Such an implication is of course very consonant with a view of the masses as mostly foolish. The remedy that the folkish philosophy provides is to establish an ideal state structure whose constitution and administrative form assures that the best minds, especially political minds, will rise to lead the national community. This line of reasoning was used by Hitler to reach the conclusion that in the folkish state the ultimate decision will be taken by one man (Hitler 1943, 449).

For this reason Hitler advocated a transfer to the folkish state of a principle that worked well for the Prussian army. This is the hierarchic principle of "authority of every leader downward and responsibility upward" (Hitler 1943, 449–50). Authority and responsibility are code words for command and obedience. Hitler claimed that this principle made the

Prussian army the most wonderful instrument of the German people. The implication was that the same principle extended to the entire nation would make it most powerful. And the added implication is that the whole civilian population will become as powerful as the army or, one might say, will itself become like an army. Hitler's followers accepted his leadership dictum officially at the general membership meeting of the Nazi party in Munich on May 22, 1926, at which time the new party program assigned unlimited power to the führer (leader or guide).

Hitler elaborated his conception of leadership in his speech (January 30, 1939) to the Reichstag. Being proud of recent Nazi economic achievements and foreign policy successes, he was quite unwilling to attribute them to any chance factors such as an increase in the prevalence of "genius and energy" (inherent leadership and action potentials) in present as compared to past times. What he basically meant by this was that the racial level or quality of the blood in German veins has not radically changed during his six years in power to account for the recent and dramatic accomplishments. Instead, he attributed the recent rising achievements to the new and better way in which such personality values as genius and energy were being utilized to the full thanks to the implementation of the leadership principle at all levels.

This attribution was straight out of his ideology. The leadership principle assures that all persons are positioned in their proper and most efficient slots and that persons of genius reach top leadership spots. Consequently, the national store of genius is being put to better use than in the past. In like fashion, as a visionary political genius becomes the supreme leader, his political acumen in giving focal expression to the newly unified will of the people guarantees maximal efficiency. From now on, the energies of the masses are given a coordinated direction and are shaped into efficient action. (Despite Hitler's claims, in reality there was a wide discrepancy between the ideology of leadership and the practice of leadership in the Nazi state. Rather than being appointed from above, many leaders were self-selected, and the situation of competing leaders under Hitler resembled at times a chaotic royal court.)

Since Hitler claimed that the efficient utilization of all the members of the folk is the basic racial assumption that underlies the leadership principle, further elaboration of his concept of personality worth is appropriate. Just as the concept of race differentiates peoples on the basis of an inherent biomystical value, so the concept of personality differentiates individuals within a given group on a similar basis. Personality worths are inherent abilities as well as limitations that are determined by nature and defined by blood. The resultant differences in force of personality are therefore ordained by Providence and should be respected by each individual. The different personality merits are actually talents, aptitudes, dispositions, and capacities for many things. They involve a whole variety of skills that are not distributed equally among different individuals. In a democracy, these individual differences are not supposed to hinder opportunity. But in a totalitarian state based on a racial ideology, these different so-called personality worths among individuals are looked at in a special way. They are viewed as an aggregate of usable values that represent the entire racial potential for culture creation and consequently should be under the exclusive control of the folkish state. This particular viewpoint holds that this aggregate of racial worth, these varieties of skills and abilities taken together, comprises the state-building and culture-producing potential of the folk. That is why an efficient utilization of this aggregate was of crucial value in past history and would continue to be so in modern times.

The whole concept is racial to the core. It pointedly refers to differences in human (possibly even subhuman) levels of functioning between different stocks of people as well as within the folk itself. Since the all-important factor of personality worth is distributed unequally among races, some races are superior and some inferior. And since personality worth is also distributed differentially among individuals of the same folk, this stratification within a single folk can become the Achilles heel of the nation given the monumental potential for stupidity that Hitler believed to be inherent in the German masses. If the distribution of personality merits is not systematically organized so as to extract the maximum value from each individual, then too many persons would be placed in wrong slots where they not only cannot contribute by putting their natural skills to use but they can even do harm. Unless such mismatches between personality merits and between assigned roles are avoided, the folk will fail to realize its racial potential. Consequently, its cultural fate, both material and spiritual, will suffer. The members at large of the folk cannot accomplish their racial destiny on their own. It is indispensable that they have guidance, meaning a führer to steer them right. This is why the most meritorious of all personality values is the providential genius of political leadership. This is the superior personality quality that can insure that all other personality worths are indeed being utilized to the full. So powerful is this exceptional gift that its bearer, because of the force of his personality, receives a spontaneous recognition of it from the ranks of the folk comrades.

The leadership principle carried with it an outright rejection of democracy as antiracial and spiritually corrupting. By ruling democracy out, Hitler signaled not only a rejection of stupidity but also a condemnation of cowardice. Cowardice seemed to have crowded out heroism among democratic leaders even in Germany because they did not rise on the basis of personality merit. In vain would one search for an indomitable strength of will among these bankrupt leaders. Thus, looking critically at twentieth-century German history, Hitler preached that the democratic leadership in Germany showed cowardice in decision making as it hid behind the skirts of the so-called majority (Hitler 1943, 82). The majority of people are after all merely befuddled cowards. When their kind of cowardice spills over from the masses to the leadership, it could spell national ruin. As Hitler put it, the world is not for cowardly people. Providence has no use for people unwilling to fight for their existence. In the long run, decline is inevitable with any system that relies on majority decisions and consequently places cowards at the top. The opposite pole of cowardice, the strength of will to fight to survive, can be secured only when ridiculous democratic practices are scrapped and truly folkish ways are used for leadership selection.

Since leadership plays such a fateful role in the life of the folk, Hitler found it necessary to describe several qualifications for a leadership role. In leaders, character should outweigh academic or alleged intellectual suitability. A natural talent for leadership (a talent to make commands obeyed) should take precedence over abstract knowledge. Although knowledge per se is not incompatible with leadership, energy (an ability to generate and sustain action) is more important. Also more important are such leadership qualities as integrity, courage, bravery, and determination. This list of high-sounding qualities seems to reflect a leader's strength of will and ability to make decisions. It is this decisiveness that galvanizes everyone's, but especially the masses' energies, so as to generate effective action. This is why Hitler concluded that in a time of crisis a single energetic man of action outweighs ten feeble intellectuals. Such a leader must be free from numerous prejudices, including any gratuitous, nonsensical code of social morals. Such freedom implies having a clear vision of the actions necessary for the nation's survival and strength, never clouding this long-term historical view with fashionable social conventions, passing interests, or even sheer momentary trivia. This prescription accords with the rest of his January 30, 1939, speech in which he spoke of extending the nation's living space and of the Jewish question. These formed key ingredients in his ideology and were considered by him as fateful issues in German history. Indeed, his attending to these very issues in the context of a discussion of leadership is most significant. It was a signal that he, the supreme leader, was ready to tackle these most momentous, emotionally laden, critical issues decisively, without prejudices or moral compunctions. From his standpoint, he had the right to risk all, counting on Providence to insure that he would gain all.

The indispensable need for potent leadership was connected in Hitler's mind to a very critical view of the masses. While he reserved an exalted role for the supreme leader, his opinion of the masses of followers was far from flattering and resembled the popular ideas of Gustav Le Bon. Hitler probably came by these ideas through secondary sources such as the popularization of Freud's summary of them. Because of the impact of Le Bon's concepts, it would be helpful at this juncture to summarize some of his basic notions.

In describing Le Bon's influence on Italian Fascism, the American political scientist A. James Gregor underscored that the Italian Fascists found especially appealing the notions that the masses are prompted to action by images and that they share collective hallucinations (Gregor 1969, 51, 67). In simpler words, the masses react emotionally rather than intellectually; hallucinations shared by contagion lead them to act in unison. In Italian Fascistic ideology, too, the masses are pliable and inert and need to be shaped by a dominating leader or a small governing elite in order to give direction to the masses' emotional reactivity. Therefore, a recurrent theme in the thinking of Italian Fascists which emerges in Gregor's descriptions is a dichotomy of sentiments and reason that originally had been pointed out by Le Bon (Gregor 1969, 120, 200). Le Bon asserted that the crowds operate mostly unconsciously and are motivated by emotionalism, which he termed "sentiments." In contrast, select individuals operate more consciously and through "reason." Le Bon concluded from this that consequently history itself is characterized by a never-ending battle between reason and sentiments. Moreover, history demonstrates that the destiny of nations has always been determined by what happens in the heart of the masses, which, as noted, is mobilized by sentiments. Since the crowd, i.e., the mass followership, functions through sentiments, it is easy to conclude from Le Bon's work that the operation of reason, which is attributed to select individuals, falls mostly within the realm of leadership. But Le Bon's book largely deals with the psychology of the followership—the crowd (Le Bon 1897).

Psychologically speaking, the crowd operates with mental unity, which catches all members by contagion. This collective mind of sorts is different from the way people think and act as individuals. The crowd is suggestible and hypnotizable. It shares collective hallucinations and can be aroused through sentiments to an exaggerated emotional state. Sentiments was a term that Le Bon used to denote basic emotional reactions clustered around the simplest of images. Sentiments have the double character of simplicity and exaggeration, and that is why crowds—like women—go at once to extremes. Le Bon regarded sentiments as an atavistic residuum of the instincts of primitive man, which retained their power for strong arousal. This arousal is easily evoked by simple symbolic and visual ideas or images. It is never accomplished by complicated intellectual discussions. Crowds can differ in disposition according to national origins. Latin crowds are more reactive and more "feminine" than Anglo-Saxon crowds. Two key concepts of Le Bon were "will" and "faith." Will is more characteristic of leaders, while faith typifies more the followers. The mark of an effective leadership is the ability to evoke the formidable force of faith among the followers. Faith can move mountains. A strong-willed leader who is able to evoke faith is likely to be perceived as having a mysterious quality called "prestige," which is readily felt by the masses. (Nowadays Max Weber's term "charisma" is more in vogue.) At any rate, it is not difficult to conclude from Le Bon's discussions that a strong-willed prestigious or charismatic leader can wield enormous effects over the masses.

At the heart of Hitler's conception of leadership lies a very sharp dichotomy between the leader and the mass of followers. This difference is based on an innate huge gap in personality worth between the former and the latter. The leader is motivated by reason, by will, and is a master of manipulating words. He is also masculine (which goes along with strength of will), and he has a keen racial consciousness that enables him to understand clearly not only the full potential of the German folkish spirit but also the mortal threat of the Jewish anti-folkish otherness. Thus, another leadership qualification was the acquisition through Le Bonian reason of a Weiningerian racially conscious scientific understanding of Jewish racial defects. It has already been mentioned that in his secret conversations Hitler did acknowledge his high esteem of Weininger. Weininger's ideas reinforced in Hitler's mind a view of the Jews that stresses their racial inferiority in cognition and racial talent at being parasites. But Hitler sharpened these ideas. His new understanding of the Jewish racial difference exposed not only the alleged Jewish inferiority but also the presumed Jewish danger of putting into evil use the deadly racial talent to exploit the national achievements of others. In line with Weininger's conception, Hitler also regarded the supreme leader as a genius who fully understands the many lives of the common people. This exceptional capacity was seen as a natural outcome of the enormous inner richness of a genius's personality, which is related to a richness of memories. Unlike the people, whose memory is next to zero, the leader retains meaningful memories that are put into a broader context. He therefore has an uncluttered historical vision that uniquely qualifies him to be the great educator of the masses. All in all, Hitler's glorification of the role of the leader clearly indicates that his cluster of ideas concerning leadership and followership borrowed as heavily from Weininger as it did from Le Bon.

But when it comes to the other side of the dichotomy, as we move away from the leader to the masses of followers, the story becomes much less exalted. In contrast to the leader, the masses of followers are motivated by emotions and sentiments; they operate on faith and are gullibly responsive to word manipulations. Moreover, and this is of crucial importance, they are also feminine. This is an assertion of Le Bon's to which Hitler added the particular feminine attribute that was emphasized by Weininger: lack of higher intelligence. Because of their sheer stupidity, the German masses fail to appreciate the magnitude of the Jewish danger both from the outside and internally. They consequently need guidance if they are to survive. In sum, the characteristics of the masses as seen by Hitler amount to a lethal compilation of the basic mass notions of Le Bon with the gender notions of Weininger. These influences contributed to a further sharpening of the dichotomy of leader and followers and reinforced Hitler's conviction that implementation of the leadership principle is a must for survival. He was convinced that the danger to the existence of the folk stems not only from outside enemies but also from within Germany, where the fickle masses dwell. The implications of all this were ominous indeed. When Le Bon's feminine masses become even more feminine in the specific Weiningerian sense of limited cognition, then they also become, Providence forbid, more Jewish. And being even a little bit like the despicable Jews is being racially inferior. This dire implication accords quite well with the basic racial assumption that personality worth is distributed differently not only among races but even among individuals of a single folk. Clearly the masses formed a dilemma for Hitler, whose predicament was well discerned by the family therapist and psychohistorian Helm Stierlin.

Stierlin noted that in relation to the German people, Hitler appeared ambivalent. The ambivalence involved a contrast between the German nation or folk and the German masses. As a folk or a nation, the Germans connoted power, culture, racial superiority, idealism, and a spirit of sacrifice: "But, to the extent that he viewed them as masses, he judged them contemptuously as unstable, stupid, corrupt, unprincipled, weak, and easily dominated" (Stierlin 1976, 109–10). Stierlin went on to quote from *Mein Kampf:* "The receptivity of the great masses is very limited, their intelligence is small, but their power of forgetting is enormous" (Hitler 1943, 180). From this Stierlin concluded that essentially Hitler voiced here the notions of Le Bon concerning the crowd. However, Hitler's references in the quotation to low intelligence and enormous forgetfulness, as well as Stierlin's entire summation of Hitler's view of the masses, fits better a blend of both Le Bon's and Weininger's ideas.

In detecting a split in Hitler's attitude toward the German people as a marvelous folk yet stupid masses, Stierlin was on to something. His own hypothesis was that Hitler's paradoxical attitude reflected a basic ambivalence toward the primary love object, his mother, who was now resurrected in Germany. That is why he needed not only to adore and idealize Germany but also to castigate and debase it (Stierlin 1976, 110).

The question still remains, however, what does it all mean ideologically and what kind of an underlying psychology does such an ideology reflect? What we are dealing with here is an ideological split of a people's self-image into a glorious nation that is nevertheless composed of stupid masses. Stripped of its ideological attire, the remaining verdict is that the Germans are brilliant dummies. It is that kind of self-image that reverberates with ironic connotations. It suggests that only through brilliance could people become such perfect suckers or that only with a fool's luck could they manage such brilliant achievements. This basic split image of the German collectivity was not unique to Hitler. Germans had a whole heritage of historical perceptions of Germany in past generations as glorious in scientific and cultural achievements but too stupid to unite politically. Germany could beat hands down both France and England combined in its history of music-making but not in its acquisition of colonies. Germans did indeed excel in metaphysics, but it was too bad that they were not also as pragmatic as the British. The ideological repository of the German collective seems to have included this kind of a split self-image, at least since the eighteenth century.

Psychologically speaking, this split image can be bridged by a defensive switch from one pole to its opposite. This comprises the well-known mechanism of switching from an inferiority complex into overcompensation. In this case of underlying German perceptions as reflected in Hitler's ideology, the overcompensating switch is from stupid, weak, and corrupt masses into a cultured, powerful, and racially superior nation. Thus, instead of being permanently saddled with the murky psychological state of being sunk in a fundamentally split self-image, a defense of overcompensation provides a way out of the malaise of ambivalence by a speedy move from feeling inferior to feeling superior. But there is even more to it than that. Given the German flare for metaphysics and the traditional predilection of Germans to flirt with absolutes, the switch reaches even more extreme dimensions. In the realm of absolutes the nadir of inferiority is complete impotence, while the peak of superiority is nothing less than omnipotence itself. The former is, of course, scorchingly shameful and utterly unacceptable while the latter is gloriously exhilarating and saturated with ravishing pride. In Hitler's ideology, the providential leader is the great overcompensator who effects this absolute switch. He therefore becomes equivalent to a talisman in the national psyche. He now has protective magical qualities such that, as long as the nation wears him around its neck, all ventures can be conducted safely. Thus, the leader now has an "ego quality" to use Fenichel's term (1954b). My understanding of Fenichel is that ego quality refers to a special ability of persons, powers, and objects outside one's own ego to be a part of and an extension of one's own ego. Therefore, in spite of their being located outside the ego, all of these beings or objects are nevertheless still shared by it. Somehow one's own ego succeeds in partaking of them. This of course is magical thinking. By endowing external objects with one's own ego quality, one imagines that one is able even to siphon off any of their envied characteristics. How much all of this stands for an extension of self at the price of a diffusion of self remains a good question. Clearly all this represents a retrieval of the lost powers of an omnipotent infant narcissism, an omnipresent animism, and also a kind of diffused magic that disregards the boundaries that separate self from nonself. But this is what makes it possible to cross over from one self to another and partake in it. And it does pay off to connect magically with a miraculous leader who serves as a talisman. By clinging to such a talisman, which stores a mighty power and also has an ego quality to boot, everyone could now feel safe by virtue of a protective magical insurance. And it was this added ego quality of the talisman, that mysterious special relationship that allows for sharing the power, that also made the mystical connection and magical participation possible. Thus, the leadership principle has in effect offered the added advantage of magic as an answer to the racial existential question. The basic question was how on earth could the flawed Germans, the brilliant dummies of sorts, ever face up successfully to the danger posed by the Jews.

We have seen how, with a blend of concepts borrowed from Le Bon and Weininger, Hitler was presented with the dilemma of what to do about masses who hold racial promise that can be realized provided that their inherent stupidity can be neutralized. And we have seen that his answer was to provide the masses with that kind of an exceptional genius leader who also is a blend of Le Bon's and Weininger's ideas. Two discussions in *Mein Kampf* demonstrate how central for Hitler were these borrowed notions that were part of the zeitgeist before and after the First World War. One passage that was mentioned before relates to his soul's struggle resulting in his greatest personality transformation. As his "reason" resisted his "sentiments" to go easy on the Jews, he not only had become a scientifically informed anti-Semite but also had been transformed from a person who functions by sentiments (a follower) into a person who operates by reason (a leader). The ascendancy of "cold reason" at the end of Hitler's so-called "bitter struggle" can be taken to signal a capacity to lead by cold logic without moral compunctions (Hitler 1943, 55). Le Bon's notion of the importance of reason as a leadership function has already been highlighted here, and it was later underscored by Hitler in his speeches.

The particular flavor of the term "reason" as used by Hitler can be gleaned from pertinent examples taken from his speeches. In a speech of August 1, 1923, he warned of the danger of "the dictatorship of a Jewish lord of finance" and declared: *"We want to be the supporters of the dictatorship of national reason, of national energy, of national–brutality and resolution, Germany can be saved only through action, when through* our talking here the bandage has been torn from the eyes of the last of the befooled" (de Roussy de Sales 1941, 66). Hitler's clever use of words with strong and well-known political associations clearly suggests that his central message in the above quotation was that, in the face of the dangers of a Jewish dictatorship as well as a communist dictatorship of the proletariat, he was summoning the opposing force of his dictatorship of National Socialism. He went on to assert in the speech that Germany could be saved only through action and that his movement would bring redemption as the will of Germany proved stronger than the spirit of international Jewry. The speech, therefore, contained a few of his standard leitmotivs, such as the mortal dangers, the fooled masses, and the promise, no less, of redemption. But the list of remedies started with "national reason," which was linked to energy, brutality, resolution, and, a bit later, action. From the way "reason" was cross-connected here with other loaded terms it most likely stood for an action-oriented analysis of the racial situation without allowing any form of tender-heartedness to interfere with the folkish state's national interest.

The Hitlerian concept of "reason" was further clarified in a September 3, 1933, speech. In discussing nature, Hitler indicated that higher achievements come only by placing the powers of many in the service of a single idea, a single conception, and a single will so as to unite them in a single action. It is reason that counsels individuals to sacrifice a part of their individual freedom and subject themselves to a single will. The right of the stronger to subject others to his will is seen in nature and can be regarded as the sole conceivable right because it is founded on reason. Hitler also discussed the key notions of command and obedience within the German folk and among different races. Within the German folk, the relationship of command and obedience was to be determined by the different personality values of the folk members. Association of Aryans with other races was to be based not on the mixture of blood (which would be sinful of course) but on an organic community of purpose by which he meant a practical cooperation as needed. In this context Hitler reached the conclusion that the supremacy of the master people should not be arbitrary and must be controlled by "a noble reasonableness" (de Roussy de Sales 1941, 199–200). So "reason" is the reason why in the final analysis one people must be ready to assert its will over others!

A further implication of this emphasis on dominance leads toward a tautological justification of the leadership principle. But there is something else to it. The subjugation of the many under the will of the few, or even the single leader, goes back to the notion of the right of the stronger, which can be found in nature, or to the notion of the capacity to subdue, which was given by Providence. For Hitler this natural right was founded on reason. Consequently "reason" became a distorted Darwinian concept of survival of the racially fittest. It is a survival of only those nations or folks that are able to concentrate their working capacity by means of placing the energy and action of the many under the overall control of the single will of an exceptional personality. "Reason," therefore, implies a successful struggle for collective survival by the uncompromising imposition of the leadership principle.

We now come to the second passage from *Mein Kampf* that also demonstrates how heavily Hitler borrowed from zeitgeist notions. This particular passage clearly fuses concepts that are derived from both Le Bon and Weininger by attributing femininity and a longing to be dominated to the masses, who are overwhelmingly motivated by emotion rather than reason. In a famous passage in the second chapter of the first volume of *Mein Kampf,* Hitler declared:

> The psyche of the great masses is not receptive to anything
> that is half-hearted and weak. Like the woman, whose
> psychic state is determined less by grounds of abstract
> reason than by an indefinable emotional longing for a force
> which will complement her nature, and who, consequently,
> would rather bow to a strong man than dominate a weak-
> ling, likewise the masses love a commander more than a
> petitioner and feel inwardly more satisfied by a doctrine,
> tolerating no other beside itself, than by the granting of
> liberalistic freedom with which, as a rule, they can do little,
> and are prone to feel that they have been abandoned.
> (Hitler 1943, 42)

That a woman has an "emotional longing for a force which will
complement her nature" was a commonplace idea of the time that
Weininger (1906, 26–52) wrote about in his laws of sexual attraction,
which stem from the rules of gender complementarity. Weininger even
claimed that highly masculine men exert greater influence on other men
(Weininger 1906, 51–52). Likewise, Hitler's emphasis on the craving
for a strong commander (a feminine desire for a manly man) bearing a
single doctrine (satisfying the need for simple images) is a reaffirmation of characteristics that both Weininger and Le Bon attributed to the
masses. Weininger attributed to them femininity and low intelligence,
while Le Bon described them as feminine and being swayed by simple
images. Hitler's advocacy of only one admissible "doctrine, tolerating
no other beside itself," did indeed keep matters simple and thoroughly
totalitarian.

Hitler was probably a borderline personality with a deeply split
ego as asserted by Robert Waite (1977, 356–59), but he was by no means
stupid. He had the gift, so important for leaders, of sensing accurately
the mood of the masses. In response to a longing that he detected among
the German masses, he evolved into an erotic dominator, a cross between a feared rapist and a beloved seducer, of his German audience.
His speeches frequently culminated in just about an orgasmic frenzy. In
symbolic as well as metaphorical language, it is possible to suggest that
with a towering grandiosity, unbending will, and stiff posture Hitler served
as the erect public penis which again and again thrust at the receptive

German audiences and threw them into explosive excitement. The prolonged Nazi rallies usually led to peak experiences in which the mesmerizing Hitler was able to stand apart from the intoxicated crowd, while at the very same time meshing with it in an exalted union. The well-crafted staging was no mere coincidence. Hitler's entire conception of leadership called for such acts. The situation called for someone from among the people who knew them perfectly well exactly because he was certifiably one of them, i.e., someone who had "ego quality" that could be magically shared. At the very same time that special someone had also to stand apart from the people so as to emerge into the unique position of a spellbinding dominator and talisman.

We discussed two passages from *Mein Kampf:* one concerning Hitler's personality transformation and switch from sentiments to reason, and another concerning the need of the feminine masses to be dominated by a strong-willed leader. Taken together, the two suggest that Hitler actually used the doctrine of the force of will as the glue that bound Le Bon's and Weininger's notions together. To reiterate, if the masses are as feminine as Le Bon and Weininger suggested and in consequence their judgment is deficient and shaky, then perforce the masses need and love to be dominated because domination brings with it clearer convictions and a strengthened will. Hitler's diagnosis was that the masses suffer from an inherent deficiency in strength of will, which in turn creates a natural yearning to be dominated by a strong-willed leader. Such a leader does not need to rape his people into submission. He shows strength and they yield happily. Thus, given feminine masses, a strong-willed masculine leader uses reason cunningly to control the emotions/sentiments of the multitudes. What Hitler sensed correctly was that it takes two to tango and that his personal success would be due not only to his overwhelming drive for power but also to the masses' willingness to dance. History bore him out. He fully outlined his conception of leadership in *Mein Kampf,* which was published in 1925 and 1926. Later he followed it faithfully during his reign in the 1930s and 1940s. The masses were receptive indeed. In retrospect it seems that he rightly sensed that many Germans longed for the pleasure of being dominated.

It was at a speech on May 10, 1933, that Hitler drew clear distinctions between the leader and the masses (de Roussy de Sales 1941, 162–72). He portrayed the average man as limited in his capacity to see the connection between his daily experiences and the fate of the community as a whole. Consequently, political and moral crises or even an impending national collapse are not sensed by the average man unless they affect his pocketbook. The people remain woefully ignorant even of life and death issues. This limited understanding on the part of the masses blinds them to the destructive effects of internal splits in Germany. Hitler believed that the whole nation was damaged by a warfare, or class struggle, which had been caused by selfish employers' organizations, by trade unions that were incited by Marxism to use the general strike as an instrument of war for the destruction of the state, and finally by the state itself, which no longer was an objective institution standing above the parties. Hitler regarded it as unfortunate that during these dangerous times the ordinary German was inclined to fix his gaze on international economic aid instead of looking squarely at his own internal life. For him the answer lay in the elimination of the domestic infighting that he equated with a state of impotence. Any future aggressive international ventures could be launched only from a unified and immeasurably strengthened internal power base.

His prescribed remedy came, therefore, as no surprise. A state leadership must be set up that is independent of any one stratum of society so as to form "the dictatorship of the people, i.e., the dictatorship of the whole people, the community." This general prescription was immediately personalized: "I am perhaps more capable than anyone else of understanding and realizing the nature of the whole life of the various German castes . . . Fate in a moment of caprice or perhaps fulfilling the designs of providence, cast me into the great mass of the people, amongst common folk. . . . So fate has perhaps fitted me more than any other to be the broker. . . . I am an independent man. . . . The masses are certainly often dull. . . . Because I know this people better than any other, and at the same time know the rest of the people, I am not only ready in this case to undertake the role of an honest broker but I am glad that destiny can cast me for the part" (de Roussy de Sales 1941, 169–72). The occasional "perhaps" rings false.

The gist of Hitler's message is that the new authority, meaning himself, will be independent of momentary currents of contemporary opinion. Hitler saw in his leadership something akin to the Weiningerian conception of a man of genius with a visionary ability to distinguish lasting meaning and value from the transitory flow of petty events and opinions. Weininger's ideas concerning the genius and the timeless man filled the zeitgeist and were profusely floating in the air. And Hitler who was inundated by these ideas was thoroughly convinced that he himself, who has retained his memories and placed them in significant contexts, was going to be independent of the momentary. He could therefore rightfully state: "I am an independent man."

In this connection it is also worth noting that being an independent man was associated in Hitler's mind with heroic thinking. As he asserted in a later speech on September 1, 1933, "to save a nation one must think heroically. But the heroic thinker must always be willing to renounce the approval of his contemporaries where truth is at stake" (de Roussy de Sales 1941, 197). This means that at a certain point the heroic leader stands alone, having only his iron will to sustain him in determining the truth and making independent decisions that could save the nation. The inherent promise in this speech during his first year in power was that, through his independent and heroic thinking Germany could be saved.

The implementation of the leadership principle signified an enormous strength and power surge that comes from a homogeneous unity of the collective. As Hitler put it two days later in another speech: "Man as an individual, whatever powers he may have in himself, will be incapable of higher achievements unless he can place the powers of the many in the service of a single idea, a single conception, a single will, and can unite them in a single action" (de Roussy de Sales 1941, 199).

The enticing reward that Hitler held before the people in return for their subjugation to the hierarchy and uniformity of the leadership principle was the promise of magic power. Risky ventures could be embarked on with invincibility because the implementation of the leadership principle worked like a magic power formula. The formula was deceptively simple and could seem like reiteration of traditional notions. It opposed internal splits within the group members and commanded them to express their unity through the focal medium of the supreme leader. Nevertheless, it was a far cry from merely being another repetition of a typical call for unity by party leaders or union leaders. Hitler was not singing a traditional unity song; he was exploiting deeper concepts than those of the standard notions of harmony's being preferable to working at cross-purposes. His magic power formula was meant to satisfy the strong yearnings for national health and effectiveness. Even though the deeper concepts were fished out of the zeitgeist pool, they seemed fresh rather than trite. They tapped a yearning for and faith in doing things in such an intuitively right way that something clicked, and the general public thought itself transcended into a new dimension of a hitherto unmatched potency. In such precious moments of magic, it matters not whether this new dimension is perceived as external Providence or as an internal ego-surge. Either way it is a matter of faith that triggers a metamorphosis. The magic occurs when certain perceptions combine to create the clicking, i.e., the "it feels right" conviction whereby a person senses that he finally gets to play a truly competent role.

But it should be borne in mind that when something seems to click and magic is ushered in, the impact is wholistic. Wholistic frequently means that the whole is more than the sum of the parts. That "more" is viewed by its adherents as the outcome of a creative group process that generates something extra; examples in the Nazi period are vitalism, mysticism, and even pure racism. Wholistic can also mean a psychological regression to a less differentiated state: the less differentiation the more wholism. Either way it is felt as something distinctly magical. For those who experience it, the sense of magic has an overall quality to it that does not derive from any conscious analysis of how it can be broken down into its various components. Nevertheless, for the purpose of this discussion, it may be helpful to look at some of the major components that contribute to the overall feeling of potent transformation.

A necessary contributor to the final sense of magic is the basic conviction that the very essence of a historical malady is finally being tackled in earnest. This perception is necessary for a sense of mastery. The appearance of trying to avoid real problems or to offer fake solutions is enough to spoil the magic. But Hitler did not make that mistake. When he castigated internal splits and divisions, he was rendering a basic verdict on German history. National disunity meant dismemberment, shrinkage, devastating wars (religious or otherwise), exploitation by powerful nations, vulnerability to internal enemies, and enfeeblement across the board. In short, internal splits were the fully proven historical recipe for impotence and catastrophe. It was a simple idea or image in the best tradition of Le Bon. As the diagnosis of internal splits rang true, the prescribed cure of a powerfully imposed rigorous unity looked valid. By and large, therefore, Hitler succeeded in conveying the conviction that this time the true essence of Germany's historical misfortunes was being confronted head-on without the least signs of weakness, half-heartedness, or buckled knees.

This brings us to another major ingredient of the magic: the issue of who is doing the confronting. Obviously it was not yet another coward in the mold of the leaders of old, since the convincing was done this time by the grand seducer of indomitable will. It thus seemed to the receptive audience that at long last the real problems were being handled correctly by the right heroic person. He was the acknowledged folkish genius; hence for a change the national efforts were directed in the smartest possible way. He towered above all, personifying the grandiose national extended self. By being aligned with him and directed by him, each individual not only beheld the grandiose national self in the person of the leader but was also able to partake in a share of this might and grandeur. And it was this sense of sharing that enhanced the magical feeling of a benevolent transformation.

This perception validated the racial notion of personality worth upon which the leadership principle has been founded. It was taken to be a rule of nature, so that compliance carried with it the invincible force of nature. This put the power of faith behind the leadership principle.

The German racial bias assigned the greatest potential to the German race by virtue of a superior biological endowment of the group. By the same token, the selection of the ideal supreme leader by force of personality was also anchored in the notion that the leader was biologically the most gifted individual. The unity of the leader's will with the people's will was therefore a powerful fusion of group and individual merits. This combination guaranteed that the collective racial potential would now be actualized. Put differently, the Nazi belief in German racial superiority reinforced the elementary feeling that the leadership principle would generate a power surge. To reiterate, since Hitler's leadership notions were based on a principle of racial efficiency, raw racism, which was prevalent in Germany, contributed mightily to the belief that magic potency was at hand.

Racism, however, included a set of virulent prejudices concerning the existence of the negative and menacing Jewish race. The existence of the Jews acquired a far greater metaphysical significance than merely the convenient availability of a scapegoating opportunity. The Jews served as a major explanation for why this world was diseased and totally messed up. By blaming the Jews, the Nazis were not just providing excuses for their own feelings of impotence, but were also seemingly taking major action toward regaining omnipotence, or at least mighty potency. To them, dealing with the Jews through cold reason without sentiments represented the start of a necessary extirpation of disease and a symbolic expression of fast healing and regaining of health. Another way of putting it would be to say that a racially correct diagnosis was already equated with taking action. Since a correct diagnosis seemed to constitute half the cure, the process of self-help had already taken its first action. And action, which is the antidote to inaction, possessed a magic quality for a people who were frustrated by a sense of helplessness in the face of a seemingly unfair history.

There was one more magic ingredient, however, thrown into the mix. It promised satisfaction of the voracious appetite, fulfillment of the limitless greed, the gobbling up of the rest of the world, and the guaranteeing of winning in a winner-takes-all global game. In this sense of cosmic avarice, even the acquisition of an extended German lebensraum would represent merely a down payment. The German master race was going to become master of the globe. It mattered not that foreigners regarded Hitler as a madman who was obsessed with the dream of "today Germany belongs to us and tomorrow the whole world." What did matter was that a belief in racial superiority legitimized a superior appetite at the expense of inferior others. Hitler's rhetoric made the big grab or the hitting of the universal jackpot seem within reach. The voracious appetite could be satisfied only by initiating national action. And this scooping up of everything, this residue of an infantile urge to swallow all, has retained its old and magical essence. This was the final wondrous ingredient that, when it was added to the total mix, made magic click.

The avarice for world domination was reinforced in Hitler by the popular spread of the fabricated ideas that were contained in the infamous forgery concerning a Jewish conspiracy for world domination known as *The Protocols of the Elders of Zion,* also known as *The Proto-*

cols of the Wise Men of Zion. We have already discussed other ideological aspects that entered into Hitler's conception of leadership. In this connection we have unveiled the lethal interaction that took place when Weininger's ideas were paired with those of Le Bon. Of equal impact was the outcome of the pairing of the notions of the *Protocols* with Le Bon's ideas.

As noted in chapter 2, Gustave Le Bon's book on the psychology of crowds, which came out in France in 1895, had deeply influenced the following generations (Le Bon 1897). It was a timely book coming out as it did during the fin-de-siècle days of the nineteenth century corresponding with the well-noted phenomenon of the emergence of mass man. This phenomenon was to remain a major preoccupation of the twentieth century. Le Bon's work left a deep impact on Sigmund Freud and served as a major impetus for his writing a book on group psychology in which he acknowledged his indebtedness to Le Bon. Robert Waite (1977, 122) was one of several authors who emphasized that many of Hitler's propaganda techniques for enforcing his will on the masses appeared to come from Le Bon whose book was translated into German in 1908. He therefore concluded that "Hitler's indebtedness to Le Bon bordered on plagiarism." Clearly Hitler, who was always fishing for usable ideas and images in the zeitgeist pool, was unconcerned with issues of copyright. Once he reused these ideas and manipulated them for political impact, they were all his anyway. And Le Bon's ideas were readily available. It is quite likely that many Germans, including Hitler who came by many ideas through secondary sources, had learned about Le Bon's ideas through Freud or through popularized reports about Freud and Le Bon. At any rate, it is obvious from reading *Mein Kampf* that the book is saturated with Le Bon's ideas. Hitler was most definitely impressed with Le Bon's notions of the peculiar psychology of the crowds.

It was Konrad Heiden who underscored the great importance of the pairing of Le Bon's ideas concerning how to influence and manipulate the masses with the lethal notions of secret conspiracies for world domination that are embedded in the anti-Semitic *Protocols of the Wise Men of Zion.* The first chapter of Heiden's perceptive book *Der Fuehrer* includes a very poignant analysis of some of the undercurrents of nineteenth-century Europe that heralded the coming of the more predominant twentieth-century condition of mass man and global politics (Heiden

1944). To make a long story short, Heiden focused on the *Protocols* as an actual blueprint for world domination. Peel away the anti-Jewish layers and you are left with a world domination manual for the use of clever and ambitious politicians who are keenly aware of the new opportunities that have opened up in the modern era of mass man. And the all-important means to this grandiose accomplishment are elaborated not only in the *Protocols* but also in even greater detail in Le Bon's book. The book's basic message is that if you know the psychology of the crowds, you already know how to manipulate the masses. In other words, the major historical lesson to be drawn from the book is that in this new age of mass man, political control of masses on a previously unprecedented scale has become quite possible. And as the means of manipulation widened in scope, so did the ambitions. This is the all-important lesson to be drawn as the infamous *Protocols* were paired with Le Bon's work. The horrendous lesson was that nothing less than world domination could now be coveted.

It was clear to Heiden that the true sense of the *Protocols* is the conviction that world domination is possible if one succeeds in tapping the underlying magical current of modern society. This magical current creates the same thoughts among the masses who expect great things from their rulers. It is this very expectation that makes great things much easier to accomplish. Heiden therefore traced in great detail the history of the different developmental stages of the evolution of the *Protocols* from their various sources. He noted especially the crucial contributions of the French lawyer Maurice Joly, who discovered what Heiden termed "the secret disease of his epoch" (Heiden 1944, 6). The disease is the new aspiration for world domination, an inherent secret in the mechanism of contemporary existence. The secret spirit of the age is that men can easily be satisfied and dominated by a clever mind. Joly understood the meaning of domination in relation to the modern masses and their state of mind. The example of Napoleon III before his downfall showed that conspiracies, crimes, and power only make the masses admire their rulers even more (Heiden 1944, 7). Subsequently this new understanding fell upon fertile ground in tsarist Russia, where the Ochrana secret police manufactured the latest versions of the *Protocols*. It was part of a counterrevolutionary conspiracy to forge a new state power based on the passions of the people.

The Protocols of the Wise Men of Zion consisted of a forgery promulgated by the Ochrana, the tsarist secret police. They were actually a Russian compilation and elaboration of earlier versions that had appeared in France and Germany. The central theme of this fabrication of alleged historical protocols is that elderly Jewish leaders conduct secret meetings in which they plot to gain world domination for the Jews. This theme of a secret Jewish conspiracy to rule the world represented among other things distorted interpretations by anti-Semites of the significance of the first Zionist congress, which was held at Basel, Switzerland, in 1897 (Cohn 1970, 112–13). The earlier and different versions of it circulated during the first decade of the twentieth century. More elaborate versions followed. Commenting on the arrival of the *Protocols* to Germany in 1919, Alfred Rosenberg stated that "millions suddenly found in them the explanation of many previously unexplainable present-day phenomena." This reaction accords with the best tradition of the dawning of a new "insight" in the form of a paranoid "ah-ha" effect. The "revelatory" *Protocols* spread throughout Europe and finally reached the United States, where they were published a year after Hitler's rise to power courtesy of Henry Ford. The American version of *The Protocols of Zion* included a selection of anti-Semitic articles that were published by Henry Ford's paper the *Dearborn Independent* during 1920–1922. This particular edition of the *Protocols* was privately published without identifying the publishing house (Marsden 1934). It also had the slogan "United We Stand, Divided We Fall" preceding the book's title. Clearly the automobile tycoon Henry Ford was not flouting a union slogan but sounding the alert for people to band together so as to oppose a secret global conspiracy. Bearing in mind the earlier discussion of Hitler's ominous perceptions concerning not only what the Jews do but also how they do it, it should be mentioned here that the *Protocols* specified not only goals but also methods of implementation. The wide popularity and persistent influence of the *Protocols* in advocating new ideas concerning both goals and means suggest that they were successful in tapping something important that belonged to the spirit of the time.

We are finally able to bring together the major ideological influences on Hitler's notion of leadership and in the process conclude our discussion of the ingredients that contributed to Hitler's magical impact on his followers. As we now juxtapose the various ideological components that Hitler embraced, we arrive at an explosive formula. We have already noted how horrific was the outcome of the pairing of Le Bon's with Weininger's thoughts. The blending of their ideas yielded a particularly dichotomous conception of the leader versus the masses. The cognitively limited masses who operate through imagery, simple ideas, and contagion (according to Le Bon) were now also seen as devoid of memory, feminine, and impressionable (according to Weininger). To Hitler this meant that the masses were feminine because they were racially inferior to variable degrees due to limited personality values. And because of this saturation with femininity, the masses craved domination and desperately needed a uniquely strong-willed leader. It is that kind of leader who knows how to use reason and how to evoke faith through clever manipulation of the masses while catering to their sentiments. Hitler followed Le Bon in this. But by seeing himself as a masculine mind of significant memory and historical vision, he also claimed the mantle of the Weiningerian genius, who understands people's lives better than anyone else, and who by personal merit has every right to manipulate the inferior masses. Moreover, he even has a holy duty to do just that since the masses are too inept to take care of themselves. In sum, pairing Le Bon with Weininger yielded the dichotomy of manipulatable, gullible multitudes and of a genius single leader whose complete independence and freedom of action carried with it fantastic prospects.

We have also just witnessed how deadly were the results of Konrad Heiden's pairing of Le Bon's notions with the ideas of the *Protocols of the Wise Men of Zion*. The outcome of this pairing was that to the knowledge of the impressionable character of the masses, as attested to by Le Bon, was now added a new awareness of the general masses' secret craving for world domination, according to Heiden's interpretation of the *Protocols*. The lesson learned from Le Bon that mass manipulation is now possible on an unprecedented scale was being applied as the new updated means to reach the most ambitious target as identified by the *Protocols*: world domination. This provoking combination of means and goals, which was arrived at by combining Le Bon with the *Protocols,* was potentially very explosive.

When all these three sources of ideological influence are allowed to interconnect, the lethal outcome is indeed worthy of a Hitler. His melange of borrowed zeitgeist notions can be added together to yield a powerful combination of leadership concepts, which he advocated with fanaticism. The resultant formula can be paraphrased and summed up briefly in the following manner: Take a Weiningerian genius, who is not only fully aware of the Aryan racial superiority but who also knows the Jewish enemy for what he is, and who is a supreme leader of unmatched strength of will; endow him with elementary yet potent knowledge of manipulating the feminine masses as taught by all three sources but mostly by Le Bon; use the leader's will to evoke the followers' faith, which, according to Le Bon, can move mountains; finally, dangle right in front of the submissive people the very alluring prospect of world domination, which is the most coveted secret aspiration of both leaders and followers as can be learned from the *Protocols,* and the results will work like magic and are guaranteed to shake the world.

Hitler knew how to mingle ingredients so as to produce magic. The tackling of the proven historical maladies, the genius leader, the deep racial convictions of German natural superiority as well as of the need to deal with the Jewish disease, and finally the seeming feasibility of reaching everywhere and grabbing everything—all of these coalesced into a feeling of faith that was put at the disposal of the supreme leader's will. And a united single will was the executive principle that endowed action with magic potency. Thus in an April 8, 1933, speech, Hitler asserted that Germany could possess unheard-of strength through an inner will tempered like steel. Consequently it was the adoption of the leadership principle, which consisted of loyalty and blind obedience, that gave the movement the power to surmount everything. Similarly in a January 15, 1936, speech, he reaffirmed the conviction that only a single will could sweep the whole nation with it. If a leadership has the courage to make its will into that of the nation, it could reform the German people for centuries (de Roussy de Sales 1941, 159–60, 343–44). Clearly Hitler regarded the strength that comes from fusing the nation into a single will as limitless in time. In other words, the implementation of the leadership principle yields eternal omnipotence. No wonder that the cry "one Reich, one Folk, one Leader" became one of the most heralded slogans in the Third Reich.

It was a magic power formula. The projected fusion of the entire people into a unity of a single will created a sensation of a power surge.

The old days of impotence due to internal splits were now history. They were replaced by a flashing sense of elation as the act of fusion reinforced feelings of a grandiose national self projected by the leader. The followers, on whom the magic power formula worked, experienced a wholistic sense of might and well-being. Capitalizing on this faith, Hitler was not tardy in indicating where, if not always how, the new power would be applied.

Two major goals formed Hitler's two-track course of action. These were the solutions of the Jewish problem and the problem of population density with limited space. For health and security, a full purification from Jews by a variety of means was necessary. For self-sufficiency and for the sake of taking a major step toward world domination, the acquisition of a larger lebensraum was necessary. Both necessities were targeted as the just rewards of mighty power that comes from competent leadership. Neither could be accomplished without the genius at the helm who considered them a matter of justice and honor. Justice implied the correction by might of past historical wrongs. Honor implied that action was imperative since inaction was tantamount to dishonor and unbearable shame. The time was coming to stake all and see what magic could do.

4

The Expansion of the Living Space

We need have no fears for our own future. I shall leave
behind me not only the most powerful army, but also a
Party that will be the most voracious animal in world
history.

There comes a time when this desire for expansion can no
longer be contained and must burst into action.
                    —Adolf Hitler, *Hitler's Secret Conversations*

We have seen that Hitler, the self-appointed political genius, prescribed
the leadership principle as the indispensable magical tool for implementing all the requirements of racial destiny. Moreover, by mid-1933 he
presumably had become that folk-appointed supreme leader that the leadership principle so clearly mandated. Being the right person in the right
position, he knew what was happening and what had to be done to effect
national recovery. At long last the degrading national impotence was
being neutralized by the establishment of the leadership principle at all
levels of the central nervous system, so to speak, of the folkish state. As
the national energy was thus being restored and the power to act fully
centralized, the time was finally coming to do what was so long overdue: to unleash the radical actions necessary to implement a total metamorphosis akin to nothing less than rebirth. This longed-for national
resurrection implied a complete psychological switch from a feeling of
impotence to one of near omnipotence. It was within this psychological

framework that the ability to take ultimate actions assumed new and unprecedented meanings of potency and invincibility.

What Hitler had in mind, as indicated earlier, was a two-pronged action that was mandated by his ideology. In his weltanschauung of a psychophysical racial health, both courses of action were closely interwoven and interdependent. What he specifically wished to do was to reach out for world domination by expanding the German living space, or lebensraum, while at the very same time cleansing the earth thoroughly of Jews and everything else they stood for such as bolshevization, poisoning, racial decay, enslavement, and death. The cleansing of the living space could produce greater homogeneity and internal unity, which translated into greater power, because the will of the more homogenized collective becomes even more unified and focused. Similarly, the expansion of the living space could produce more material resources but less oppressive crowdedness. These new conditions were bound to lead not only to greater wealth, but also to lesser internal dissension and greater internal harmony, as the physical and psychological impacts of deprivation and crowdedness were alleviated. Once again it was expected that the increased resources and internal unity would generate greater power with which to face whatever enemies were still left, both within and without the mighty and expanding folkish power base. In other words, using the catapulting power of the leadership principle, which was now implemented throughout the folkish state, the providential magician on top was going to multiply this power geometrically by a dual and mutually reinforcing action. The two linked and forceful courses to follow were the cleansing, as well as the expansion, of the existential "must": the lebensraum. Underlying both courses of action was the desired metamorphosis from extreme weakness to the heights of strength. While the urge to purge accentuated the desire to do away with sickness and to eliminate impotence, the drive to expand focused on rectifying historical injustice and on exercising power. Rudolph Binion correctly emphasized the great importance of this "double track" where one political track ran to Auschwitz, the other to Stalingrad. He also speculated that for Hitler personally, the Jewish track was of greater importance for satisfying his own unconscious needs (Binion 1979, 85). Be that as it may, the two main political courses formed an inseparable ideological package deal. This was so because Jews, Marxists and other enemies, both within and without, were all the same and were all presumed responsible for Germany's diminished size and strength.

From the very start, the notion of the dual application of the newly won national magic power involved the riddle of limits versus limitlessness. The expectation that things would progress in stages implied a limited beginning (expanded German living space) as well as a limitless end (world domination). The true limits of cleansing and of expansion were left somewhat vague yet ominously open-ended. It was not entirely clear how far cleansing could go before the diseased national body, not to mention the whole sick world, would be considered finally free from racial infection. It was not specified how many Jews and others must be extirpated by whatever means before the feeling of security, which comes from an integrated sense of psychophysical health, sets in. Nor was it spelled out how long this cleansing process would last, as it was most likely going to be prolonged by the concurrent process of the expansion of the living space. The latter process, after all, inevitably involved the enlargement of areas to be cleansed as well as possible increases in the number of "disease agents," which would need to be identified and removed from the expanded area by whatever a method left to be specified. Hitler set out to cleanse not just the national body but all of Europe, even the world, otherwise the disease would not be licked. Thereon hinged a contradiction as discussed by Binion (1983). Theoretically, German expansionist interest lay in exporting its Jews to potential enemy countries (France, England, the United States), thereby weakening those countries. Yet by making other countries less receptive to accepting Jews, the Nazi policy of exporting anti-Semitism compromised the policy of exporting Jews. But Hitler's messianic anti-Semitism nevertheless impelled him to export anti-Semitism while doing France (etc.) the favor of killing French Jews at Germany's expense. Such contradictions, however, could be ultimately resolved as events would move in the direction of limitless, rather than limited, goals. "Removal" of the Jews could thus progress from pressure to emigrate to forced expulsion and finally to extermination.

Looming large over the whole question of limits was the issue of how much should the living space expand. What would constitute justice? How far should German boundaries expand? If the expansion were to proceed in stages, would it someday encompass the whole world after an anticipated intercontinental settling of scores with America? Whatever the limits were going to be, their mere hovering over the racial ideological horizons constituted a dizzying stuff for the leader and also for the masses.

Such questions, which were implied in the ideological package deal of Nazism, were not really meant to be answered by the increasingly homogenized masses who were supposed just to put their unquestioning faith at the disposal of their leader's will. The people were simply expected to respond with a leap of faith and get caught up with an elation that comes about as they make a dash from the confines of realistic power toward the domain of illusionary omnipotence. This represents a fascinating psychological phenomenon. Very deep in the recesses of their minds, the people may occasionally still have sensed that such a gigantic power grab was impossible and that it would mean that somewhere down the road the next so-called collapse would inevitably come. After all, since this enchanting magical cure by Hitler for the ignominious collapse during the previous world war was constructed at the expense of reality, it consequently carried with it the seeds of the next collapse in a second world war. People may have had dim realizations that when the myth of omnipotence would be finally punctured, the horrendous consequences would most likely involve the recurrence of a major catastrophe, a repetition of the trauma. But any such dim realizations fell far short of the German people's ability to apply the brakes to the unfolding process. Apparently there was an irresistible collective need to relive the trauma of the First World War as indicated by Binion (1979, 117). Under this enormous pressure, the shocking defeat had been mishandled by self-defeating psychological reactions such as paranoid explanations of what happened coupled with grandiose dreams of future revenge. So potent was this need to heal the narcissistic open wound—caused by the self-image of defeat and collapse at the end of World War I—that future reality gave way to present magic. A collapse, after all, would not constitute anything that had not already happened in the past to poor torn-apart Germany. But the joy ride of omnipotence in the here-and-now felt truly unprecedented and wonderfully overwhelming. To live through this wondrous group experience, if only once, meant that each person would receive personal metaphysical validation. Each person would finally know that he had truly lived life to the fullest, to the point of transcendence. And only *der Führer* could enable the people to accomplish such a feat. He, and he alone, was commissioned by Providence, i.e., by both nature and the folk comrades, to launch the German nation onto the path of greatness through a quest for the limitless.

Hitler's preoccupation with the necessity of an adequate living space was pervasive indeed. When delivering his ringing speeches, he loved to throw numbers around showing how shortchanged Germany was by comparison with other countries when total area and population density were taken into account. There was much more to this than mere tendentious propaganda for the purpose of whitewashing aggressive geopolitical intents. Underlying this constant obsession was a self-righteous and compulsive search for justice, which was driven by a basic sense of insecurity about national health and survival. Historical wrongs had to be corrected not only for the sake of justice but also because their occurrence put into question Germany's future and the ability of the Germans to survive. When it is understood that an expanded lebensraum was meant to be the effective answer to a constant underlying dread about one's sheer existence, it is also understood why it could never work. The geographic diagnosis of an inadequate living space may have represented a reshuffling of the location of insecurity away from the internal psychological realm into a highly symbolic external geographic one. Similarly, the expansion cure may have served as a geographic answer to psychological problems. Such illusory shifts, which are embedded in psychogeographic fantasies, are notoriously unrealistic.

An early clue as to the psychological loadings and ideological importance of the lebensraum issue appears in the second chapter of the first volume of *Mein Kampf* (Hitler 1943, 30–34). Hitler was discussing the deplorable lack of national pride among the Germans. This issue led him to focus on the importance of "the infinite number of separate memories of the greatness of our national fatherland in all the fields of cultural and artistic life" to inspire national pride. He focused this discussion on errors of omission and of commission in education. German education suffered not only from "the negative sin of omission" of memories of German greatness in all fields of endeavor, but also from the added "positive destruction" of even the little that is being taught. In other words, the education omitted most of what should be taught, while at the very same time it distorted and destroyed that which was taught. No wonder therefore that such a dismal teaching failed to instill national pride in children. Who was to blame for this failure? "The rats [politicians, Bolsheviks, Jews, and whoever else Hitler meant by rats] that politically poison our nation gnaw even this little [what is left of nationalistic education] from the heart and memory of the broad masses." At this point, in order to make the situation more vivid for his readers, Hitler drew an imaginary picture of how a three-year-old boy grows up. The picture may contain autobiographical elements.

The imaginary scene that Hitler portrayed involved a family life in a crowded basement apartment. A working family of seven lives in two stuffy rooms. One of the five boys is a three-year-old: "This is the age in which the first impressions are made on the consciousness of the child. Talented persons retain traces of memory from this period down to advanced old age. The very narrowness and overcrowding of the room does not lead to favorable conditions. Quarreling and wrangling will very frequently arise as a result. In these circumstances, people do not live with one another, they press against one another. Every argument, even the most trifling, which in a spacious apartment can be reconciled by a mild segregation, thus solving itself, here leads to loathsome wrangling without end" (Hitler 1943, 31–32). As the loathsome quarreling without end continues among the parents, it includes brutal attacks and beatings of the mother by the drunken father. The impact on the child is to contemplate life with horror by the time he is six years old. He is therefore "morally poisoned" and "physically undernourished" by the time he goes to school. As life goes on in this fashion and the parents keep denigrating the teachers during talks at home in front of the children, by the time the boy becomes fourteen or fifteen years old he despises all authority, ranging from his teacher to the head of the government. Within the next few years, he gets embroiled in criminal activities so that his education receives its last polish in the house of correction. In the meantime, his dear bourgeois fellow men are utterly amazed at his lack of national enthusiasm. This last barb was a typical sarcasm to which Hitler frequently resorted when he wanted to accentuate an ideological point. And the ideological point he raised at the conclusion of his discussion was the necessity for total reeducation of the people: "*The question of the 'nationalization' of a people is, among other things, primarily a question of creating healthy social conditions as a foundation for the possibility of educating the individual"* (Hitler 1943, 33–34). Embedded here is a totalistic vision of how to manage society in the folkish state. This central theme was later explored and analyzed by historian George Mosse (1977) in *The Nationalization of the Masses*. He emphasized that in this totalistic management of society, the regular liturgic and cultic forms disguised the pragmatism of daily politics and became a "magic" believed by both leaders and people. Moreover, he ascertained that this form of secular religion enabled its adherents to act out their hopes and fears by viewing the world through myths and symbols (Mosse 1977, 15, 214). Actually, Nazism, the new form of secular religion to be practiced arduously and ceremonially on a daily basis, included many millenarian, apocalyptic, Gnostic, and Manichean features, as was well illustrated by James Rhodes (1980).

While this story has been used as a basis of psychobiographical speculations by many authors, our primary concern is with its ideological significance. Hitler's description contains about seven ideological points, some of which he delivered in repeated messages, while others were transmitted in telegraphic language. The first point concerns the rats. These are most likely the failed leaders and educators, Jews or politicians under Jewish influence. Since their deadly impact falls upon German education they most likely represent an internal weakness and the enemy within Germany's borders. What is implied here is that to whatever degree the existing rank of rats includes the old style and failing German political leaders, these leaders should be removed.

The second point concerns the quarreling family members and by extension the wrangling masses. Their behavior is not smart; they denigrate the child's teachers while raising up a criminal child who lacks valuable memories. The implied verdict is that the people fail miserably in coping with the hardships of life not only because of failed leadership but also in consequence of the basic fact that the masses, rather than being bright, are actually stupid.

The third point relates to the description of the young boy or "citizen" as morally poisoned and physically undernourished. This kind of combined damage to both mind and body alludes to an underlying assumption of psychophysical integrity as the cornerstone of folkish health. To the degree that the psychological and the physical remain inseparable, a magic promise of health and well-being is held out at the same time that a totalistic practice of control is deemed necessary. It is this inseparability of the physical from the psychological that justifies exercising full state control over all behavior, which affects both. Since infecting the mind affects the body and vice versa, totalitarian measures are needed for reasons of folkish health.

The fourth point deals with disrespect toward all authority, be it teacher or head of state, as one of the reasons for the nation's failure. Hitler fanatically insisted on absolute obedience to all meritorious authorities, especially the supreme leader. For him, therefore, the loss of respect toward all authorities, which resulted from the flawed education, represented a serious undermining of the leadership principle central to his ideology.

The fifth point, which emphasizes the importance of memories, requires a lengthier discussion. The lessons drawn by Hitler from his portrayal of a miserable family life are supposedly anchored in the earliest impressions and memories that talented persons can have. In essence this is a reference to the capacity for memory. But Hitler also spoke about the infinite number of separate memories of the greatness of the national fatherland. This is a reference to the content of memory or its meaning. These references bear the influence of Otto Weininger, whose ideas created such a splash in Vienna in the early twentieth century. Hitler was no lover of Jews, but, as discussed in chapter 3, Weininger was one of the very few Jews whom he appreciated, as indicated by Hitler's secret conversations (Trevor-Roper 1953, 116). Weininger contrasted the poor memory of the average person with the exceptional memory of the genius. In a related fashion, he contrasted the meaningless drift of the ordinary person in the momentary stream of events with the ability of the genius to endow his experiences with meaning and thus make them timeless and memorable. After pointing out that the genius excels in imparting meaning and value to events, Weininger suggested that the genius is the only timeless man, that a nation orients itself by its own geniuses, and that the timeless men are those who make history (Weininger 1906, 138). The sensational ideas of Weininger were floating in the zeitgeist, from which Hitler is likely to have drawn them. Therefore, when Hitler depicted the life of an ignorant boy who lacks meaningful memories, he positioned himself in the role of a talented boy who grew up to become a true genius as an adult. In contrast to the boy in the imaginary scene, Hitler, in his own eyes, is a person who remembers meaningful impressions from the very age at which memories begin to form. In that sense he identified himself as a different kind of small boy who grew up to write *Mein Kampf.* And when the adult Hitler thus implies that even his (manufactured) boyhood memories were so meaningful that they carried the seeds of momentous lessons for the conduct of the nation, he basically identifies himself as a Weiningerian political genius. He thus merits being the supreme leader because he is that timeless man who can impart value to events and define a meaningful destiny for others.

The sixth ideological point that is embedded in the narrative deals with the impact of overcrowding. Quarreling and wrangling result from the narrowness and overcrowding of the room, which precludes reconciling arguments by means of a mild segregation, which would have been possible in a more spacious apartment. One may conclude that an inadequate family living space was instrumental in fostering the conditions that hinder proper education and produce fateful results. The core national memories are not being instilled in the people, and one of the consequences is that they lack pride. Moreover, people who do not live with one another but press against each other are not likely to work in unison, which dooms them to national impotence. It is important to note that Hitler emphasized the memories that would make a person proud of being a member of the nation. Thus, when he implied that insufficient family living space leads to internal division, disunity, bad memories, and lack of national pride, he was talking not only about one little family but about the larger national family, which was also biologically related. It is important to emphasize here that for Hitler, lack of national pride was a designation of an extreme state of racial ill health. Corrective measures for this mortal sickness were literally a dictate of proper racial consciousness—which he already possessed.

This brings us to the seventh ideological point, which is the nationalization of the people. The implied lesson from Hitler's portrayal of a failed family life is that inadequate living space fosters improper education. In turn, this bankrupt education produces persons who are devoid of significant memories and who therefore lack national pride. What is more, the inadequate living space gives rise to a quarreling citizenry, which fosters disunity and does not respect any leadership prin-

ciple. The remedies to these situations, which seem to suggest themselves from the text, are proper leadership and adequate living space,
where people could "live with one another" (with the added proviso that
non-Aryans need not apply). The additional remedy, which was proclaimed by Hitler, was the nationalization of the people by creating
healthy social conditions. For this reeducation program to accomplish
the totalistic behavioral and thought control that Hitler had in mind, a
folkish state would have to be created. That future totalitarian state would
succeed in nationalizing the masses, instilling pride and health in them,
and mobilizing them under a providential political leader who would
inspire them to enlarge their living space.

Hitler clarified his stand concerning the sensitive issue of living
space in a speech he delivered on March 7, 1936, before the Reichstag
(de Roussy de Sales 1941, 362–83). He bemoaned the fact that sixty-
seven million Germans lived in a very restricted and only partially
fertile area. This represented much less ground per capita than the Russians had. It would therefore be in the interest of the rest of the world
if Germany succeeded in securing the necessities of the struggle for
existence. Well-fed people are more sensible than hungry ones. There
is no better proof of the innate love of peace of the German people
than the fact that in spite of its dense population it has secured for
itself only a modest share of space for living. Very significantly, Hitler
broadened his subject matter to Europe at large. He asserted that in
spite of their quarrels, the European people are related to one another
and not separable spiritually, culturally, or economically. It was time
for the European family of nations to use the wisdom of constructive-
ness and apply inner state laws externally. Inner state laws are what, in
an earlier speech, he termed laws of cool, considered reasonableness.
In his worldview, however, only the laws of the folkish state can be so
regarded. Now Hitler was asserting that in the space of a restricted house,
such as Europe, it would not be a sound idea to keep the community of
nations under different principles of law. Different laws and legal principles will produce in those suffering from injustice an accumulation
of will and energies driven by resentment. On the other hand, among
those who cause the injustice, these inequities will produce an accumulation of psychosis and fear. What he implied by this threat was
that unless the house of Europe were to be consistently governed by the

laws of the folkish state, the ensuing injustice would result in dangerous instability.

Hitler was alluding to the need to create a spiritually, culturally, and economically unified community within the restricted European living space. This was to be accomplished by exporting and imposing the German inner state laws onto neighboring European states. It would be a peace-loving act by a peace-loving people and would successfully eliminate growing tensions, which were otherwise bound to explode into future international conflict. These tensions increase because of different developments in various countries. In wrongfully treated Germany, the masses accumulate energies while the leader accumulates the willpower with which to guide these energies. By contrast, in the guilty countries, which mistreated Germany, psychosis and fear mount. It would therefore be better to have a constructive settlement of historical disparities that stem from past mistreatments before they continue to develop and reach a boiling point. The outwardly reasonable Hitler was of course a master at delivering peace-loving threats. Moreover, his attribution of psychosis and fear to others, rather than to Germans themselves, was in the best tradition of collective projection. In voicing these sentiments, he was speaking for many Germans and not only for himself. And being set on the lebensraum course, he went on to assert, "I tremble for Europe and the thought of what would happen to our old, overpopulated continent if the chaos of a bolshevistic revolution should be successful through the outbreak of this destructive Asiatic world conception, which strikes at all hitherto recognized values" (de Roussy de Sales 1941, 373). This is no longer the vision of the guardian of the German living space who contemplates expansion to Middle Europe. By now it is the enlarged vision of the guardian of the living space of Middle Europe fearing an Asiatic and racially foreign destructive world conception, and consequently envisioning a preemptive expansion into Russia's Eurasian space in the name of self-defense.

It is interesting to note that as Hitler was contemplating the big dream of reforming the European continent by an expansion of the German living space, he trafficked concurrently with megalomania and with humility. The grandiosity revealed itself as he promised to demand of history at some future date to recognize that he was acting not only on behalf of Germany but also for the preservation of European cultural civilization. Thus he thought of himself as the omnipotent master of history who is able to summon it to serve him at will. He was going to demand of history itself to ratify after the fact that his actions were indeed whatever he had already asserted them to be. The willpower of such a person should therefore reign supreme to compel people and history. So powerful is the will that sheer willing makes anything happen, i.e., a form of the omnipotence of thought where mere thinking materializes action. Yet no matter how grandiose the leader who summons history to his command, he nevertheless ended his speech with a most humble plea. He entreated his listeners (de Roussy de Sales 1941, 383): "I now ask the German people to strengthen me in my faith and to give me, through the strength of its will, further individual strength with which to fight always courageously for its honor and freedom and to be able to take care of its economic well-being. And especially to support me in my struggle for a new peace."

What we witness here is how the flow of eloquence creates the appearance of false modesty that reverses traditional Nazi roles. Hitler is now the one who operates by faith, like Le Bon's crowds, while the masses are now the providers of a strength of will as if they were the supreme Nazi leader. Suddenly Hitler is the humble follower through faith guided by the indomitable will of the masses. But this is just a fleeting, though deliberate, deception of the masses in order to allow them to share momentarily in supreme glory. It also renews the mandate to rule which *der Führer* receives directly from the people. Nevertheless, there is not really a serious question as to whose will shall take care of honor, freedom, economic well-being, and peace—a collection of flowery euphemisms that stand for lebensraum. The expansion of the living space through the strength generated by a unified will is too serious a matter to be left to "the confused and excited masses of people," to use Hitler's own phrase earlier in the speech (de Roussy de Sales 1941, 367). With his clever lip service, Hitler, "the humble follower of the followers," has reasserted that he is the true leader of the masses. Theirs is the faith. His is the will.

The magical and greedy grab for expansion, which would involve the redistribution of the world, was perceived and justified as a redress of an intolerable injustice. The most prominent symbol of the injurious injustice that was inflicted upon Germany was of course the *Diktat* of

Versailles, which became akin to a generic term standing for all past wrongs done to Germany. Since it seemed only right to redress past wrongs, the drive to expand powerfully and magically was viewed as a traditional quest for justice. As Sigmund Neumann put it, "to be a 'Have-not' nation made the quest for redistribution of worldly goods a moral issue" (Neumann 1965, 8). But it was more than that. It was also an issue of tapping into the realm of magic in order to influence events. There is an underlying link between ideas of magic and notions of primitive justice, which requires greater elaboration. Whenever people resort to magic, they implicitly acknowledge that they wish somehow to redistribute the good and the bad in this world with greater power than the way normal rules and realistic constraints usually allow. The magical power grab is really a grab for an ultramanipulative ability that transcends traditional realistic limits. Yet a limitless power in an infinite universe would be too diffuse to remain psychologically effective. It would simply be too open-ended as well as too structureless to permit defined and directed actions. It would not be possible for a person to operate within such an amorphous state and still feel safe because he would no longer feel linked to the familiar world. A different way of stating this principle would be to say that although magic is conjured up in order to change the face of the earth, it is not summoned for the purpose of dispensing with the earth altogether. However, what magic is meant to do is to tilt the existing power equation in favor of the practitioner of this art (Hitler) or his client (the German folk) or both (when a psychological fusion of the two takes place). Thus the ultimate aim of magic is to grant the practitioner or his client a greater share of good fortune. In black magic, the complementary aim is to inflict malfeasance and all sorts of misfortune on others. Psychologically, however, this damage to others entails a gain to self. This point relates to the archaic notion of symmetry embedded in the concepts of justice. For now, however, it is worth noting that in the Middle Ages malfeasance was regarded as one of the favorite pastimes of witches who dabbled in black magic. But in Nazi ideology the old image of witches was eclipsed by the Jews, who were seen as the timeless inflicters of the worst malfeasance of all: blood pollution. Thus they did ultimate damage, but always to their own advantage. With this particular assertion, Nazi ideology reinforced and replaced the earlier Christian view of the Jews as timeless inflicters of the worst malfeasance of all: killing Jesus. The old religious hatred for the alleged Jewish killing of the Son of God could now find new racial expression as hatred for the agents of decomposition who destroy everything of value and for whom nothing is too precious to escape destruction.

Since magic is not designed to operate in an unfamiliar universe beyond recognition, a limit is imposed on the game, so to speak. The limits insure that the psychological universe, meaning the individual self as well as the extended collective self, must remain viable. They thus insure that any magical manipulations would not change the world so much that it would defeat the basic purpose of magic to begin with, which is to provide better fortune and greater security in the still familiar world. These limits are achieved by restricting the ultramanipulative game to fixed quantities. What this means is that the magical game is actually a zero-sum game: the quantitative changes of fortune and misfortune cancel each other out.

This assumption of limits consists of fixed quantities of both "goodies" and "baddies," with the actual allotments left to chance, God, nature, or as is the case with Hitler, to a manly grab for magical ultramanipulative abilities in the name of destiny. This is not a new idea in western civilization and is not peculiar to German culture. It is an old assumption, which can be detected even in some of the ancient Mesopotamian roots of western civilization, as will be demonstrated later. At present, suffice it to say, the Jewish Talmud for instance includes such sayings as "ten measures of beauty descended to the world, nine were taken by Jerusalem and one by the rest of the world" or "ten measures of talk descended to the world, nine were taken by women and one by the rest of the world." What we have here is a fairly benign expression of admiration for Jerusalem's beauty but a less benign imputation of prattle to women. But the framework of these expressions concerning the distributions of the "goodie" of beauty as well as of the "baddie" of overtalkativeness, reveals that same basic assumption of a zero-sum game governing the universe. Whatever comes one's way has to come from what there is in this world. Therefore if there is more in one place, there is less in another. This applies to all tangibles as well as intangibles such as happiness, wealth, and power. This is the untranscendable constraint that insures that no manmade magic or human ultramanipulativeness could change the world beyond recognition.

The pitfall of this notion of fixed quantities that governs the world of man is that it can easily turn into something nasty as people become manipulative and even turn into something lethal when they grope for magical redistributions of whatever exists. Existence, or the human condition, can then be perceived as a Darwinian struggle for justice: namely, the improved and more favorable distribution of all material as well as psychological assets. Since the additions and subtractions of tangible as well as symbolic fortunes among people add up to zero, every one person's good fortune is another person's bad fortune. Similarly, a misfortune that strikes in one place benefits others elsewhere. This can lead to a Manichean and a paranoid view of the world.

If the world is thought to work in such a manner that one can improve his lot only at the expense of others, then one may readily develop a paranoid attitude toward others. There is no great need then to wonder what the others may be up to, since at some level one knows what one is up to oneself. After all, if this is how the world really works, then one should not trust others not to seek unfair advantages through extraordinary means. And no means are as extraordinary as the total mobilization of a compact and united nation to effect a magical redistribution of the fixed quantities of both good and bad fortunes. In such a world, hypervigilance provides an existential advantage. What is more, a touch of paranoia is commendable since it makes one more prudently cautious. Finally, doing unto others first what they would do unto you becomes a dictate of survival and therefore of justice. Thus it is just to survive even as others must perish in a world of fixed, scarce resources. It was the zero-sum game premise of Nazi magic that made it so Darwinian by dictating the survival of the manipulative fittest.

Of course peoples throughout history have not always behaved according to the basic assumption of fixed and limited quantities of worldly largess. But this more civilized model never held full sway or we would have been closer to utopia. Just think, for instance, of how much nicer the world would be if rival national groups could either divide a land equitably or live together peacefully on the same land. Put succinctly, what if "goodies" could come many peoples' way with the sum total of all changes landing squarely in the plus column rather than good and bad changes canceling each other out? Then there would be no need to quarrel over living spaces for the sake of "autarky" or absolute independence and self-sufficiency. Sharing would be perceived not as a loss, but as a mutual gain because it fosters interactions to create a larger pie for all. People could afford to be altruistic without being seen as self-sacrificing because "to give" becomes psychologically equated with "to receive." Think of the demise of nationalism as we know it in this kind of a "new, improved" world. Nations could afford to be benevolent and even altruistic toward each other. Moreover, the demand for sacrifice would cease because there would no longer be a lethal basic assumption of both magic and justice that stipulates that to gain or secure life, it is necessary to sacrifice a life.

Even though humanity rises on occasions to this civilized level, the psychological equation of "to give" with "to receive" has been only inconsistently held while the archaic principle of "a life for a life" largely prevailed. Only too frequently the basic assumption of a zero-sum game gained the ascendancy. People jockey around to gain the "goodies" of longevity and health (sometimes symbolized by wealth) while relegating the "baddies" of sickness and death to others. In this desperate shuffle, magic prowess could appear as a timely help in tilting the worldly distribution in the desired direction. People with ultramanipulative knowhow could be expected to seek extra advantage at the expense of others. Could this be fair? On the fixed quantities assumption, the answer would be that if we do it, then it is fair, but whenever others do it, it is foul. As a matter of fact, when others do the same thing to us, it is so patently unfair that it constitutes injustice. This is a good example of the double standard of perception that characterizes narcissistic persons according to Erich Fromm. And it was not for naught that he viewed group narcissism as one of the most important sources of human aggression (Fromm 1973, 200–205). Another way of putting it would be to say that in a world that is seen through a narcissistic tunnel vision, only one's self or one's group has any rights. If these rights are encroached upon, all corrective measures, no matter how aggressive, seem justified.

This brings us to the issue of primitive justice. The basic conception of justice in its most archaic origins is thoroughly symmetrical. The symmetry of justice can easily be sensed in the historically prevalent moral code of the *Lex Talionis* or Law of Talion. This is the old biblical law of "an eye for an eye," which has been so influential in western concepts of justice. It carries with it a sense of psychological satisfaction that is derived from the symmetry of the dictate. The punishment is made to fit the crime. Yet the biblical code of "a life for a life" is actually derived from an older Mesopotamian heritage that had already promoted highly symmetrical notions of justice. Among the more famous examples are the laws of retribution in the code of law of the Babylonian king Hammurabi, which dates from the first half of the eighteenth century B.C. This code contains explicit examples of the eye for an eye or bone for a bone principle. Similarly, the twelfth century B.C. Middle Assyrian laws from the time of Tiglath Pileser I include the principle of a life for a life. For example, if a man strikes another man's wife and causes a miscarriage then in retaliation his own wife will be forced to miscarry. But if the other man's wife died as she was struck then the offending man himself would be killed. What was of paramount importance was that the principle of compensating with a life for a life would be upheld. This principle has been bequeathed to western culture mostly by the Bible. The ancient and psychologically potent primitive origins of the basic conception of symmetrical retribution retained a tremendous drawing power that causes people to regress to both magic and cruelty under personal stress and historical duress.

There is indeed an element of magic that is imbedded in "commonsense" justice that requires that the punishment be made to fit the crime. The crudest but seemingly logical way of creating a perfect fit is to replicate the damage on the other side of the scales. It is as if the victim who lost an eye regained it through the newly removed eye of the perpetrator. In reality it is of course not so, but psychologically it feels that way. The other person's loss is thus one's own gain, and justice is therefore done not only *to* the perpetrator but also *for* the victim. Psychologically speaking, the victim does get something out of the perpetrator's loss, but there has to be symmetry; the punishment has to fit the crime.

When we bear in mind how symmetrical the primitive notion of justice is, we begin also to realize that this very symmetry imposes a zero-sum game rule on the distributive act of justice. Justice is retribution through redistribution. But so long as the psychological retribution and legal redistribution operate on a principle of symmetry between crime and punishment, they also operate on a principle of symmetry between losses and gains. Crime is a victim's loss and therefore an offender's gain while punishment is an offender's loss and therefore a victim's gain. They must fit or there is no justice. But is justice nevertheless a bit elastic? Can it still be distorted or tilted? The answer every so often seems to be yes. Ultramanipulativeness in the best tradition of magic could give more justice to some but more injustice to others, all within the confines of totaling all the distributive changes into the sum of sheer zero. Not only did it seem that justice could be influenced, but it also seemed only just and proper that those persons with extra initiative or extraordinary abilities receive a greater reward, i.e., a greater share of justice. This, for instance, had been a cornerstone in Hitler's conception of the rules that govern the economic sphere. And in his famous speech of January 27, 1932, at the Industry Club in Düsseldorf, he insisted on the extension of this principle of individual differences in abilities and compensations in the economic sphere to the political sphere as well (Domarus 1990, 1:93). He averred that the logic and justification of the whole idea of private property is based on inherent individual differences in "personal value" as well as in "achievements." The administration of different achievements in the economic sector was therefore properly left to different individuals since men are not equally valuable. Hitler called for the application of the same principle to the political sector, an application that would, of course, have rendered men politically unequal. But his obsessive focus on differences in the force of personality was not only antidemocratic but also a reckless plunge into a magical concept of personality. Its major derivative—the power of the will—was ultramanipulative to the core. The apex was the charismatic leader with the greatest force of personality, who was willing and able to wrestle from fate greater justice for his people.

The greater justice that Hitler sought was a greater living space for the German master race. Magical prowess on a national scale was going to correct the gross injustice of the despicable Versailles peace treaty, which had been signed on June 28, 1919. In the eyes of the German public, this treaty unfairly left Germany weakened and shriveled in size after having been defeated only by treachery in the First World War. The territorial loss stood as the prime example of Germany's having been unfairly wronged. Indeed a depressing as well as enraging sense of injustice kept inflaming the German public ever since the military capitulation in 1918. It rankled deeply and remained persistent. Rudolph Binion suggested that during Hitler's early career, which culminated in the abortive Nazi putsch of November 1923, the future führer left undisclosed the full meaning of his mission to deliver Germany from defeat. Expressly it meant canceling the Treaty of Versailles: "But it implied, beyond this, retrieving the lost victory—an implication close to the surface of all his early speeches and writings, yet never quite drawn in those first years" (Binion 1979, 23).

"Retrieving the lost victory" in the eastern front of World War I was indeed on Hitler's mind during his highly symbolic staging of the signing ceremony of French surrender in World War II on June 21, 1940. He arranged for the signing to take place at the very same *wagon-lit* of Marshal Foch in Compiègne where, on November 11, 1918, at the dictation of Marshal Foch, the German emissaries signed the armistice that effectively ended fighting. The journalist William Shirer provided an apt description of the elaborate special preparations that went into releasing the original train compartment from the confines of a walled museum as well as the ceremony that followed (Shirer 1968, 975–79). At a conscious level, this historical play signified the long overdue redress of the injustice of the earlier defeat on the western front during World War I. But it can be postulated that at an unconscious level, it signaled psychohistorical replays that were fairly fused together. One replay was not merely the present redress, but rather the retroactive reversal, of the unjust defeat on the western front, turning it into the meritorious victory it was meant to be—and thus finally winning World War I. And the complementary replay was the equation of the present victory with inevitable future victories, which were yet to come and which will resuscitate past victories. This was the dream of the retrieval of the lost victory in the east during World War I, as was suggested by Binion, except that this time around it could serve as a springboard toward world domination. Yet this other replay signaled the resumption of the old and heady dash toward a catastrophe. Since the battle in the west was but an initial stage of securing the rear prior to the major drive to the east to acquire an extended living space, the folly of biting off more than one can chew still lay ahead. Binion (1979, 106) correctly pointed out that an unconscious reliving of a trauma requires that the second experience be distanced from the first. In the case of Germany, this distancing in-cluded underestimating Russian military strength in 1941 after it was overestimated in 1914. Indeed, this unconscious distancing of the two events in order to prevent a conscious identification of the two suggests that the whole project was unconsciously programmed for failure. Pre-sumably the present victory in France promised even more victories to come in the east. As Binion stated, "at that aural frequency, 'living space' signified the eastern conquest of 1917–1918 and stirred associated vi-sions of German continental sufficiency and invulnerability" (Binion 1979, 69). But underneath the promise of expansion lay the threat of the next collapse. And the threat usually overtakes the promise at that point in which reality catches up to magic.

However, before we pursue this point further and analyze the com-pulsion to repeat a trauma, we need to say a few more words about the issue of rectifying injustice through magical prowess. In the zero-sum game type of justice, which is secured by ultramanipulativeness, what is foul for self is nevertheless quite fair to others. A stunning illustration of this is provided by the fact that in early Nazi speeches and political campaigns a favorite subject for discussion was a comparison of the unfair Versailles peace treaty, which was imposed by the allies, with the earlier and presumably generous peace treaty of Brest-Litovsk, which victorious Germany had concluded with Russia on March 3, 1918. Ac-tually the Russians were forced to cede Poland, the Baltic states, and part of Byelorussia to Germany and Austria-Hungary. They also gave up certain territories to Turkey. Furthermore, they were forced to recog-nize the independence of the Ukraine and Georgia from Russia. Later on Germany also demanded a large indemnity. These were harsh terms, but luckily for the Russians the Brest-Litovsk treaty was canceled after the allied victory in the western front in World War I. The Treaty of Versailles, which was signed on June 28, 1919, also imposed territorial concessions on the vanquished Germans, who found it hard to swallow defeat. Alsace-Lorraine was returned to France. West Prussia and the Polish corridor and part of Upper Silesia were given to Poland. Danzig was established as a free city. Following plebiscites, certain cities and territories were given to Belgium and to Denmark. The Rhineland was to be occupied for fifteen years and permanently demilitarized, while the Saar was to be administered by the French for an equal period of time on behalf of the League of Nations. Germany lost its overseas colonies and most of its navy. It had to pay reparations and accept and acknowledge war guilt. These terms were also harsh even though, somewhat luckily, Germany was later on helped in the financing of its reparation payments. The Germans were left feeling enraged over the severity of the terms.

But the terms that Germany itself had imposed in Brest-Litovsk were neither wise nor generous. Noting that this treaty gave Germany one third of Russia's population and cultivated land, half her heavy industry, and almost all of her coal mines, John Weiss (1996, 210–11) pointed out that only the German social democrats opposed these draconian terms and that this thrust into Russia demonstrated that the drive for lebensraum was a goal that preceded the Nazi period. In this connection, A.J.P. Taylor concluded that a moderate peace with Russia, which would have really ended the eastern war, would have also saved Germany from catastrophe in France. But Gen. Erich Ludendorff was committed to the Greater German dream of *Mitteleuropa* and therefore imposed on Russia a peace treaty that deprived her of a territory nearly as large as Austro-Hungary and Turkey combined. Consequently a force of one million German soldiers was needed to collect the plunder of Brest-Litovsk. This force could have turned the scale in the war in the west instead of being wasted on continuing to carry the burden of the "war on two fronts" (Taylor 1962, 177–78). But the folly and harshness of it all, not to mention the unconscious quest for an inevitable defeat at the end of the road, did not consciously register in the German mind. The reason for this is that psychological issues of magical prowess and primitive justice reverberated beneath the passionate concern for an adequate lebensraum. And in that kind of worldview, securing greater justice for self by ultramanipulative abilities is mandatory while any resultant injustice to others is irrelevant. By contrast, any injustice that befalls oneself is of course extremely relevant and represents the unfair ultramanipulative machinations of others, which must be redressed by any means. Hitler stated it emphatically in a speech of April 20, 1923: "We may be inhumane, but if we rescue Germany we have achieved the greatest deed in the world! We may work injustice, but if we rescue Germany then we have removed the greatest injustice in the world. We may be immoral, but if our people is rescued we have once more opened

up the way for morality!" (Baynes 1942, 1:60). This was the bare essence of the post-Versailles moral code: seeking justice to self no matter
what the traumatic cost to others. And it resonated well among the German masses grieving over the defeat in World War I. It thus came to be
that in early Nazi political propaganda and campaigns, as the harsh terms
of the Treaty of Versailles imposed by the allies on Germany were unfa-
vorably contrasted with the harsh terms of the treaty of Brest-Litovsk,
which Germany forced upon Russia, what is foul for self was nevertheless deemed quite fair to others. Such is the nature of seeking primitive
justice by magic powers. It carries a huge component of group narcissism. The delving into magic prowess to secure justice betrays something else too. Since reality can be expected sooner or later to overtake
magic and demolish it, the compulsive resort to ultramanipulative powers so as to get closer to omnipotence may also betray a repetition compulsion of a trauma.

There is indeed a flavor of ongoing traumatic encounters to living
life in a psychological world in which the succession of crimes and punishments fuses into an expectation of the repetition of the same basic
damage. It all goes back to early formative stages in the development of
a rather precarious sense of self. The psychological origin of the primitive sense of justice, with its rigid adherence to a tight fit between crime
and punishment, lies in, and is derived from, early splits and projections
within a fragile and only partly integrated self whose boundaries are
hardly fixed. And because the boundaries that separate the inside world
from the outside world are very permeable during such early times, "bad"
wishes or impulses are easily projected onto outside objects. The projected elements do not really have to travel far because the permeability
of the boundaries makes the inside and the outside overlapping and partly
interchangeable. In this semi-amorphous state, when the line between
feelings and actions is still blurred and when there is not yet a clear-cut
distinction between wish and wish fulfillment, a thought is indistinguish-
able from a deed and an impulse can be equated with an accomplished
action. Put differently—and in this connection Hitler's doctrine of the
will comes to mind—sheer willing makes it so. Consequently, that which
one wished to do to others and therefore presumably "did" to others is
attributed to these others on the outside who now seemingly wish to do
the identical thing to oneself. Hence there is an imaginary and near-

perfect fit between what one is tempted to do and what one fears will be done to oneself.

This is, therefore, the crossroads of magic and justice, where a magical will and symmetrical retributions meet. As if by poetic justice, it is the very same projected stuff that was originally externalized by the self, which now returns to haunt that very same self. And it is in this reencounter with the formerly projected aggression that one's own original drive—the crime—now returns as fear of the very same thing in a new form—the punishment. It is thus possible to detect in this reenactment rudimentary "uncanny" qualities in the Freudian sense.

The reencounter is based on a symmetrical principle of recurrent damage, which includes a hidden component of a repetition of trauma. In the blurred world of infantile existence, painful stimulations by either external or internal sources give rise to fear and to aggressive impulses, which in turn evoke new fears of retaliation akin to a repetition of the original trauma. It is very important to note that both the projective element and the repetitive element, which are imbedded in the principle of retaliation, involve the blurring of the lines between outside and inside. Through projection, the self loses touch with parts of the "inside" in order to retain a self-image of goodness and safety as well as to shore up the boundaries between the good inside and bad outside. In like fashion, through repetition, in which one's new punishment is but a reincarnated return of one's old crime, the threat arises of a painful reconnection with an archaically split psychic world where both good and bad float across blurred boundaries. The mere prospect of such a reconnection is bound to be painful. This is because, in the rudimentary psychic universe, the reigning primordial feeling is that one's own self includes all and is the originator of everything. It would therefore be impossible in that kind of a psychic universe to aggress toward the outside without being simultaneously invaded by it. Consequently the early and rudimentary psychological universe is a universe of fear and trembling where every aggression that goes around must come around in a repetitive succession of traumas. This exposes the primitive origins of Hitler's thinking; Hitler's claim regarding each Nazi aggression that it was retaliatory or preemptive might not have been just standard diplomatic duplicity. A striking example is his claim that the attack on the USSR was preemptive when in fact it had been in the cards since the early 1920s.

These symmetrical aspects of the psychology of a primitive sense of justice become even more pertinent for the current discussion when one recalls what a paramount role in Hitler's ideology was played by the need to stay forever on the alert against the enemies outside as well as inside. This constant dual alert on Hitler's part resonated with the people. It tapped into certain primordial currents of emotion that were long ago adopted as basic assumptions of the German group. Once again the development of group psychology tends to overwhelm individual psychology. Most members of national or ethnic groups are fated to remain locked into the primitive basic assumptions that define their current group identity.

It should be underscored that these currents of emotion go back to an early stage of development of a yet very fragmented sense of self with its primitive projective maneuvers, which include the splitting off of aggressive impulses. These preverbal primitive maneuvers can therefore be described only through the use of a metaphorical language. In these maneuvers, hostile bad chunks of "not me" are externalized in the form of bad "them," who are now likely to inflict the same harm on good and innocent "me." The primitive origins of these operations are what makes them so symmetrical. The formerly but no longer bad "me" and the currently bad "them" are at bottom the same thing. Similarly, the wish to transgress or act badly and the accompanying fear that this very same and familiar act of aggression will come back as retaliation are also nearly identical. Such dreadful feelings can subsequently receive national expression in mytho-historical terms where the bad Slavs seem to threaten to overrun the good Germans as the Germans once overran the Roman empire. Originally, though, this is how things work at an infantile age where there is no clear distinction yet between wishing and doing as well as no distinction between a clear sense of self and a clear sense of others. Raging attacks are therefore conducted to push the outside farther away as well as to wall it off so that it may no longer impinge so easily and so brutally on the inside. This walling off is accomplished primarily by means of projections. Through projections of bad split-off parts of the self, two goals can be seemingly accomplished. On the one hand, the purged good self is now more homogenized and less fragmented after the expulsion of the internal bad parts. And on the other hand, the bad "others" now reside mainly on the outside because the extended boundaries of the purified and more cohesive self have been fixed with greater clarity. If one substitutes "Germany" for "the self" in these last two sentences, one gets a classical psychogeographic solution to the malaise of the Germans in the form of a dual prescription for racial purges and for territorial expansion.

There is, however, one more missing element in this depiction of the infantile residues that underline the recurrent lebensraum drive. In these earliest stages of development, orality reigns supreme. In the primitive world of fuzzy boundaries, both universal delight and cosmic rage are funneled through the mouth. This means that the rage attacks and angry strikes at the blurry and threatening outside take the form of an oral aggressive gobbling up. It is interesting to note that when discussing Hitler's rhetoric, Binion (1979, 57–58) pointed out that Hitler's oral aggression intoned symbiosis with his followers. This too implies a link between aggressive orality and the fuzzy boundaries of a primitive psychological state.

Paradoxically, however, this extension of boundaries by oral incorporation serves to transport "badness" from the outside back to the inside. Consequently, the expanded and seemingly more cohesive self still remains vulnerable from within. Paradoxically, therefore, it continues to bear the burden of internal splits. Theoretically speaking, if the primal oral mode remains fixated and is not surmounted, it could lead to a succession of gobbling victories turned into internal defeats. All this primordial orality may have been reinforced by the national starvation complex of 1914–1918/19 in Germany. The overwhelming orality suggests that the underlying psychological loadings of the lebensraum drive for geographic expansion fit an infantile organism without fixed ego boundaries, which can omnipotently expand without limits but which is also frightened of being invaded and devoured. The defensive/aggressive oral response of gobbling up the threatening outside only transfers the danger back to the inside. The need to regain safe internal homogeneity or goodness creates a desire to expel the inner threat ("poison" in Hitler's language) back to the outside. It all represents an ongoing effort to fix more securely the boundaries of an expanding self, an effort that can find at future times a new psychogeographic expression in drives to redraw the borders of an expanding country.

There are three points that should be borne in mind with reference to the above. The first is that such a persistent condition of traumatic vulnerability creates a demand for something or someone close to omnipotence as protection. This need was answered by the leadership principle: the führer was the magic talisman of the nation who provided this protection.

The second point is that the early psychological states described above are preverbal even though for obvious reasons they were given a verbal expression here. To be retriggered later, they need to be reinforced and channeled after language has already set in. This process was aptly described by Vamik Volkan (1988), who illustrated how "suitable targets of externalization" are developed and shared. These are symbols and images of enemies who serve as both visible and legitimate targets for projecting aggression outward. These targets are rooted in postverbal childhood experiences of land, language, music, dance, and heroes. These experiences create primordial emotional ties, which give rise to the kind of sentiments that are simpler and more basic than sentiments that arise from the more complex adolescent and adult ties. It is at that basic level of emotional ties that elements of the childhood experiences of foods, colors, and familiar smells, sights, and sounds (including storytelling), come to symbolize either all good beings or all bad beings—namely, allies or enemies. The latter symbols now serve as suitable targets of externalization. But both the positive and negative shared ties that give rise to common symbols form the foundation upon which new layers of more complicated perceptions and thoughts can be added. Eventually, therefore, the symbols become layered with more primitive and magical images lying below the more sophisticated thought. It should be underscored that this intricate process, which culminates in the formation of allies and enemies, is part and parcel of group development and group identification. Besides being born to their parents, children also are born into the larger group that will shape them as it did their parents before them. Individual psychology tends to be subsumed here by group psychology, which affects the process throughout and solidifies the distinct psychocultural characteristics of the members of each group.

The third point is that in the old psychology of oral incorporation, in which the self habitually swallows more and more chunks of the world, excessive oral activity served as a vehicle for expanding the ego boundaries. And it was this older psychology that now fueled the newer psychogeographic drive to expand the country's borders. For this to have happened, "borders" must have played a very enigmatic role in German history and not only in a literal geographic sense. Borders can include border symbolism, which carries with it intrapsychic significance, as was dully emphasized by Avner Falk (1974; 1983). He suggested that political borders as well as geographic features such as rivers and bridges can unconsciously symbolize internal boundaries. Crossing "borders" in both a literal and figurative sense is therefore very significant. It may represent loss of ego control over impulses and the breaking down of interpersonal barriers such as the incest taboo. It can also signify a return to the crucial early issues of separation and individuation. The psychological importance of actual and symbolic borders makes them a prime concern of the group. That is why Falk asserted that a country's borders are not necessary just for military security but are also unconsciously needed to overcome the fear of loss of ego boundaries. That is also why Volkan (1988, 93) maintained that the sharing of ethnicity within a group can provide emotional borders, which protect the self by more clearly defining the enemy (Volkan 1988, 93). For the Germans, this was a particularly complicated issue because of their lack of national boundaries throughout their history. Even Bismarck's "unification" gave them no such boundaries as it included non-Germans, such as Danes and Poles, and left out Germans all over the European map. Thus there was a lack of coherent German identity throughout history. The dispersion of Germans across Europe intermixing with other people, and for that matter the fuzzy divides (whether linguistic or ethnic) between Germans and their kindred neighbors, was problematic for a coherent sense of identity and tended to foster an unflattering self-image.

When the German quest for justice through territorial expansion was discussed earlier, it was stated that the compulsive resort to ultramanipulative powers could betray a repetition compulsion of a trauma. It therefore behooves us now to take a look at some of the psychoanalytic explorations of this important phenomenon. In reporting the results of these explorations, it would be necessary to include some of the technical psychoanalytic terms that are used. Freud's preoccupation with the concept of trauma stemmed both from metapsychological concerns and from clinical interests. He was concerned with underlying theoretical issues with regard to the different roles of the pleasure principle and the reality principle. And he was also interested in the subsequent clinical manifestations of unresolved traumas. He viewed trauma as a major break through the ego's stimulus barrier by a sudden and overwhelming stimulus. It results in a total flooding of the ego. Henceforward the terrorized and overwhelmed ego is incapable of adequately carrying on its normal functions of discharging tensions as well as binding energies that result from excitations. Freud's reflections led him to a major stipulation: "Enough is left unexplained to justify the hypothesis of a compulsion to repeat—something that seems more primitive, more elementary, more instinctual than the pleasure principle which it overrides" (S. Freud 1955b, 23). He further hypothesized that the traumatic breach in the stimulus barrier can also take place when extremely unpleasant excitations from within are treated as if they originated not from the inside but from the outside. The purpose of such an intrapsychic maneuver was, of course, to activate the shield against external stimuli as a means of defense against internal stimuli as well. Freud regarded this specific maneuver as the origin of the defense of projection (S. Freud 1955b, 28–29). The implications of this assertion are that, in some instances, projection serves as a major last-ditch defense against a traumatic breach in a barrier that is designed to shield the ego from being flooded by internal stimulation. As for belated clinical manifestations of traumas, Freud speculated that in the cases of traumatic neurosis dreams go "beyond the pleasure principle" and represent not the fulfillment of wishes but something earlier—an obedience to the compulsion to repeat (S. Freud 1955b, 32–33). The purpose of this repetition is similar to that of some aspects of children's play: "In the case of children's play we seemed to see that children repeat unpleasurable experiences for the additional reason that they can master a powerful impression far more thoroughly by being active than they could by merely experiencing it passively. Each fresh repetition seems to strengthen the mastery they are in search of" (S. Freud 1955b, 35).

All in all, Freud's major assertions were very rich and thought-provoking. To sum them up, he suggested the occurrence of breached barriers and inundation from both the outside and the inside, the interchangeability of the defensive functions of the stimulus barrier as a shield against external as well as internal stimuli, the resultant loss in the ego functions of binding energies and modulating discharges, the consequent rise of a new compulsion to repeat the trauma in an attempt to secure a belated mastery over it, and finally, the regressive and primitive nature of this reparative effort, especially the major resort to projection. In a larger sense, his ideas seem to suggest that major traumas damage not only stimulus barriers but also ego boundaries and that living without secure demarcations of both the outside world and the inner world subjects a person to a regressed mode of existence, which is characterized by infantile terrors.

Freud's notion that the repetition compulsion of traumas represents belated attempts at mastery was picked up by Fenichel. In his discussion of traumatic neuroses, he emphasized that the repetitions of trauma represent a throwback to the more archaic ego, which was unable to anticipate the future and which mastered the outer world by active repetition of what had been experienced passively. Thus, in cases of traumatic neurosis, the repetition is in a certain sense twofold. There is not only a repetition of the original state of being overwhelmed but also a repetition of later attempts at a new, archaic, and undifferentiated type of mastery (Fenichel 1945, 120–21). In this connection one may truly wonder which repetition will win out: the repetition of being traumatized and victimized or the repetition of gaining mastery. Of course it could be both but the dismal prospect of being locked in a vicious cycle of a compulsion to repeat a trauma—under the guise of overcoming it—does suggest itself. On the whole, Fenichel emphasized how "overwhelming" was the task of a belated mastery of the intruding excitation, and his choice of this particular term suggests that the repetitions delivered more trauma than mastery. Moreover, in accordance with psychodynamic principles of clinical practice, he suggested that reactions to trauma are likely to involve associative connections between the trauma and infantile conflicts that become activated (Fenichel 1945, 124). This means that through associative connections new traumas are piled over old ones with increasing ferocity. The issue of associative connections has additional implications, which will now be discussed in relation to the ideas of Anna Freud.

Freud's daughter, Anna, provided important elaborations to his basic concept of trauma. She averred that there actually existed not just one stimulus barrier against environmental stimuli but rather two protective shields against two types of dangers threatening from both the inner world and the outer world. She also asserted that even harmless external happenings can be given threatening meaning on the basis of existing internal constellations (A. Freud 1967, 236). In other words, preexisting associative connections may determine whether an event is perceived as traumatic or benign. Another important point which she made was that external traumas can be turned into internal ones if they symbolize the fulfillment of either deep-seated anxieties such as fear of annihilation or the fulfillment of wish fantasies, be they aggressive, such as wishing someone dead, or sexual, such as wanting to seduce somebody (A. Freud 1967, 241). This proposition, that those external traumas that are highly symbolic can be turned into internal traumas, is important. It serves as a reminder that at the symbolic, or fantasy, level the outer and inner worlds are very closely related and may represent the flip side of each other. And the bigger the excitation and the more jarring the excitement, the closer is the link and the likelier the possibility that both worlds will shade into each other. Such is the power of a traumatic onslaught that it respects no boundaries. It also seems highly probable that whatever form the perceptual resolution of the dichotomy of external versus internal trauma assumes is dependent on the preexisting associative connections. No less important was Anna Freud's suggestion that differences in adaptation to stimulation may be connected with characteristics of the external, often communal, situation (A. Freud 1967, 238–39). The far-reaching implications of this last suggestion were that the subject of trauma, including repetition compulsion, is applicable to group psychology.

This application was carried out within the newly developed field of psychohistory. In a milestone paper, which was originally published in 1971 and which became a classic in psychohistory, Peter Loewenberg (1983) researched the impact of the trauma of the First World War upon the Nazi youth cohort. A cohort was defined by him as "the aggregate of individuals within a population who have shared a significant common experience of a personal or historical event at the same time" (Loewenberg 1983, 246–47). World War I had a traumatic impact on this youth group because of the shared experiences of the absence of the fathers, the exhaustion of the mothers who were recruited into the work force, and the hunger and ill health of the neglected children. Loewenberg discovered that the impact of the war on the Nazi youth cohort was to reinforce the tendency to use the archaic psychic mechanisms of splitting and projection in coping with self and world. Moreover, there was a greater tendency to submit to the authority of a total, charismatic leader. Hitler thus served as an idealized father to these youth who were ready for a repeat world war: "Thus, the repetition was to seek the glory of identification with the absent soldier-father, but like all quests for a fantasied past, it had to fail" (Loewenberg 1983, 279). Most important, the new trauma of the Great Depression in the early 1930s retriggered the anxieties that were experienced during those traumatic days on the home front. This regression to the fixations that were established during the war fostered an embrace of National Socialism as a repetition and fulfillment of traumatic childhoods. The historical result of this embrace was that the regressive illusion of Nazism ended in a repetition of misery at the front and starvation at home. The gist of Loewenberg's brilliant exploration was therefore that, for the Nazi youth cohort, the trauma of the home front of World War I, which was relived and reinforced by the trauma of the Great Depression, created its own repetition in World War II.

A penetrating analysis of the traumatic impact of World War I on the German population at large, on Hitler personally, and on the interaction between the two was conducted by the psychohistorian Rudolph Binion (1979) in his book *Hitler among the Germans*. The book broke new ground in exploring the subtle connections of psychobiography with group psychohistory. In the introduction to the book, Binion defined traumatic experience as the kind that is too painful to be assimilated. He reiterated that, in traumatic neurosis, the attempts to come to terms with a traumatic experience take the form of reliving it by contriving new experiences that unconsciously stand for the original trauma. The purpose of this reliving of a traumatic experience is to control and master it after having been overcome by it the first time around. So compelling becomes this pursuit that it overrides all other ideals, interests, or inhibitions. As Binion put it, "anyone suitably traumatized can massacre innocents, especially by remote control. The afflicted ego reverts to earliest, purest self-will" (Binion 1979, xii). At this juncture Binion made some intriguing psychological hypotheses concerning both Hitler and the Germans. He suggested that a prominent corrective tendency in traumatic reliving is to ward off the traumatic blow, which is delivered nonetheless. He also suggested, however, that another corrective tendency can win out if enough guilt is felt. This was the tendency "to convert the blow into a punishment due, to make the misadventure over into a misdeed that is then expiated." He went on to explain that, when this takes place, the whole enterprise of unconscious reliving defeats itself or becomes a repetitive, lifelong, desperate, futile routine. In essence what he was saying was that a repetitive pursuit of expiations through punishments, which is motivated by guilt, secures only more punishments but never the desired mastery that the guilt-ridden person does not feel that he deserves. And concerning this particular self-defeating tendency, he boldly hypothesized the following: "This traumatic mechanism will be seen to have operated not only with Hitler individually but with Germans collectively" (Binion 1979, xii–xiii). Such a conclusion would seem less daring had Binion written a book on Jeremiah among the Israelites. Surely the traditional Jewish heritage includes in it a view of history that habitually anticipates the next catastrophe. An eternal historical cycle of sin, punishment, repentance, and forgiveness is followed by sin and the inevitable start of a new cycle. Only the advent of the Messiah at the end of days, after disastrous pre-messianic cataclysms, supposedly will break the vicious cycle. Binion, however, was not analyzing Jewish history. He was exploring German history and dealt with it from within the framework of German culture. Yet what he unearthed turned out to be quite "Jewish." It all goes to show that Jews do not have the sole claim to cycles of martyrdom and that any people, including Germans, who are saddled with an undigested trauma, may respond to the guilt-inducing narcissistic blow by seeking belated mastery in a fashion that courts disaster.

   At this point it is important to reflect upon the fact that when dealing with highly intricate and at times inferred characteristics of human behavior, such as unconscious reliving of traumas, there is no one rule that fits all cases. Sometimes the most powerful impulses can also be the most elusive ones. This is why there is really no clear-cut determination as to how many forms of trauma there are or how many kinds of reliving. This is also why psychohistorical verdicts of trauma repetition may seem like the old scientific fallacy of asserting the consequences after the fact. Nevertheless, when on face value a certain individual or group conduct seems irrational, inexplicable, or terribly self-defeating, a psychological model that fits it into a coherent pattern can provide the best understanding of such a behavior. But it should be remembered that very potent but also very elusive factors of human behavior can manifest themselves in a great variety of ways. Indeed Binion (1986) himself, upon further reflections on the mechanism by which an individual or a collective trauma can be relieved, opened the door for wider applications and more versatile interpretations than the ones that his earlier conception allowed. He asserted that a trauma does not necessarily represent a single sudden blow, that it can be relieved as well in pieces as in whole, and that it need not necessarily escalate during repetitions or include the expiation of guilt. Furthermore, the mechanism of reliving a trauma may not be designed to secure eventual mastery but can be a mechanism of aimless repetition the way physical processes repeat themselves without psychic determination.

All this means that there are a number of different options available in the search for an explanation that provides the best fit in any particular situation. It therefore becomes possible to apply the concept of a German repetition compulsion to more than the latest trauma of the defeat in World War I. Any internalized but unacceptable and scorching self-image that is capable every so often of flooding the psyche can be seen as functionally equivalent to trauma or at least akin to it. This includes also the unacceptable self-image of being that kind of person who would allow a trauma to be inflicted upon him. In other words, trauma can beget such a negative self-perception that it acquires its own independent traumatic impact. This could lead to the hypothesis that the notion of an ongoing trauma can allude not only to shocking events as such but also to personality characteristics that oppress the self. One such example of an outstanding personality feature with the power to traumatize could be a shared inner concept of a self-defeating fatal flaw in the German national character. Such a deeply ingrained self-image concerning one's personality makeup can act like a trauma. Not only does it serve as a perpetual narcissistic insult but it is also capable of inducing guilt. This insulting perception of an inherent character flaw that keeps programming failures seems to be related to what George Bailey called the "almost factor" in German history:

> In order to understand the cult of Bismarck-worshipers you have to weigh the "almost factor" in German history.

> Except for Bismarck's half-century, German history is
> an unbroken chain of failures-by-a-hair, of maddeningly
> near misses and no cigars: the Germans *almost* reformed
> the Catholic Church, the Hanseatic League *almost* pre-
> vailed, the peasants *almost* succeeded in their uprising in
> 1527, the Hohenstauffen emperors *almost* consolidated and
> centralized the Holy Roman Empire, the Frankfurt Parlia-
> ment of 1848–1850 *almost* created an integrated ethnic,
> democratic German state, and so on—frustration feeds on
> itself and perpetuates itself in myth. (Bailey 1974, 32)

What we have here is a perception of a fatal flaw, which habitually leads
from a tantalizing "almost" to a maddening failure. Psychologically
speaking, the glorious "almost" represents something like the potential
elation of a liberation from impotence while the inglorious failure seem
to certify a punctured omnipotence. There is an implicit recognition in
such a perception of self that German identity can at any time revert
from the overt to the covert and expose its flip side. This psychological
verdict appears to be based on certain facets of German history. There
were truly phenomenal German accomplishments in the arts and sci-
ences but also actual shortcomings and disappointments. The latter included lack of German colonies, a splintered German homeland, German
political immaturity, and lack of British pragmatism. And it was this
perceived flaw that created the split self-image of Germans as both brilliant and dumb (see chapter 3). In turn the guilt induced by such a perception could have generated recurrent action that aimed to eradicate
the fatal flaw or inner catastrophe but was doomed to repeat it. The
German drive toward the east for the purpose of grabbing a greater
lebensraum was a classic example of the futility of such compulsive
ventures.

Our point of view is therefore that there has been something compulsive and repetitive inherent in the notion of the expansion of the living space. It was something that had to be done, yet this "must" was in
some fashion a repetition of past colonization, Teutonic knights and all.
The theme included an unavoidable escape from coercive narrowness
into the freedom of vast landscapes. Paradoxically, such a fleeing forward could always present at the end of the line that very same thing

that one was fleeing away from. The whole venture looked like corrective lashing out in an attempt to escape from a traumatic condition that was supposedly imposed by the injustice of others, but was also possibly allowed to happen through the ineptness of self.

On the surface, everything was done with confidence. As Hitler provided Germans with some clues concerning the coming venture, he stuck to his traditional mottoes. These included the magic power formula of total unity, the increased strength at the home base, and the coming application of this strength abroad. In a speech at Augsburg on November 21, 1937, he declared:

> To-day we are faced with new tasks, for the livingspace (*Lebensraum*) of our people is too narrow. The world seeks to evade the examination of these problems and the answering of these questions. But that it will not be able to do. One day the world will have to pay attention to our demands. I do not for one second doubt that just as we have been able to raise up the nation at home so, too, abroad we shall secure the same vital rights as other peoples. I do not doubt that this vital right of the German people will in its turn one day be understood by the whole world.
>
> I am convinced that the most difficult part of the preparatory work has already been achieved. It only remains for all National Socialists ever and again to recall the principles by which we have grown great. If the whole Party and also the whole nation stand united behind the leadership, then this leadership, relying on this common strength of a people of sixty-eight millions expressed in the last resort by its army, will be able both to defend with success the nation's interests and successfully to accomplish the tasks which are set before us. (Baynes 1942, 2:1370)

It was all said with an apparent supreme confidence, but the denial of any doubts smacked too much of an affirmation through negation, that is, betraying the deeply hidden doubts by allowing the subject to be even mentioned only within the context of total denial. Manifestly there was every expectation that in the coming big grab for more living space, Germany would be victorious and would enjoy the rewards of winner takes all. But latently there may have been hidden doubts and fears that defeated Germany would lose all.

Eventually the biggest and most decisive move came: the German invasion of the Soviet Union on June 22, 1941. This was the heart and soul of the old historical drive toward the east to secure a vast living space. From its very start, it was conceived as a "double track" mission (Binion 1979, 85) "for a final accounting with the Soviet Union and Jewry" (Goldhagen 1996, 147). Six days after the start of the invasion Joseph Goebbels, Hitler's propaganda minister, inserted the following note in his diary:

> Europe is closing ranks under our leadership. The entire continent is undergoing an awakening. Small and great nations alike are joining us. It is impossible to know yet where it will lead.
>
> In any event, we shall go forward, forward, forward, until the great hour comes. (F. Taylor 1984, 435).

What we have here is a sense of trepidation that arises from not knowing where events are leading and is reacted to by dashing forward, forward, forward toward the great hour. In this heady stuff, one gets a distinct impression of someone swept by an overwhelming current, hoping to go forward in a magical swim rather than to go down and sink. The relentless rush forward suggests a flight from something traumatic no less than a dash toward victory. This rush also represents a resort to perpetual action, which precludes ever being permanently locked into a defeat. This is somewhat like the strategy of a gambler who keeps betting "double or nothing" in the hope of eventually emerging victorious. Somewhat similarly, Goebbels and his compatriots plunged into the framework of ceaseless action as a defense against the dread of not really knowing where events would lead even though at the end it should be a great hour.

At any rate, it took only half a year longer to run into more definite clues as to what the great hour would finally bring. Throughout late November and early December of 1941, the overextended and exhausted

German armies reached the limits of their capacity and were then repulsed at the gates of Moscow and thrown back. It was therefore already possible to forecast the eventual defeat of Germany in the Second World War. Thus, the great hour was destined to be still another trauma. Consequently Goebbels wrote on November 16, 1941, in the magazine *Das Reich* that "the Jews wanted the war and now they have it" (Gilbert 1989, 267). In this connection he added that the führer's prophecy of January 30, 1939, that if the Jews succeeded in plunging the nations into a world war it would mean the annihilation of the Jewish race in Europe was now coming true. It was all self-serving propaganda and a rewriting of history. The decision to kill all of Soviet Jewry was made either at the end of 1940 or in early 1941 and was the beginning of the wider Holocaust that followed. It was an outcome of the inherent logic of the Nazi ideology and not merely a belated response to a reversal on the eastern front. But the toughness of the Bolshevik foe must have inspired new dreams of vengeance and reinforced the old desire to gain magical potency by killing the Jewish disease agents. Thus the ideologically interrelated two tracks—the expansion of the living space and the purification of the national organism from Jews—were being mingled in concrete actions that enormously complicated the German war effort. Indeed Martin Gilbert's (1989) history of the Second World War is replete with descriptions of the enormous ongoing effort to deport and exterminate the Jews in spite of the fact that it detracted from the German war effort.

Nazi Germany had finally unleashed in full its murderous psychology of desperation. The tougher it became to wrest more living space from the Soviet Union in the face of its stupendous "Bolshevik" resistance, the more essential it was to fortify the national body with magical strength. Only purification from the Jewish disease could possibly provide the kind of boost to health and might that was now needed if Germany was to prevail after all. But as with the passage of time it looked more and more as if Germany was not going to prevail, there was a mounting Nazi determination to go down in an apocalypse. Everything possible was going to be done to insure that the impending trauma would not be confined to self but would fully engulf the other as well. This inner logic of the unfolding events was inherent in the worldview of Nazi ideology. Justice demanded an Aryan victory and a Jewish defeat. But if, for whatever reasons, magic no longer worked while the fateful laws of nature decreed that the Germans simply failed to prove themselves capable and worthy of arrogating for themselves a superior lot on earth, the task was still not finished. The Jewish menace had still to be dealt with. The Jewish danger had always been in the forefront of the psychological field of vision even in the midst of the great fight for lebensraum. And this is where the Holocaust came in. Extermination of the Jews would at least make certain that even an Aryan defeat did not result in Jewish victory. What is more, this genocidal extirpation of disease, it was believed, could still benefit humanity at large, even if it was too late for the Germans in their inability to retain an extended living space.

5

The Folkish State

It is the duty of the State to cultivate harmony between the
political and private life of the people—neither more nor
less.

—Germany Speaks

The National Socialist Student Union Association put
university students into brown uniforms and taught them to
sing such old party songs as:

Sharpen the long knives on the pavements,
so they'll cut the bodies of priests more easily!
And when the hour of retribution strikes,
we'll be ready for every sort of mass murder.

—The Hitler File

In promoting the idea of the folkish state, Nazi ideology aspired to
build up an ideal state form that would maximize the people's chances
to actualize the full potential of their inner folkish spirit. A precondi-
tion for a lasting future success of this endeavor was for the folkish
state to integrate the people into a united community of folk comrades
or kindred souls who share a common racial awareness. For that lofty
purpose to be accomplished, it was necessary to implement the leadership principle throughout the folkish state. Hitler's reasoning had been
that since this principle rejected the democratic mass idea in favor of
the idea of personality, it virtually guaranteed that the best minds in
the so-called *Volksgemeinschaft* or folkish community would rise to

leading and influential positions. Hitler's statement in this regard speaks
for itself:

> *The best state constitution and state form is that which,*
> *with the most unquestioned certainty, raises the best minds*
> *in the national community to leading position and leading*
> *influence.*
>   . . . From the smallest community cell to the highest
> leadership of the entire Reich, the state must have the
> personality principle anchored in its organization.
>   There must be no majority decisions, but only respon-
> sible persons, and the word "council" must be restored to
> its original meaning. Surely every man will have advisers
> by his side, but *the decision will be made by one man.*
> (Hitler 1943, 449)

This rejection of the supposed failed ways of democracy coupled with a
return to the imaginary older tribal method requiring that the decision
within a council be made by one man was presumed to uphold a supposed humanistic promise. Democracy deserved to be rejected since for
Hitler it was as dirty and as false as the Jew. "Democracy" could, however, hold a true humanistic promise if it were redefined in proper folkish
terms. Thus, in his speech of November 8, 1938, Hitler redefined "democracy" in this clever bit of verbal fancy-foot dancing:

> In our opinion, democracy implies a regime supported by
> the will of a people. I became Chancellor of Germany once
> in compliance with the rules of parliamentary democracy . . .
> and today I received the complete approval of the German
> Volk—let Mr. Churchill doubt this if he pleases. I did not
> eliminate two democracies this year, rather, I destroyed, as
> the epitome of a true democrat, two dictatorships! Namely,
> the dictatorship of Herr Schuschnigg and the dictatorship of
> Herr Benes. . . . I am merely the advocate of my Volk! . . .
> Besides that, I am not a head of state in the sense that a
> dictator or monarch is, I am a leader of the German Volk!
> . . . Mr. Churchill and these gentlemen are delegates of the

English people, and I am a delegate of the German Volk. The only difference here is that Mr. Churchill received only a fraction of his people's votes while, I may confidently say, I represent the entire German Volk! (Domarus 1992, 1238–39)

In this brief sample of Orwellian "newspeak," the sarcastic Hitler is "the epitome of a true democrat" while democratic Austria and, even more so, Czechoslovakia are each a "dictatorship," which deserved to be destroyed by him. But he was dead serious when he pitted himself against Churchill to judge who was a more authentic delegate of his people. Churchill represented but a fraction of the people, while Hitler imagined that he represented the entire folk.

In these statements it can be readily seen that the racial ideal of what a true democracy would be is based on some mystical notion of representing the will of the entire people. And in Hitler's ideology, this expression cannot take place unless society is ordered and led by the force of personality to begin with. Then, and only then, is a human community "redeemed from the curse of Mechanism and becomes a living thing" (Hitler 1943, 446). The folkish state was thus more than an organization. It was a living organism, which promoted the people's community or *Volksgemeinschaft*. And it successfully accomplished this in accordance with the people's separate personalities and collective will, with an emphasis on the latter.

Thus, Nazi ideology aspired to a blissful union of individual contentment through collective merging as if there were no contradiction between the two. The contradiction was conveniently brushed aside through the supposition that no personal satisfaction was possible for individuals anyway except through the collective. But in spite of this cozy presumption, there had been an inherent contradiction there all along, as the requirements of the national collective completely preempted the rights of the individual. Nevertheless, Nazi ideologues were eager to promote their discrepant ideals as if they reinforced one another rather than negated each other. Under the umbrella of the *Volksgemeinschaft*, the folk community, everything was supposed to cohere naturally in pleasant harmony. Some of the peddlers of this harmony may have been aware of the fraud. And some people did not buy it. But many did. Yet we know from psychology that blissful ignorance of contradictions is a defensive maneuver where a supposedly benevolent unconscious spares people conscious pain. It therefore behooves us to take a closer look at the inherent contradiction.

On face value, the hallmark of life in a true people's community according to Hitler is that it is organic. This means that the entire collectivity, rather than being put together like a thoughtless machine, is united like a conscious living organism. Above all the organic promise, so to speak, is a promise of meaningful connectedness. Instead of the alienation of modernity comes the rootedness in the people's historical past. Instead of the isolation of industrialized life comes the ongoing and available friendliness of folk comrades. Instead of mechanistic existence comes a vitalistic way of life that is characterized by intentionality and will. Instead of atomism, which is the epitome of meaningless disconnectedness, comes the consciousness of being a meaningful part of an organic community to which one is linked by blood, by history, by love, and by choice in a thousand ways. The people yearned for this antidote to alienation. And the leadership principle, which was akin to the central nervous system of the folkish state, promised them that the yearning would be collectively fulfilled yet in an individual and humanistic fashion. Was not each person going to be plugged into a slot that suited him by nature rather than by the coincidence of birth and the vagaries of internal class splits? Was not each individual going to be selected for a proper position so as to play a fitting economic, political, and even artistic role according to his natural inclinations as determined by his inherent personality worth? Was there not room for every single person to fit comfortably into the collective racial framework which was so marvelously able to accommodate individual differences exactly because the greatest personal bent of each folk comrade was the identification with that living and breathing organic whole? What could be more humane and democratic than that? And it would have been self-evident that this is truly democratic if it were not for the fact that the term democratic, rather than denoting accurate expression of the will of the entire people, acquired the distorted antipersonality principle of rule by numerical majority. This kind of a distorted outlook, which disregarded the value of personality, implied that democracy itself is in effect anti-individual. For if democracy were truly to mean the cultivation of people's inherent personalities while each individual enjoyed a glorious connectedness with the all-important organic whole, then the *Volksgemeinschaft* would be instantly recognized as the most humanistic form of existence that delivers that fulfillment, which in present-day democracies remained only an empty promise. In short, there had never been a more natural and spiritually rewarding way of life than the Nazi-promised life in an organic community established in the folkish state through the implementation of the leadership principle. But this principle, which required unquestioned obedience from everybody, rested on the cozy assumption that there was no inherent contradiction between each person's "will" and the will of the leader.

All along there was an inherent tension imbedded in the establishment of a folk community. The rigid implementation of the hierarchical leadership principle in the organic community led to a unity that held a dual promise. The first promise of the unity was the assurance of individual connectedness for everyone; no one was going to be left out leading a meaningless, isolated existence. The second promise of the unity was the creation of magical mass power. It was this power part of the formula, the means to get it and the goals that it would serve, that proved to be preponderant in the Nazi state.

Power is what tilted everything in the direction of mechanism and atomism in spite of the existence of the overall organic umbrella. Since the desire for and promise of power was there all along, it pushed things in a certain direction. For power one needed industrialization regardless of how alienating it was and how it disconnected the individual. For power one needed mechanistic existence imposed from above regardless of how deadening and antivitalistic it was for each person. For power people had to be shunted into slots where more production was needed, not where their personalities would find it most natural to be. And for the sake of power, people who were unhappy with their current and past employment were compelled to remain locked into it all in the name of their common will and individual choice. These inherent contradictions were well exposed by David Schoenbaum (1966), who pointed out that Nazi social theory denied equality but at the same time asserted it. While the premise of the *Volksgemeinschaft* was the natural (racial) superiority of all Germans, the premise of the leadership principle was the natural superiority (personality merit) of only some Germans. As a result the attempt to square the elite leadership principle with the equality principle of the national community was akin to an attempt to square the circle. In practice, opting for industrial rearmament won over other goals (Schoenbaum 1966, 59, 245–46, 251). It can be concluded from this that power, including military power, assumed top priority.

As for the immediate as well as long-term goals of power, they varied. They ranged from the quest for some form of a German hegemony over Europe to outright world domination and from extirpating Jews by social isolation or by expulsions to doing away with them by outright extermination. In short, these goals of power, which received the utmost national priority, reinforced the tendency to generate power by any means, period. Consequently, the exalted unity of the promised organic community came to serve more the needs of creating collective power rather than the individual need for spiritual connectedness or the need to overcome the alienating impact of modernity. Thus, the revolt against modernity that fueled the initial rise of Nazism was subsequently quashed by the victory of the Nazi movement. The major reason for this was that modernity, which came to be identified first and foremost with modern means of production no matter how mechanistic, was necessary for power. This is the reason why the ideal of voluntary connectedness in an organic community fell casualty to the reality of coercive practices within the same community. In the process, the united whole retained the term organic but assumed definite atomistic and mechanistic features. In sum, the discrepancy between ideological claims and mundane reality created a dilemma. Meaningful organic connectedness could not be maintained without loss of power, while the generation of power by an atomistic linking of society could not take effect without sacrificing organic connectedness.

A feature of Nazi ideology that tried to escape between the horns of this dilemma was the well-emphasized credo that the individual is nothing but the nation is everything. Its implication was that true individual fulfillment is impossible anyway unless a person is enmeshed in the united whole. In other words, nothing is more alienating or less meaningful for a person than to detach himself from the central significance of the collective to which he belongs. To try and reach personal fulfillment in this individual and detached condition is a meaningless and self-negating exercise in futility. What Nazi ideology implied was that a person's "groupish" self is not merely his extended national self but is actually his only self. Thus, by narrowing the psychological space of identity and denying the feasibility of any individual fulfillment outside the framework of the collective, Nazi ideology did away with the notion of autonomous persons seeking on their own initiative either individual or group experiences, according to their varying needs and preferences. What the ideology left standing instead was the notion of a collectivity that is the only agent capable of actualizing the personality potential of its members. The paradigm here was that once the magical mystical link of connectedness between the individual and the group is successfully established, the collectivity unlocks the individual capacity for personal fulfillment, which can be defined only as a personal sharing of the collective life. Left to his own devices, the individual is incapable of unlocking this capacity and is therefore denied participation in the exalted experience of mystical union that comes through such a collective sharing. He thus remains a wasted personality or an individual nothing who tragically missed the chance to become everything through his folk.

By this co-opting or even preemption of the psychological space of personal identity by the psychological realm of collective identity, the contradiction between the requirements of unity for connectedness and the requirements of unity for power was seemingly resolved. The roads toward achieving both goals were supposed to be identical rather than one being organic but the other atomistic. By the same token, all roads led to the same place: a united *Volksgemeinschaft* fast secured by the folkish state. The state formed the all important means for achieving the sacred goal of a true folkish community. As Hitler (1943, 393) stated in *Mein Kampf: "The state is a means to an end. Its end lies in the preservation and advancement of a community of physically and psychically homogeneous creatures. This preservation itself comprises first of all existence as a race and thereby permits the free development of all the forces dormant in this race."* There it was—the old promise of a psychophysical integrity—destined to be realized through the homogenizing by the state of the creatures who belong to the folkish community. In consequence, the generation of national power could now proceed under the banner of the organic whole while people were expected to delight in the discovery of personal fulfillment by becoming individual nothings only to be reincarnated as folk "everythings." To reinforce the people's predilection of moving in this direction, Nazi ideology routinely called for sacrifice. In essence this was a call for the sacrifice of individuality and even of life itself for the sake of the whole. That is one meaning of readiness to sacrifice on behalf of the group—voluntarily becoming an individual nothing for the sake of the national everything. A related meaning is the transformation of the entire masses into pure energy. The implications of this method of generating ultimate power merit further discussion.

Richard Koenigsberg compiled various statements by Hitler concerning sacrifice and provided a summary of the basic themes (Koenigsberg 1975, 43–46). He concluded that Hitler stressed the necessity of the sacrifice in the individual in relation to his country, species, state, community, people, and the demands of Germany, stating, "You are nothing, your nation is everything." Hitler also asked the Germans to work for the community, to be the servant of the nation and think only of the nation. Finally Hitler expressed a belief in the value of a willingness to die for the country, calling this act the "crown of all sacrifice." The following statements from *Mein Kampf* were included in Koenigsberg's compilation but are quoted here at greater length:

> The Aryan is not greatest in his mental qualities as such, but in the extent of his willingness to put all his abilities in the service of the community. In him the instinct for self-preservation has reached the noblest form, since he willingly subordinates his own ego to the life of the community and, if the hour demands, even sacrifices it. (Hitler 1943, 297)

> This state of mind, which subordinates the interests of the ego to the conservation of the community, is really the first premise for every truly human culture. From it alone can arise all the great works of mankind, which bring the founder little reward, but the richest blessings to posterity.
> . . . What applies to work as the foundation of human sustenance and all human progress is true to an even greater degree for the defense of man and his culture. In giving one's own life for the existence of the community

lies the crown of all sense of sacrifice. It is this alone that
prevents what human hands have built from being over-
thrown by human hands or destroyed by Nature. (Hitler
1943, 298)

Care must be taken not to underestimate the force of an
idea. . . . For what made men die then was not concern for
their daily bread, but love of the fatherland, faith in its
greatness, a general feeling for the honor of the nation. . . .
Therefore it is really necessary to confront the master
book-keepers of the present *material republic* by faith in an
ideal Reich. (Hitler 1943, 437)

The italics by Hitler in the last sentence refer to the Weimar Republic
and to the would-be Third Reich respectively.

Even a cursory look at these quotations reveals that sacrifice, sometimes in combination with other loaded terms such as love, faith, or
honor, is identified as an indispensable instrument for the building of a
culture as well as for its preservation. It thus forms a required element
for racial survival and self-actualization. Moreover, the act of sacrifice
serves as a testimony to such an inspired faith in an ideal that it generates the necessary will or willingness to do anything. Consequently the
will to sacrifice consists of the final step in completely bridging the gap
between ideas and actions no matter how extreme either of them is. It
was no coincidence that the notion of the sacrifice was tied by Hitler to
faith, honor, and love. Faith serves to propel people to action. Honor
legitimizes the action and also makes it inevitable in order to avoid shame.
Finally, "love" has a dual role. It is the "horizontal" love for family and
for folk, which endows the action with fanaticism, while it is also the
"vertical" love for the leader, which accepts the direction of the action
as prescribed by the leader. All of this suggests that the issue of "sacrifice" is one of those fateful issues that deals with national ultimate stakes.
Consequently, readiness to sacrifice, not only others but also oneself,
can sometimes serve as a danger signal, especially at times when a nation turns a blind eye to objective reality and instead finds itself in the
grip of a shared group fantasy.

"Sacrifice" has loomed large on the German psychohistorical

agenda in the first half of the twentieth century. This subject was puzzling indeed to Hermann Rauschning, a minor player in the unfolding drama of the 1930s. He was a Nazi who left the movement and moved to England, where he wrote a series of books warning the west of the dangers of Nazism. However, his accounts and opinions remain historically controversial, and in fact he was exposed as a fraud who falsely claimed to have conducted confidential conversations with Hitler. Nevertheless, part of his analysis of the unfolding events was insightful. David Schoenbaum (1966, xxi) characterized Rauschning's 1939 book *The Revolution of Nihilism: Warning to the West,* as the book that "described the Nazi revolution as the novelty it was." In that book, Rauschning discussed the question of what was unfolding in German history in the aftermath of the First World War and during the Nazi era: was the Third Reich a promising new order or was it a holocaust in the making for Germany itself? His own judgment was that the very same thing that was celebrated by the Nazis as the rebirth of the nation was what he himself regarded as a permanent revolution of sheer destruction. This disparity in perception, between the German public's illusion of rebirth on the one hand and his own personal holocaustal vision on the other hand, caused him to wonder what in actuality is make-believe and what is reality, in the Nazi movement specifically and in German history generally.

Such crucial questions cannot be subjected to a genuine national enquiry unless honest criticism is allowed. But in reflecting upon the fact that in Nazi Germany criticism was regarded as the worst of crimes and as high treason, Rauschning also recalled that already twenty years earlier, in the aftermath of the defeat in World War I, he witnessed a similar "bad psychology." This "bad psychology" consisted of a conviction that maintaining the national will to resist requires the nation be kept in ignorance of the frightful gravity of its situation. It was a conviction of the need for a fixed resolve and unquestioning faith combined with contemptuous belittlement of the moral forces of the nation. He poignantly contrasted this bad psychology of unquestioning faith with the practice of other nations that succeeded in increasing their resolve by facing the truth. This finally led Rauschning to ask the pertinent question whether it was a quality peculiar to the German that his readiness for sacrifice can only be maintained under illusions.

Rauschning seems to have hit upon a major psychological strand that characterized the Nazi revolution, which was seen by him as "dynamic," that is, perpetual and capable of energetic movement toward total nihilism and the destruction of all values. His diagnosis of nihilism implied, of course, that the revolutionary promise was an illusion. And now he hit upon the psychological underpinning of this destructive trend. The psychological strand that he detected consisted of a progression from a totally unquestioning faith leading to complete illusions that culminates in the maintenance of sacrifice. To this one may add that in the Nazi ideology, the sequence of faith-illusion-sacrifice leads from the domain of feeling to the domain of action. And in the process, the self-sacrificing person meshes into a glorified all-powerful collective that will triumphantly march on to eternity. Rauschning thus sensed that both Nazi ideology and pre-Nazi psychology led to and culminated in a notion of sacrifice based on illusionary premises of rebirth. He therefore proclaimed, with great exasperation: "It seems to be our destiny to have to repeat the same mistakes with a berserker's infatuation" (Rauschning 1939, xiii). To him the whole notion of a sacrifice based on illusion seemed like a renewed invitation for a catastrophe. It is interesting to note that in the last two paragraphs of *Mein Kampf* Hitler seems to have engaged in a denial of this very possibility: "A state which in this age of racial poisoning dedicates itself to the care of its best racial elements must some day become lord of the earth. May the adherents of our movement never forget this if ever the magnitude of the sacrifices should beguile them to an anxious comparison with the possible results" (Hitler 1943, 688). This is the bombastic finale of his book, and it was meant to deliver an ideological punch. But its format betrays an underlying dread. The "results to sacrifices ratio" of this format pits future victory and future hegemony against sizable but worthwhile sacrifices. It totally rejects the possibility of a repeat collapse that would make the sacrifices worthless. Consequently, while it reiterates that Germany will become lord of the earth, it also offers a preemptive denial that the required sacrifices will be catastrophic.

Why was any sacrifice deemed essential on the road to racial paradise? The answer partly depends on which meanings are attached to the word. There are many meanings of the term sacrifice. Belt tightening, for instance, can be called "sacrifice." But the readiness for sacrifice that Hitler demanded from his followers leaves no question as to his meaning. Inspection of the above-mentioned collection by Koenigsberg (1975, 44–46) of Hitler's statements about sacrifice shows that his underlying meaning of sacrifice is dying: the readiness of each individual to give up his life for the sake of the collective. The images that Hitler conjured up involved regiments going to their death singing *Deutschland über Alles in der Welt,* the joyful sacrifice through faith of the most precious blood, giving one's life for the community as the crown of all sacrifice, dying not for daily bread but for love of, faith in, and honor of the country, young men sacrificing their young lives freely and joyfully on the altar of the beloved fatherland, and finally the notion that, for German boys and girls, life must mean sacrifice.

It is clear that subscription to these images by the masses, especially the young generation, laid the foundation for successful application of the leadership principle. The willing sacrificers were going to be obedient subjects indeed to the supreme leader. His will was to be their will because his will represented the will of the entire nation. In Nazi ideology, the notion of the sacrifice implies that any individual will, which separates the individual from the group, is a misguided will and is the faulty product of a mechanistic civilization. In contrast, the individual's willingness to sacrifice self for the nation represents that admirable individual will that is an outcome of salutary total identification with the nation. That kind of will, which is based on faith, is the authentic product of the healthy environment of an organic culture. Subordination of personal ego to the collective is the hallmark of the folkish state, while its realization and proof lie in the total readiness of all members of the folkish community to die at the leader's command because his was the guiding brain of the folkish organism.

It is time now to reiterate some of the highlights of Hitler's ideology in order to illustrate how the ideological matrix culminated in the notion of sacrifice. Since the individual is nothing while the nation is everything, each individual should be willing to give his life for the sake of the collective. This is especially true at a time of mortal danger to the national organism when things are not as they ought to be. The national organism should have nonpolluted blood, which makes for a healthy soul—a psychophysical integrity of mind and body where the power of the will prevails. This would result in magical powers and invincibility.

Unfortunately, however, the national body is afflicted by polluted blood and is therefore in a degenerative state and lacks the necessary strength of will. The responsible parties for this decay into death are the universal agents of decomposition: the Jews. It is therefore an absolute must to do something about the blood poisoning immediately. The essential cure for this affliction is the implementation of the leadership principle—the magic power formula, which results in "one Reich, one Folk, one Leader." It generates mighty energies that enable the nation to restore its health by purging the Jews and by expanding its inadequate living space. But this power surge, by generating human energies on a mass scale, requires total readiness for ultimate self-sacrifice as a necessary condition. Then, and only then, can the leader of will move mountains with the masses' faith.

Hitler's notions imply that the readiness for sacrifice transforms the masses into an effective instrument of unlimited resources, since those who are willing to die are ready to do anything. In his ideology, readiness for sacrifice signals total malleability of the masses to the point of becoming pure energy. And this brings us back to Rauschning, who regarded the entire purpose of the Nazi philosophy to be that of serving as fuel for energy (Rauschning 1939, 23). This was consistent with his view of the Nazi revolution as a revolution of nihilism that annuls all values including its own ideological credos. But this was not entirely true. Unlike his socialistic principles, Hitler's racial principles (especially the ones concerning the Jewish danger) were nonnegotiable and were not meant to disappear once they served as fuel for action. However, while Rauschning's assertion was incorrect with regard to the Nazi ideology in toto, it was fairly correct in many ways. These included those features that were valued only as useful myths that raise the people's energy level and mobilize them for mass actions. Energy was indeed one of the sacred goals of Nazi ideology, and it was the readiness for sacrifice that signaled the psychological point of transformation of people into readily usable human energy. The premium placed on the concept of energy was also related to key characteristics of Nazism such as dynamism and permanent revolution, which were discussed by Rauschning (1939) and by Neumann (1965) and which stood for a continuous self-propelled action in an incessant state of warlike mobilization and readiness.

Thus, the dominance of sacrifice in the folkish state was in effect the triumph of mechanism. The folk comrades of the people's community were effectively atomized so as to become a rich storehouse of energy available for use. And the energy was supposed to be turned on and off with the precision of a machine. (In reality the Nazi machine never ran smoothly or precisely.) Claims continued to be made that the *Volksgemeinschaft* was a living organism, but its modus operandi was highly mechanistic. As for the folkish state, it evolved into an elaborate organization as befits a totalistic state, which tries to control all aspects of life for the purpose of generating a mighty power. The outcome of it all was a glaring discrepancy between the ideological celebration of the living organism and the actual practice of mechanism and atomism.

This did not mean, however, that the atomized masses always caught on to the true reality. But sometimes they were aware of how oppressive totalistic regimentation was and did recognize that they functioned like small cogs in a huge machine. On some such occasions this awareness was expressed through humor. For instance, in one well-circulated joke, a busy Nazi family life was described. Each family member was enrolled in a state-sponsored organization. The father belonged to the SA, the mother to the National Socialist Women's Association, the son to the Hitler Youth, and the daughter to the German Girl's League. The time of every single family member, whether young or old, was confiscated entirely by an endless series of mandated meetings and organized activities. The question arose as to when do the busy family members ever get a chance to meet with each other. The surprise answer—at the annual party rally in Nuremberg. This was a telling joke indeed. It is even possible to perceive it as a humorous sequel to Hitler's portrayal in *Mein Kampf* (1943, 30–34) of the wrangling family that lacks national pride. In the present sequel of sorts the educational deficiencies that were exposed in Hitler's earlier portrayal have been fully corrected. This time around, the story is of a family that took full part in the process of the "nationalization" of the people, which Hitler promoted as the desired remedy. The results, however, were not as enthralling as Hitler would have expected them to be. Actually the stinging joke illustrates quite poignantly what happens when, through regimentation, the entire nation is maneuvered from above to play the role of everyone's family. Not surprisingly, this form of imperialism with regard to private time preempts the immediate nuclear family. This is why, in discussing this joke, Sigmund Neumann (1965, 192–93) spoke of the Nazi dictatorship's practice of undermining the family by training children to report on their parents and by the elimination of separate spheres for private and public life. The underlying bottom line here was no private domain, ergo, no family domain.

For Hitler, however, this process represented not the destructive preemption of the domain of the immediate family but rather the integration of all into a one big happy family. His private conversations clearly allude to this famous joke in a defensive attempt to put his own slant on it by treating it not as a joke but as a serious statement. In the process he let the cat out of the bag by stating what it was really all about. He made the following statements at a dinner conversation on July 6, 1942:

> In the course of our many electoral tours my companions and I have got to know and to love the Reich from Berlin to its uttermost corners. As for the most part I was invited to take my meals *en famille,* I also got to know intimately Germans all over Germany. There I used to meet whole families, in which the father would be working in our political section, the mother was a member of the Women's Association, one brother was in the SS, the other in the Hitler Youth, and the daughter was in the German Girl's League. And so when we all meet once a year at the Party Rally at Nuremberg, it always gives me the impression of being just one huge family gathering.
>
> The Party Rally has, however, been not only a quite unique occasion in the life of the NSDAP but also in many respects a valuable preparation for war. Each Rally requires the organization of no fewer than four thousand special trains. As these trains stretched as far as Munich and Halle, the railway authorities were given first-class practice in the military problem of handling mass troop transportation. (Trevor-Roper 1953, 458–59)

There it was. The overbusy members of the preempted immediate family finally get to meet once a year in one huge family gathering of the National Socialist German Workers' (Nazi) Party at Nuremberg. But for Hitler the primary value of this family gathering or party rally was that it served as a valuable preparation for war.

What happened in reality was the dissolution of separate spheres for private and public life, which Sigmund Neumann spoke about. In other words, when the nation is everything but the individual is nothing, his immediate family is reduced to nothing as well. The small family was left with no autonomous functions, but only with the officially sanctioned collaborative state functions of keeping workers content, encouraging the young to become warriors, and incubating a new supply of future soldiers. Indeed, as the pressure to produce new babies and future soldiers increased after the outbreak of World War II, a break from traditional family patterns took place with the official encouragement of girls "to present the Führer with a child" (Bleuel 1974, 226–27). It was reported by Bleuel that one such determined girl wrote home from a Labor Service training camp warning her family: "You better not beat me if I come home with a baby, or I will denounce you!" This is a prime example of a child who has been indoctrinated to report her parents and who grew up in a folkish community that systematically dissolved the private domain, switching loyalty and identification from the private nuclear family to the public national family.

At any rate, wishing to present the führer with a child was quite consonant with the notion that in the *Volksgemeinschaft* the whole nation is the family while the führer is the symbolic father of all. Not that there were not plenty of girls around who wrote love letters to the führer dreaming of his becoming the actual biological father of their child. But in actuality the führer had to remain a symbolic mate. As Richard Grunberger reported, good German maidens were resolved to make the führer the gift of a child by means of the *Lebensborn* (Spring of Life) program, which enabled willing single women to be impregnated by SS men. Clearly such practices added up to a relentless pressure on the nuclear family. Grunberger discussed the Nazi party rally joke as an illustration of the phenomenon of women finding themselves in a situation of "political widowhood" because the active party involvement prevented their husbands from using the home for more than bed and board. He maintained that this was only one aspect of a whole array of pressures that eroded family cohesion. These included prolonged national service periods out of home by both boys and girls as well as structural changes in the workplaces involving widespread industrial employment of women, more overtime, and irregular shift work as well as work that required being continually absent from home except for weekends (Grunberger 1972, 255–74). Obviously the folkish state did its utmost to preempt the nuclear family by incorporating it into the larger folk community and channeling its labor for the dual purpose of propagation and production, which would both be necessary for fueling future wars.

Since behavioral and mind-control measures were so frequently sugarcoated with the notion of love of the nation, the masses did not always catch on to their true import. There was, after all, the reward of exhilaration each time an individual, who participated in one of those oft-recurring marches and parades, fused with the crowd to become one with the whole nation. Similarly, there was a great sense of exuberance each time that an inspired person, who felt ready for self-sacrifice, experienced the psychological death of his individuality being resurrected in the eternal life of the collectivity. It was, after all, through this willingness to undergo the self-asserting act of self-sacrifice that each insignificant and largely impotent individual moved away from powerlessness toward omnipotence. But the enormous metamorphosis due to these dialectical experiences involving rebirth through willingness to die was an illusion that hid the reality of self-destruction. Yet the energies that are released by such a powerful illusion, which leads from feelings of faith to willingness to sacrifice, are enormous. So is the price. Mass sacrifice for any goal, not to mention an unrealistic goal, is too tragic a price. But it is illustrative of the enormous mobilizing power of certain illusions, such as the conversion of individual death to rebirth into an eternal collective life. It is indeed like converting all matter into energy. Self-sacrificing people are supercharged with energy and are completely available for any kind of an immediate action. It was basically this boundless action potential that Rauschning termed "dynamism." Nothing can hold back the determined self-sacrificer. Such sacrificers are the best followers a totalitarian ideology can recruit.

Thus, in Hitler's ideology, sacrifice represents a self-initiated action that is deliberately induced as a necessary step to acquire collective omnipotence or at least greater collective might. There is a clear element of magic in all of this. The magic is derived from the complete fusion of the would-be sacrificer with the leader and with the nation, which enables each person to partake in the larger glory of the national grandeur. The magic also flows from the tremendous boost given to action potential by the emotional readiness for sacrifice, which is psychologically equivalent to a conversion into a state of pure energy. And finally the magic is also derived from the compelling power of the symmetrical principle of justice, which mandates glorious compensation for the self-inflicted losses. What is more, the magical impact of trading with fate under this archaic principle is being further augmented by the fact that in this unique instance what is being traded is blood. Blood, as we may recall, was the magic content of the folkish container, and with its magical impact it could reward its protectors with racial thriving for all eternity. But it was still necessary every so often, especially at war times, to engage once again in the joyful sacrifice of blood—the stuff of life and the miraculous essence of the race. Its sacrifice was expected to yield priceless returns while its connection to war was mythologized and glorified. That is why Hitler stated: "In October and November 1914, we had there received our baptism of fire. Fatherland love in our heart and songs on our lips, our young regiments had gone into battle as to a dance. The most precious blood there sacrificed itself joyfully, in the faith that it was preserving the independence and freedom of the fatherland" (Hitler 1943, 201). Independence and freedom were thus the kind of invaluable gains that justify the most painful of losses—the loss of the precious blood.

The general idea that sacrificial losses of life can benefit the collective was not a Nazi innovation and was not really new. We already know that the issue of the sacrifice is related to the magical dimensions of the symmetry of primitive justice. As we may recall, the quest for justice required that punishments should fit crimes. However, it also allowed for ultramanipulative interventions in the distribution of the worldly gains and losses of assets—both material and symbolic. And nowhere is that distribution more crucial than in the gains and losses of lives. The principle of "a life for a life" was a cornerstone of symmetrical justice, but it too was somewhat elastic and subject to ultramanipulative influences. And one of the most manipulative maneuvers available for influencing the distribution of lives is the self-initiated loss of life that is the outcome of sacrifice. A loss cannot stand by itself. In the symmetrical and primitive system of justice, the introduction of a loss in one place exerts an irresistible or magical pressure to produce a gain in another realm. Any sacrificial losses of lives are therefore destined to yield healthy dividends in longevity and health for the rest of the collective. Since biblical times, and even earlier, human sacrifices have been offered to the gods in an attempt to cajole them to abide by the requirements of justice and therefore to repay a life for a life. The repayment to the whole group in the currency of "life," and with additional dividends, could include health, longevity, propagation, growth, and anything else that is life-enhancing for the collective. It could also include victory, the successful sacrifice of others, where the deaths or lost lives of the enemy symbolically stood for life gains for one's own group. Every so often the currency of "life" seemed to be a good investment. Metaphorically speaking, the best stock in the stock market of justice was death by sacrifice of human life. The symmetrical rules of justice were compelled to compensate the dearest of losses with the most precious of gains. It is no coincidence that, in present day financial parlance, making a lot of money in the stock market is characterized as making a "killing." The choice of language here betrays an implicit zero-sum-game assumption that is not the economic reality of the market but sometimes appears to be the psychological reality. It is as if one could not make a handsome profit in the stock market unless it was preceded by someone else being killed financially so that his loss now becomes one's gain. In the game of nations this kind of primitive psychology is far more lethal than in the stock market. The quest for national justice in the international arena legitimizes any and all ultramanipulative measures. All is fair in love of führer and war of expansion; it includes enslavement or even genocide.

We have already discussed love of the leader and faith in him in relation to self-sacrifice. But war is a form of magical intervention that utilizes the ultramanipulative act of sacrificing others no less than the act of sacrificing self. In some magical fashion, through intrapsychic compulsion, the disaster that is inflicted upon others through war translates into added security and prosperity for one's own group. War is thus presumed to shore up fixed boundaries that clearly demarcate who gets disaster and who gets utopia. It is no wonder therefore that, from psychohistorical and psychopolitical standpoints, war has been perceived as designed to settle not only the manifest issue of real physical borders but also the latent issue of psychological borders (Volkan 1988, 124–32). Who wins and who loses has not only geographical implications but deeply felt psychological ramifications. (See the next chapter). A deadly war machine, not a living organism, is what the folkish state was actually designed to be.

An ever tighter control of this folkish greenhouse for the cultivation of warriors was being imposed by the totalitarian state. The measures of control were designed to extend to all aspects of life. They were fraught with dialectics and inner contradictions that could seem humorous at times if it were not for the fact that their intrusiveness was also backed by terror. The incessant barrage of propaganda that reached the homes, the schools, and the workplaces did not leave many hiding places into which to escape from this constant nationalization of the people. A few hardy individuals who did not escape by emigration from Germany retreated into the so-called internal emigration in an attempt to secure for themselves tiny corners of free thinking, which successfully elude the attention of the all-knowing and coercive state. The state did its best to become all-knowing. And if it were ever going to be fully successful, then it would have to become like God. Religion teaches that, since God can read what is in the hearts of human beings, it is impossible to hide from him. In like fashion, the Nazi state aspired to be all-knowing, leaving no one a possible hiding place, not even in his most private thoughts. Yet in the final analysis, the folkish state could not really be a mind reader fashioned after the godly model. All it could hope to do was to shape the mind of the people as much as possible through everlasting propaganda. Once this was accomplished, the state could indeed "read" all peoples' minds since it shaped these minds to begin with. This would have enabled the state to exercise the desired total control of both body and soul, i.e., not only of peoples' behavior but also their thinking. Dialectically, therefore, the final success of the relentless and coercive propaganda could even lead to the abandonment of terror as a means of control. The reason for this is that control by physical coercion becomes less and less necessary if the behavior to be controlled is emitted more and more voluntarily and presumably even spontaneously. Thus the final success of propaganda as a control measure could have almost rendered it superfluous. Nevertheless in view of Hitler's contempt for the mind of the masses, it seems highly unlikely that propaganda reinforced by terror would ever have been withdrawn because otherwise the masses could easily fall prey to "wrong" ideas. In Hitler's program, the incessant drive to implement utopia was meant to be, among other things, a never ending propaganda endeavor to instill faith or to manufacture spontaneity, depending on the point of view. And the folkish state was tireless in its incessant propaganda activities. Consequently, some people became true believers without any reservation, while others ignored their inner misgivings and deluded themselves that their coerced behavior was voluntary. Finally, there were persons with well-integrated identities who felt good and secure about themselves and remained fairly immune to the persistent national education.

Since women served as the vehicle for the increased production of babies and would-be warriors of the folkish state, it was necessary to instruct them about the limits of their role and the confines of their domain. Hitler clarified these issues in a speech delivered on September 8, 1934, in Nuremberg to the convention of the National Socialist Women's Association (Domarus 1990, 531–35). Sounding somewhat like an Otto Weininger with a sense of humor, he praised women for their sureness of emotion and feeling, which supplements the intellect of man. Following this put-down in the guise of a compliment, he reminded the audience that nature and Providence assigned different tasks to the two sexes. In this connection he asserted that the catchphrase "Women's Liberation" was the invention of Jewish intellect. The clear implication of this was, of course, that women would find true freedom when they fulfill the limited biological and domestic task assigned to them by nature. He went on to explain that while a man's world is the state, a woman's world is a smaller one: her husband, her family, her children, and her home. But the two worlds complement each other. What is more, the larger world could not survive had not Providence assigned to woman the care of the smaller world, her very own world. Finally Hitler arrived at the crux of the matter: "What a man sacrifices in struggling for his Volk, a woman sacrifices in struggling to preserve this Volk in individual cases. What a man gives in heroic courage on the battlefield, woman gives in eternally patient devotion, in eternally patient suffering and endurance. Every child to which she gives birth is a battle which she wages in her Volk's fateful question of to be or not to be" (Domarus

1990, 533). Women were thus told what to expect. Men's larger world of the state (and waging war) is dependent on the emotional, nonintellectual women tending reliably to their smaller world at home. As courageous men will suffer sacrifices on the battlefield, devoted women will ensure that new children replace the losses. The bottom line therefore is that the folkish state is designed to be a war machine and that consequently, and in accordance with the laws of nature, women's true liberation is being in labor.

Hitler's treatment of women was in the best tradition of the *kitsch* and death mode as described by Saul Friedländer (1984). His perceptive analysis of Nazi culture, as well as the new discourse in the late 1960s and the 1970s on the phenomenon of fascism, unveiled an underlying coexistence and link between an adoration of power and a dream of its explosive annulment. The former represented the craving for order and the willingness for submission, while the latter reflected the gravitation toward chaos and a readiness to discard all existing order in an attempt to become all-powerful even at the risk of annihilation. Friedländer maintained that this coexistence and link between the two opposites represents the very foundation of the psychological hold of Nazism. Moreover, he averred that the linking of this duality as seen in the cultural flow of ideas, emotions, and phantasms was unique to Nazism since in other modern western societies, its two concepts were kept separate. His major contention was that this underlying psychological duality created the aesthetics of *kitsch* and death.

As Friedländer pointed out, *kitsch* is a term that characterizes art and decorations adapted to the taste of the majority. It represents the harmony so dear to the petit bourgeois, who sees in it a respect for beauty and order. There is no adequate English word with which to translate the term *kitsch.* Cheap taste, ticky-tacky sentimentality, and shoddy come to mind, but they do not do full justice to *kitsch.* Very significantly Friedländer included in it expressions of the notorious everyday *Gemütlichkeit*—the German image of comfortableness, cosiness, snugness, and hominess. This inclusion serves to accentuate the contrast between the homey everyday cosiness of *kitsch* and the terror of death. It is the juxtaposition of *kitsch* aesthetics with death themes that creates a surprise response, or a frisson. What starts as comfortable *kitsch* conjures up images of death including the popular theme of the hero dedicated to sacrifice. There is therefore a *kitsch* of death, which in its grandest scale even includes a *kitsch* of the apocalypse. Consequently, Friedländer made the bold assertion that *kitsch* is a debased form of myth. He illuminated an important channel through which the emotive power of myth is funneled into the mundane life of the common man so as to create room enough for cosmic happenings. Sugarcoated as *kitsch* might be in its provision of delicious excitations in homey comfort and complete safety, it nevertheless opens the door to the influx of the mythological and horrendous. Friedländer's indication that this pairing creates the juxtaposition of such violently contradictory feelings as harmony and terror has wide-reaching implications. It is possible to conclude from this that the juxtaposition of such widely discrepant strong emotions shifts the psychological reactions onto the larger universal arena of cosmic messianic and apocalyptic forces where German romanticism can usher in its notorious demonic urges.

Hitler's portrayal of the little world of women was a good illustration of how *kitsch* can be paired with death. It began with the *Gemütlichkeit* of a woman's small world being her husband, her family, her children, and her home. This, however, led to a kitschy description of a woman who sacrifices in her own way just as a man does in his way (in war). Her way is eternally patient devotion and eternally patient suffering and endurance as she wins yet another battle for the folk's survival by every child she bears (who, if a boy, will one day be a man sacrificing in the struggle for the folk). What creates a quiver of surprise here is that a sentimental hominess has found a direct route to battle and sacrifice, to future wars and death. All of a sudden the sweetness of home becomes transformed into the ordeals of war. So there can be death in *kitsch*. And since *kitsch* and death are thus habitually juxtaposed, an express route also exists leading in the opposite direction, this time from death to *kitsch*. Robert Waite (1977, 402) cited the following triumphant announcement by Hitler's Ministry of Propaganda one week after the invasion of Russia: "In seven short days, the Führer's offensive has smashed the Red Army to splinters . . . the eastern continent lies, like a limp virgin, in the mighty arms of the German Mars." In seven horrible days, death and devastation were inflicted on Russia, and there was yet much more to come. But this death news was reported via certified *kitsch*. The frisson this time involved the metamorphosis of the conquered land into a limp (but not necessarily unhappy) virgin. In a rather mythological way, she rests in the mighty arms of the German Mars, the old Roman God of War now turned German. So the godly conquering hero got his virgin. And being a German incarnation of a Roman God, he could even reverberate with echoes of the old Holy Roman Empire of the German Nation, which remained a living German fantasy for centuries. How trite it all was and a truly debased form of myth. The portrayal of the seized land through the image of a limp virgin in the arms of a conquering German War God is a poignant illustration of how death can be reduced to *kitsch.* But when this happens, the gruesome reality of death may be obfuscated by the nonfrightening image of a limp virgin. This probably insures that no matter how horrendous death and terror are, they nevertheless remain tolerable because of their link to *kitsch.*

The pairing of *kitsch* with death and their habitual coexistence is what ensures this tolerance. And the folkish state was saturated with this mode. The folkish state thus has created a land of *kitsch* and death regulating and predisposing all its members toward the coming and highly dubious *"Gemütlichkeit"* of war and its miraculously effective sacrifices. Not even the führer escaped this fate. His last hours were summed up by Karl Dietrich Bracher (1970, 463): "After finally accepting how fantastic were his hopes for the relief of the encircled capital, and after macabre final scenes combining a Wagnerian Götterdämmerung mood with the petty-bourgeois marriage to his long-time secret mistress Eva Braun, he committed suicide with his wife on April 30, 1945." This combination of a Wagnerian Götterdämmerung mood with a last-minute, petit bourgeois marriage to Eva Braun was a classical pairing of *kitsch* with death. To his alleged mistress, Hitler presented the final interlocking acts of conventional respectability followed by death. The psychological reality and hidden logic of the folkish state caught up with Hitler just as they did with so many other Germans who collectively shared his delusions.

By no means, therefore, could the folkish state's control be confined to the little world of women. It had to include the larger world of men, which meant all functional aspects of the totalitarian folkish state. For this purpose the policy of *Gleichschaltung,* or total coordination of activities, was devised. The particular choice of this term was in itself a giveaway. Gordon Craig (1982, 326) pointed out that this is an engineering term that means "putting into the same gear." He made the astute observation that this term was sufficiently abstract and technical to mask what it might mean in human terms—the elimination from public and professional life of persons whom the Nazis regarded as dangerous or undesirable. Very aptly the historian William Sheridan Allen (1965, 209–26) described the implementation of this policy as "the atomization of society." In this reorganization of the community, all societies, clubs, professional organizations, and the like came under Nazi control. Some clubs were dissolved while others were fused together. Free unions were broken up. All societies were required to have a majority of Nazi party members in their executive committees. It was all done in the name of reproducing national unity in every governmental or institutional body. To this one may add that actually all institutions became quasi-governmental bodies through this process of coordination or synchronization. What this process actually produced was atomized individuals who faced the stark choice between solitude or mass relationship through some Nazi organization. As Allen rightly indicated, each individual related not to his fellow men but only to the state and to the Nazi leader, who became the personal embodiment of the state. This important point brings us back to the inherent connection of the coordination project with the magic power formula that was embedded in the leadership principle. The aim of it all was to forge a united single political will of mighty power that would be symbolized by the supreme leader and solely controlled by him. This underlying connection between the concepts of coordination and of will was clarified by Hitler in a speech at Munich on March 12, 1933: "It was in this city that years ago I began the struggle the first part of which can now be regarded as finally closed. What for centuries has been longed for but could not be attained has now become accomplished fact. Already a co-ordination (Gleichschaltung) of the political will has been achieved such as we have never yet experienced, and we shall do everything in our power to secure that this co-ordination shall never be lost" (Baynes 1942, 1:269–70).

Although coordination of all activities in the state was not aimed at men alone, they were nevertheless a prime target since the state as such constituted the domain of the larger world of men. Thus, men did not escape the privilege of being totally coordinated or controlled in their larger world. The process was never completed internally, as certain church bodies were not coordinated. Nor was it ever completed externally in occupied territories even though, in the long run, the whole world was destined to be coordinated. Losing the Second World War took care of that. But it was a spreading process that was designed to expand internally and subsequently also externally until it filled up all existing vacuums and controlled everything. In practice, however, the folkish state was afflicted with typical symptoms of administrative incoherence such as rival hierarchies, competing agencies, uncertain chains of command, duplication of responsibilities, reluctant pooling of information, and inadequate machinery for coordination (Caplan 1978, 234). What is more, the Nazi party did not succeed in becoming "the most voracious animal in world history" as Hitler hoped. Despite the ostensible merger of state and party, the Nazi party actually lost the battle for turf to the civil service (Schoenbaum 1966, 221). But the underlying rationale of synchronization was that of a united organization that expands within the national community by gradually bringing everything under coordination. It thus stood, at least in theory, for internal expansion on the home front, which paralleled and complemented the expansion dreams outside Germany. It is ironic to reflect upon the fact that this particular *Gleichschaltung* goal of aggressive spreading looked very suspiciously like the racist fantasy concerning the alien Jewish trait of global spreading and domination, which was so castigated in the anti-Semitic Nazi propaganda.

In the process of molding the members of the folkish community into a homogenized single collective, the folkish state endeavored to exercise total control over the arts. It would have been unthinkable to allow autonomous cultural activities. An unsupervised production of art by either misguided or malicious persons and an unchecked consumption of such art by the gullible public could open the door for a destruction of racial health and psychophysical integrity through spiritual corruption by degenerate art. Besides, it was the inherent nature of the totalistic state to control everything. After all, one never knows whether today's independent artistic trends might not be the harbingers of tomorrow's independent political actions. Art, which is so influential over people, is power. It could therefore be practiced in Nazi Germany only under the aegis of the all-powerful state.

Art has form as well as content, and both can project messages.

The Nazis were determined to control both. The form had to be clear and realistic in terms of shape and proportions. It had to be easily recognizable and readily identifiable with no hint of modernism or experimentalism. Anything that approached formlessness or displayed nontraditional forms was condemned as degenerate. Psychologically, this traditionalist stance can be seen as drawing a rigid line against chaos (formlessness) and against revolution (radical forms). It is a drawing of an ideological line no less than of an artistic one. As for the contents of art works, they all had to depict National Socialist ideals and myths, racial origins, and folkish values that were officially sanctioned by the authorities. Nothing else was permitted. When it came to the arts, not only were alien values forbidden but so were any useless musings of art for art's sake. Put differently, art's contents had to express the spirit and soul of the folk without ever being infiltrated and corrupted by the alien values of inferior races.

Art, of course, is one of the major pools that serves as a reservoir of themes and mottoes for ideological use whenever the zeitgeist catapults them to the foreground. In our earlier discussion of the role of ideologies, it was pointed out that effective ideologies promise newness, meaning "revolution," while at the very same time connecting to powerful old themes of the past. There are two major ways in which they can play on revolutionary drives. They seek the kind of newness that would reverse, revise, or improve the past as they cater to radical sentiments. Or they play on conservative instincts as they promote a newness that actually protects the current status quo by linking it with the restoration of an ideal condition of the past. The tightening control of the arts in the folkish state sent ideological messages related to this issue.

The basic Nazi approach to art did not undergo significant changes before or after the Nazi takeover of the state. But the zeal and rigidity of the new enforcement of the old conceptions concerning healthy folkish art carried a clear ideological message. Before taking over the state, it may have been opportune for Nazis to promote chaos in order to generate new opportunities for fomenting revolution. And because revolution is always something that is perceived as more new than old, even old stuff had to be sold as new. After the accession to power and the implementation of the National Socialist revolution, the Nazi new order became the established order of the day while chaos became anathema.

New revolutions against the Nazi state were therefore condemned as counterrevolutionary, as when, after the Röhm purge, Hitler denounced his victims as putschists. This basic ideological message was included in a Proclamation to the People that was read in Nuremberg by Gauleiter (regional leader) Adolf Wagner of Bavaria on September 5, 1934: "The German form of life is definitely determined for the next thousand years! For us, the nervous nineteenth century has finally ended. There will be no revolution in Germany for the next one thousand years!"

The journalist William Shirer who witnessed the occasion reported that the words provoked the brown mass in the great hall into a frenzy as thirty thousand people leaped to their feet and wildly cheered and clapped (Shirer 1985, 119–21). It was a defining moment indeed. Germany was brimming with confidence as the current myth-selling ideology affirmed · that the new was as fully established as the past ever was. But this was not the tainted recent past of a nervous nineteenth century. The clear implication was that this new German form of life was a revival of the remote past that stretched all the way back to tribal origins and a mythological racial health. And so, since it is usually the fate of victorious revolutions to turn conservative, the accent of zeitgeist manipulations shifted somewhat after the Nazi takeover. If until then more of the old stuff was presented as revolutionary, from then on more of the new was presented as the reaffirmation of the old. Consequently, neoclassicism and neoconservatism were bound to receive growing reinforcement in the statewide control of the arts. John Hanson, an expert on literature and psychology, has produced a perceptive analysis of Nazi aesthetics. He summed up Nazi art as follows:

> Fundamentally, Nazi art is the expression of a mobilization against the strains of primitivism and depersonalization in modernism. It rejects, on the one hand, non-Western modes of perception based on the art of Oceania and Africa and, on the other, the impersonal vision of the machine aesthetics. Against both it affirms (with Fascist and Soviet Art) a vigorous anthropomorphism and a cultural chauvinism based on the glorification of neoclassic ideals. Psychoanalytically, it represents a narcissistic formation against the loss of boundaries or egolessness at work in both primitiv-

ism and constructivism. Its response remains a manic
affirmation of race-consciousness on the level of the group
and a deliberate archaism with regard to technical culture.
(Hanson 1981, 251–52)

The coercive insistence on recognizable forms and traditional contents
in the arts can indeed be viewed as a reaction to fear of loss of ego
boundaries as pointed out by Hanson. In a rather narcissistic fashion,
the reaction has indeed been carried out in an overcompensatory tilt that
resulted in a manic affirmation of the superior and well-defined racial
self. Yet, in spite of this presumed superiority, the folk comrades who
comprised the master race were deemed to be in dire need of external
limits that symbolically represented psychological internal borders. They
needed outer limits or inner borders against which to bounce repeatedly
in order to reconfirm their selfhood. The entire folkish state imposed
these limits in all of its functions. In this respect the arts were no exception, and became a reflection of politics just as politics became a reflection of art. They all expressed a compulsive as well as an anxiety-laden
need for order in an attempt to fortify inner psychological boundaries so
as to ward off a dissolution of self. It is as if everything must always be
in order in Germany; otherwise both the outer world and the inner self
will disintegrate in the ensuing chaos. One could speculate that during
periods in which such anxieties reach new heights, people become more
willing to sacrifice various aspects of their individual self to the collective self. It is then easier for a determined savior to impose a "new order" because of the greater public readiness to preempt the individual
self for the sake of the collective self so long as the latter offers greater
order. It may very well be the case that the Germans have traditionally
savored order possibly in response to a perceived threat emanating from
their own dim fears of a deep fatal flaw in their personality makeup. In
offering them a "new order," Hitler the myth seller engaged in a classical maneuver: the new thing he offered was a beloved thing of old.

A specific strand of the expression of a craving for order in Nazi
aesthetics was nicely captured by George Mosse (1991). He discerned
in the portrayal of men and women in Nazi painting and sculpture a
particular standard of beauty that was designed to cement the unity of
the nation by projecting a moral code to which everyone should aspire.

That special standard of beauty, which was meant to signify that proper moral and sexual behavior, consisted of beauty without sensuality. The stipulation that beauty should be without sensuality is what ensured the aura of respectability. And respectability was crucial for maintaining security, order, and proper values as well as for taming the chaos that seemed always to threaten society from within. The pairing by Mosse of beauty without sensuality with respectability was very insightful. Respectability does indeed reflect a combination of order and conservatism. It therefore seems justified to view it as an antidote to chaos. Respectability was also a central motif of Nazi diplomacy (Beisel).

Moreover, by subtly anchoring respectability in an aesthetic standard of beauty without sensuality, the Nazis were able to keep it pretty and appealing but at the same time defanged of uncontrolled sexuality and other instinctual or impulsive behaviors. Respectability thus stood for maintaining order (beauty) and preventing chaos (sensuality). But there was something more to it. As Mosse pointed out, respectability came to reflect people's attitude toward themselves as well as their attitude toward all that was "different." It is therefore possible to conclude from his assertion that the defensive stance of respectability encapsulated the archaic split of the world into orderly good us and chaotic bad them. This primordial split received a symbolic expression in 1937 as two art exhibits opened in Munich: the Great German Art exhibition on July 18 and the Degenerate Art exhibition on July 19. Good and evil were thus symbolically pitted against each other, with "evil" winning the popularity contest hands down. This was so because the Degenerate Art exhibition included much more interesting works and because it represented what was likely to be the last chance to view such works before they were taken out of circulation. The Great German Art exhibition was designed to extol folkish virtues. But the Degenerate Art exhibition was assembled for an unusual purpose. As Mosse (1991) summed it up, the exhibit aimed to depict society's views of the "outsider." These views included such diverse images as the mentally ill, Jews, homosexuals, criminals, the physically unbalanced, as well as nervousness, exhaustion, contortions, and grimaces. In retrospect, though, it seems that this contrived attempt to teach the populace the pitfalls of degeneracy and chaos that spring from the outsider was a failure. The enormous popularity of the exhibit suggests that the attending visitors learned not only about the corrupt nature of "the others" but also about the rewards of viewing art containing sensuality, disorder, impulse, and lack of respectability.

In the final analysis, the arts were but one part of many interlocking activities which together symbolized the collective national body or *Volksgemeinschaft* and which were all controlled by the ubiquitous folkish state. These included work and hobbies, economics and finance, education and propaganda, politics and party rallies, sports and recreation, parades and marches, family and nation, and, last but not least, a führer. Although he was originally one of the people who therefore knew them well, with his providentially endowed force of personality and genius for symbolizing their collectivity, he stood there in unique glory all by himself. And it was the führer who on July 18, 1937, delivered in Munich a major speech on the arts on the occasion of the opening of the House of German Art (Baynes 1942, 1:584–92). The speech confirmed that the rules for art were part of a totalistic program. He called for a German art that would correspond to the increasing homogeneity of the German racial composition and thus represent its characteristic of unity and homogeneity. As we already know, this homogenizing process was the primary business of the folkish state in toto. It was not specific to the arts. The arts, like everything else in the folkish state, were simply coordinated. Hitler's message was therefore applicable to the *Gleichschaltung* or synchronization of everything inside the totalistic state. He basically reiterated the same message at the end of his speech when he expressed his confidence that the "value of personality" will assert itself in artistic achievements as in so many other spheres of life. As we may recall, the value of personality is a basic assumption of intraracial stratification of individuals, which is analogous to the interracial stratification of peoples. It requires the leadership principle as the basis for a hierarchical organization of individuals within the folkish state. And this was the underlying meaning of a basic slogan that he voiced in the speech: "To be German is to be clear." It was applicable to the arts, where clarity of form and contents was a must. But this German quality was also supposed to be true for all other aspects of life in the folkish state. Above all, everyone was clear about his place in the firmly established new order, which was not going to be rocked by future German revolutions.

Nevertheless, things were not as clear as all that. In the prevailing

Nazi perspective, internal revolutions had indeed ended. The German master race was not going to witness a new seizure of power within Germany. But external revolutions, meaning wars, were still the order of the day even though Hitler refrained from making this fully clear. Non-Germans were destined to witness some unwelcome changes. The destructive Jews did not qualify for *Gleichschaltung* and would therefore have to be spewed out from whatever territories the Third Reich came to control. Luckier races in the world, which were deemed to be a bit more meritorious than the Jews, would have to wait their turn to undergo subjugation and *Gleichschaltung*. But this could never have been done without the kind of war in which a Germany pitted against most of the world was bound to lose. Not even the wholesale transformation of the Germans into a united folk, energized for sacrifice at the führer's command, could change this reality. Unfortunately most Germans failed to recognize this, due to the psychological effectiveness of Nazi ideology. Little did they realize that as the folkish state cemented itself for war, it was programmed to redress a trauma by repeating it. So to be German is not always to be clear.

6

Ideology as Psychology

An effective utopia cannot in the long run be the work of
an individual, since the individual cannot by himself tear
asunder the historical-social situation. Only when the
utopian conception of the individual seizes upon currents
already present in society and gives expression to them,
when in this form it flows back into the outlook of the
whole group, and is translated into action by it, only then
can the existing order be challenged by the striving for
another order of existence.
                                —Karl Mannheim, *Ideology and Utopia*

It is time now to put together Hitler's basic ideological principles with
an emphasis on their underlying psychological meanings, which were
extracted in the course of this exploration.

First Principle: The world is permeated by an ill-understood mortal danger. At this eleventh hour, the historical clock for removing this
danger is about to run out.

The Jews are a killer alien race whose inherent nature is to destroy
its victimized hosts parasitically. Being duplicitous by nature, they are
frequently cunningly disguised and at times are even utterly invisible.
They thus represent a mortal danger to the national organism from within
and from without. By poisoning Aryan blood, they decompose the psychophysical integrity of body and soul. This fatal disconnection deprives
the sickened folk of effective use of the power of the will and plunges it

into a course of impotence followed by death. Unless the magic potency of the folkish spirit is regenerated, the Jews, who pose the greatest mortal danger to humankind since time immemorial, will win. The entire folk is both guardian and container of its precious blood. Betrayal of this holy charge is original sin, which may be punished by racial extinction. The Jewish danger, therefore, thrusts the folk into an apocalyptic life-and-death struggle, which must result not in a folkish failure to survive but rather in a destruction of the Jews and in a redemptive utopia for the Aryan race.

Second Principle: To cling to the magic substance of life is to cling to biomystical health.

Blood is the be-all and end-all of existence. It is the currency of life and death. If the currency is not devalued, it buys life. It has magic qualities that secure the integration of mind and body. This monistic magic guarantees health and longevity because it allows the mind to command the body, i.e., it lets the power of the will prevail. The blood is the sacred charge that Providence or nature bequeathed to the folk. Kept pure, it not only guarantees freedom from Jewish corruption and destruction but also ensures the material and spiritual fulfillment of the Aryan racial destiny.

Third Principle: The omnipotent leader confers magic power.

The leadership principle represents the hierarchical ordering of society according to the personality merit of its members. Such personality value is an outcome and manifestation of the inherent quality of each individual's blood. Therefore, this raw psychobiological building block lends itself to natural stratification both between different races and among individuals of the same race. Consequently it is crucial for survival that society's ordering of its members should not violate or preempt their inherent personality worth. When this ordering conforms to the natural principle of racial and personality merit, it inevitably lifts the gifted genius to the top and places all others under his command in a descending hierarchy. Implementation of the leadership principle yields a magic power formula, based on a single national will expressed through the person of the leader, who now becomes the talisman of his nation. He is the genius, the timeless man, the expert on national destiny who knows how to navigate the ship of state safely in the sea of history.

The people's faith can perform miracles and can even move mountains, but it is *the leader's will* that determines which mountains to move. When everyone's faith is aligned behind the single leader's will, all wonders are possible and sheer willing materializes results.

Fourth Principle: The urge to merge is nature's way of making people feel both good and powerful.

The Volksgemeinschaft is the spiritual outcome of the folkish state. It is an organic blood brotherhood under the rule of the fatherly leader. In this people's community, the leader is the national brain while the people are the national body. Organic connectedness prevails while mechanistic meaninglessness or atomistic isolation are eliminated or relegated to the realms of foreign and degenerate democracies. Not only is the organic connectedness of all members of the national body uplifting, but it also places the followers' faith at the disposal of the single leader's will. This cohesion generates the kind of mighty power surge that enables the folkish state to utilize its capacity for war in a quest for a new justice and a redress of old injustices.

Fifth Principle: It is only just that no one should do it to us, but we should do it to them.

Justice is the distribution or redistribution of all the material and psychic assets of this world, which are available in only limited quantities. It is also symmetrical, which means that a corollary of one's fortune is someone else's misfortune. Moreover, it is magical, which means that it can be influenced by ultramanipulative interventions. Justice is therefore Darwinian and requires constant struggle. The distribution of justice is affected not only by peoples' inherent racial merits and personality values but also by ultramanipulative ploys and magical maneuvers that tilt the distribution one way or another. This is unfortunately how, through foul wizardry, less meritorious people sometimes gain unfair advantage over more meritorious folks. Such injustices go against nature and should therefore be rectified. This kind of rectification can be accomplished by a powerful reordering of justice through potent ultramanipulative redistributions of assets, which this time are completely "fair" to us.

Being *a master race* by virtue of a noble blood and superior personality is itself a claim to justice. An inherent racial merit ordains a right to fulfill racial destiny by arrogating to oneself the lion's share of the world's material and cultural assets whenever one has the power to do so.

Sixth Principle: We can do it.

Power is the ability and hence the duty to enforce justice. Not only does it insure survival for those who possess it, but it also secures a model existence for them. And now the folk has the power to claim its blood entitlement and in the process magnify its power. The two major requisites of a growing power are wider boundaries for the national organism—to be gained by expansion—and greater homogeneity of the people to be achieved by purges. Both require initial power for their accomplishment, which in turn multiplies the power exponentially. And both serve as a prime example of what justice means.

Seventh Principle: We shall gobble up!

Lebensraum is the prize booty of redistributive justice; it is on a par with thwarting the Jewish danger. Justice is retribution by redistribution of both peoples and lands. Among the peoples the Jews are at the top of the list. It is only just to extricate the Jewish poison and to remove infecting agents of decomposition. Of the available living spaces, the eastern territories are the most inviting target in line with the old historical drive to expand Germany eastward. Expanding the living space is the epitome of justice, since Germany was too weak in the past and was therefore shortchanged in territorial extension by comparison with other European powers and their colonies. Territorial redistribution is absolutely necessary for survival since the current German living space is woefully inadequate and cannot guarantee autarky. Opting for expansion also reaffirms the self-confident judgment that the national strength has now reached such a height that grabbing in different directions is at last possible and pushing against previous limits is now feasible.

Eighth Principle: We shall spew out evil since the urge to purge is nature's way of healing.

Being homogeneous, both physically and psychologically, is a prerequisite for exercising the power of the will effectively and for restoring the lost condition of tribal health and happiness. Non-sameness (heterogeneity) within the group betrays the dangerous presence of poisonous foreign elements. Therefore the purging of material and spiritual poison by whatever means necessary in order to protect the homogeneity and health of the folk is a dictate of fate.

Ninth Principle: Sacrifice is the best investment.

Sacrifice is the apex of the fully developed folkish character that enables a mature people to become a storehouse of readily accessible human energies. And its most important use is for a bold trade-off with fate in the currency of life and death. In essence, sacrifice represents current payments in folkish blood for hefty future returns in folkish life dividends. He who loves his folk and who understands this simple equation fears not war and does not engage in futile and anxious comparisons of war's inescapable sacrifices with its fantastic results.

A cardinal verdict of Hitler's ideology consists of the grim diagnosis that the national organism would be helpless in facing its mortal danger without being aided by some form of special intervention, which appears to us to be a form of magic. This was so because the invisible or well-disguised Jews possessed devilish powers; unless stopped, they could pour out enough undetected poison to decompose both body and spirit and to sow disunion, which creates impotence. This diabolic threat of internal splits to produce total weakness could not be resisted by the masses alone. Left to their own devices, these "brilliant dummies" of sorts could not be relied upon to recognize the insidious, invisible infection infiltrating them to sap their health and strength. Only one remedy could provide the desperately needed magical cure. This antidote consisted of the implementation of the leadership principle, which worked like a magic power formula and yielded near omnipotence because it created internal unity of one will under a single leader. It was miraculous exactly because it conformed to the laws of nature, comprised of racial principles. Because the uniquely gifted person was placed at the top, the only person who was purely brilliant and no dummy, the vulnerable masses could be saved. Providence itself decreed that, under the guidance of the natural leader endowed with the racial gift of genius, power and victory were assured.

Armed with a natural understanding of racial principles, the führer and savior prescribed a formula of removal of Jews followed by national unity and culminating in conquest of land (Binion 1981, 104–5). This prescription of homogenization and expansion required purging the national organism and redrawing borders. This program, which involved much more than issues of geography or of political persecution of minorities, had the elements which could lead to a world war as well as to genocide. What was at play here regarding homogeneity and territorial expansion were definitions of the group self that provided basic security. It was the group identity, with its new portrayal of the changing status of power and boundaries, that determined how it felt to be a member of the group. This determination applied not only to external borders but also to the inner environment within the psychic territory of the extended national self. Through purification the inner space had to feel comfortable so that one no longer lived in an infectious environment, meaning inner badness in the domain of the group self. Inner badness means unharnessed instincts and uncontrolled aggressive drives, which can boomerang upon the individual self or the extended group self. By labeling inner badness as "Jewish" and offering a remedy, Nazi ideology tried to relieve the folk comrades of the fear that social interactions within the national community will be characterized by a discomfiting sense of being intruded upon by invasive and destructive "others." Although the Nazi goal was group cohesion, it also appealed to some individuals in an internal psychic sense. It helped them to avoid, by defensive maneuvers if need be, any clashes or contradictions between various parts and clusters of the self that would result in aggression turned toward the self.

No less important was a badly needed sense of comfort concerning invulnerability with regard to destructive assaults by external enemies. The geographic borders had to be fortified and made impregnable for that purpose. But the outer borders signaled more than just the realities of geopolitics. They also reflected psychic undercurrents concerning issues of identity and ego boundaries. The outer enemy could reflect the old inner self; thus the currently barbaric Slavs to the east wanted to do to the German civilization that which the formerly barbaric Germans from the northeast once did to the Roman civilization. Another fantasy concerned the Jews, who allegedly tried to enslave everybody else, which is exactly what the Germans were planning for the Slavs after the successful extension of the German living space to the east.

Put differently, both the racial myths and their concomitant geopolitical moves signify the psychological reality of a national organism at odds with itself and characterized by some kind of a schism of "two souls in one breast," to use Peter Viereck's phrase (1965, 3–15) borrowed from Goethe. Viereck was referring to an inner conflict, almost a schizophrenic split, between rationalism and force, between classicism and romanticism, and between Christianity and tribal paganism, which included the heritage of the barbaric tribal cults of war and blood. In his opinion, this old German cultural schizophrenia is what made Nazism possible (Viereck 1965, 20). At any rate, the psychological reality of a breached national organism seemed to hearken back to the conflicted world of infancy when identity is insufficiently integrated.

Since the national body was conceived by Hitler as a living organism, it was sometimes portrayed in the image of the human body. But with ever-present mortal danger, the national organism was subject to infectious assaults, which enfeebled the body and created internal splits, such as those between brain and brawn or brain and hands. The ubiquitous enemy was internal and external at the same time. It was therefore going to remain eternal unless it was to be completely destroyed, not just inside or outside, but literally everywhere. In the meantime, however, the repeated attacks by the eternal enemy wore the organism down. Perpetual impotence in the face of such a menace produced both rage and terror and created a counterpressure in the direction of action and omnipotence.

All this is of great psychological significance. The dread of an internal split betrays the dual fear of having one's boundaries penetrated and of being powerless to resist. It was to this sick and sickened, terrorized yet enraged, national organism that Hitler prescribed the leadership principle as an antidote to the ubiquitous and toxic Jewish/Bolshevik germ. What complicated his task enormously was the widely shared conviction that it was not just the national organism that was split and splintered; the whole world was actually split between the racial forces of construction and of destruction, with the latter permeating inner and outer spaces and crossconnected in a myriad of hidden ways. By this logic, therefore, as Germany was dashing toward the expansion of its living space by means of a final and just redistribution of the world, it was also fleeing forward in the direction of a worldwide split organism whose sickness could no longer be exported elsewhere. There would be no "abroad" left in such a Nazi dominated and "coordinated" global living organism. The infection could therefore no longer be eradicated by expelling it from the organism. Its mortal sickness would therefore have to be dealt with by an internal process of elimination. Consequently, genocide formed a major milestone on the road to fulfillment of the racial destiny. But since inner splits proliferate everywhere both within and without, the program for extirpating sickness everywhere required limitless expansion. In reality this exceeded German capabilities and invited disaster. For this reason, the plan to extirpate sickness while expanding bore all the characteristics of an unconscious program for failure as well as a repetition of traumas.

As the inner space of the German self turned unlivable because it was saturated with inner demons and enemies that needed to be expelled, the projection of these malevolent parts of the self to the outside made the whole world a source of danger since it now proliferated with mortal enemies of the Germans. But when the whole world needs to be taken on, a glorious victory is less likely than a traumatic repetition of defeat in an earlier world war. The aspired conquering of Eurasian spaces and domination of the world could always result in the physical destruction of Germany itself. What is more, the planned annihilation of Jewish and other disease agents was at a deep emotional level akin to psychological self-immolation. The reason the Jews were larger than life yet so real is that they were a projection of the hidden aspects of German life. After all, in an uncanny sense, all these "bad" Jews were split off "bad" parts of the German self. And destruction of some parts of the self, albeit disowned parts, is not a sound recipe for security. At an emotionally intense and unconscious level, it serves as a perturbing reminder that any part of the self can be destroyed at any time. It therefore does not eliminate the internal terror. At any rate, since at a very deep level the external physical genocide reflected also an internal psychological self-immolation, there was going to be a steep price to be paid. Only individuals who were thoroughly psychopathic could escape paying the price. For most Germans the damage done to their own identity was unavoidable. It left them well adept at not knowing what happened, which meant not being in touch with themselves.

It also left them fearful of their own impulses, with the legacy that nowadays they frequently seek a "European" umbrella for their foreign actions while being leery of activities that could be labeled as specific and independent German initiatives. When other Europeans express anxiety concerning what the Germans might do, they regard it as an anti-German bias and an inability to let bygones be bygones. But they themselves have deep anxieties concerning how they might behave should rampant inflation ever hit them again. Their scrupulous efforts to keep a tight lid on inflation are reinforced not just by economic concerns, but also by fears of a Nazi revival. The psychic damage also left the Germans oversensitive to any analysis of their psychology and personality that might suggest any form of German uniqueness. It is as if such explorations represent nothing less than reverse racism, which this time treats Germans, rather than non-Aryans, as a pseudospecies. Such explorations may look like inverted anti-Semitism where the collective guilt for all eternity is now being stamped upon Germans for actual genocide, rather than upon Jews for alleged deicide.

In describing the lethal impact of the pervasive Jewish disease, Hitler warned that the corruption it causes is both material and spiritual. By linking the fate of the two, Hitler advocated the kind of monism that provides justification for totalitarian practices. The ideal of unity implied that in practice everything without exception, whether physical or cultural, must be totally controlled. This monistic ideal included also a promise of magical deliverance from need and tension and enfeeblement. The promise here was that the aspired unity could enable the mind to have complete command over its well-synchronized body. Herein lies the power of the will: that most potent executive power whose magic rested on the supposition of an intact national organism, one with a complete psychophysical integrity.

From a psychological standpoint, however, this all-powerful unity is reminiscent of the omnipotence of early infancy when in a magical fashion sheer willing by itself materialized results. In those early and fuzzy times, the limitless self included the entire world within. But the infant gradually discovers that he is not omnipotent because others have power over him. He senses therefore some tugging and pulling inside due to developing fissures between mental representations of self and of others. Some aspects of the Nazi ideology can therefore be seen as contemporary political derivatives of infantile psychology. The obsessive fear of internal splitting is particularly relevant here. In early infancy the developing splits between good and bad parts of oneself, as well as between self and nonself, contribute to the formation of both inner boundaries and outer borders. However, with this psychological birth of the human infant, no longer does the self include a whole world subject to its mighty will. The mental legacy of all this is that splits or inner breaches that are due to internal and/or external pressures can be associated with lost magic and weakened powers. This development may facilitate collective predilections to embrace psychogeographic solutions to identity conflicts. In psychogeographic solutions, external geographic features such as borders and rivers come to symbolize internal psychological concerns such as ego boundaries and inner splits. If the history and identity of a given national group include heightened concerns with threats to unity and loss of power, then the group is likely to rely upon those particular archaic infantile features that reflect the elementary emotions of the group's basic assumptions. In this connection such features as fear, rage, and aggressive orality come to mind.

Of course the bitter infantile lesson of lost magic is not consciously remembered. Rather, it becomes ingrained as a prototypical perceptual structure into which future events can be fitted under certain limited circumstances. Clearly in Hitler's political ideology, internal splitting represented the diabolical Jewish formula for inducing impotence. This contemporary and growing disaster sounded a lot like a repetition of the ancient loss of infantile omnipotence. It is therefore highly likely that the magic power formula of the leadership principle unconsciously aimed to restore an imaginary lost omnipotence of Germans of the past. It was therefore not just a case of consciously playing politics on Hitler's part, but also an instance of unconsciously acting out psychopolitics on behalf of the masses. And the enthusiasm with which the notion of a single will was greeted by many Germans suggests that this archaic yearning to be all-powerful was collectively, albeit not uniformly, shared. The omnipotence of the single will was, on face value, a product of the unity of all the members of the folk. It symbolized the recreation of a primordial condition of lost tribal unity with its imaginary omnipotence. A group is unlikely to embark on a search for the total power of infantile omnipotence unless there is something in its history that propels it in this particular direction. In Germany, that psychohistorical "something" involved shared feelings of national impotence coupled with revered myths of past omnipotence. But it was well nigh impossible for the group to recapture absolute omnipotence in the contemporary geopolitical world.

Hitler's ideology portrayed a Manichean world. Evil was lurking everywhere in an eternal battle against all that is good. The good was a mystical/biological concept of racial superiority, which was always under threat since the omnipresent evil force of destruction imposed on it a ceaseless battle for survival. This portrayal is typical of messianic psychologies that tend to deal with the ultimate and mythical battle over the fate of the world. But some of the basic assumptions involved in the determination of who would prove fit to survive were paranoid par excellence. The world was one of misleading appearances. Evil operated on a conspiratorial basis, which not only organized and orchestrated its vile activities, but also disguised its true nature. Appearances, therefore, could serve as cleverly disguised traps for unaware victims. And those who tripped into them failed the survival test. In other words, underneath the benign-looking but misleading appearances lurked a malignant reality of evil consisting of well-organized activities aimed at inflicting sickness and death through diabolically disguised means. Sickness phobia as well as paranoid fear of imagined enemies combined here to shape the ground rules for the contest of who shall survive. Therefore, the major countermeasure had to be the education/nationalization of the people so that they could unmask the enemy in order to confront him with their united strength. Fighting mere appearances was a losing proposition. What survival really required was a fight against the hidden and well-camouflaged reality of a conspiratorial evil that plotted to subjugate and destroy all else.

Thus, Hitler's ideology projected a worldview in which a Messianic end-of-days final battle was imminent. This worldview blended three major psychological strands. The first was the rigid and absolutist division of the world along the Manichean dualism of an eternal struggle between good and evil. The second was a paranoid stance that faced a well-organized conspiracy masked by the world of appearances. And the third was phobia against infection, disease, and death. As was noted before in the chapter on the Jewish danger, this phobia signaled fear of a malignant process or a fatal flaw that already emanates from the inside.

This takes us back to the German masses once again. The issue of what is appearance and what reality, or the fear that things may not be what they seem, already existed with regard to the masses. Nazi ideology did not present them in a simple-minded fashion as the forces of good. They were a breached entity, which contained both great promise and a fatal flaw. As a folk they could be glorious, but as masses they were foolish. In spite of their splendid cultural potential due to their racial merit, they were handicapped by internal limitations such as stupidity, gullibility, and femininity, the latter possibly representing a touch of Jewishness. Consequently, even though the German masses basically belonged to the forces of good, they nevertheless comprised a split entity, which harbored within itself evil ingredients that could destroy it from within. With the forces of good so compromised and weakened, the evil methods of Jewish duping could still prove victorious. In the midst of battle, the forces of good could be stabbed in the back as evil sneaked up on them from inside. Put differently, in the murky reality of the world of appearances, even the predominantly good camp was a place of blurry boundaries whose compromised and flawed inhabitants were already contaminated. It is possible that in Hitler's view only the Japanese escaped this contamination. According to Trevor-Roper's book *Hitler's Secret Conversations,* Hitler stated that the racial instinct of the Japanese was so highly developed that even the Jews realized that Japan cannot be attacked from within but only from the outside (Trevor-Roper 1953, 255–56). There was no such luck though for the contemptible German masses, who were befuddled idiots. Living in a very confusing world, they were subjected to both paranoid and phobic fears as they faced the ultimate Manichean battle of survival/salvation for the racially fittest.

No wonder that such a condition of extreme vulnerability invited a miracle. And it came in the form of the providential single leader, a Messiah of sorts, who provided distinctions between appearances and reality or between deception and truth, and who was thus able to shore up psychological borders by imposing greater clarity on the condition of the folk and the state of the world.

The great hope of emerging with a new utopia out of the impending messianic trials and tribulations encapsulated within it the dream of recreating a lost utopia of the past. These messianic yearnings rode upon and were nourished by a deeply ingrained German national fantasy concerning the Holy Roman Empire. The notion of a Holy Roman Empire dates back to Christmas Day of the year A.D. 800, when Pope Leo III crowned the Frankish king Charlemagne at St. Peter's Cathedral in Rome and hailed him as the august emperor of the Romans. Charlemagne succeeded in establishing a kingdom that at the time included France, Holland, Flanders, Austria, Bohemia, Moravia, as well as a part of Spain and a large part of Italy. This gave rise to the notion that an empire had been created that was Roman, Christian, and Germanic in one (Reinhardt 1961, 1:43–44). These Frankish successes, however, could be construed only in fantasy as a new and holy revival of the old Roman Empire. Voltaire's oft-quoted barb that the Holy Roman Empire was neither holy, nor Roman, nor an empire, amounts to a diagnosis of the entire idea as a fantasy construction. But this fantasy involved the comforting belief that so long as the empire existed, the end of the world and the last judgment would be postponed (Heer 1968, 3). In the course of time the German component of this fantasy of a new empire was further reinforced. In A.D. 962 after the Saxon king Otto the Great entered Italy at the request of Pope John XII, the pope bestowed upon him an imperial crown. This event marked the beginning of the "Holy Roman Empire of the German Nation" although the term itself was not applied until the fifteenth century (Heer 1968, 63). And even though the empire changed forms or stayed alive only in peoples' imagination, the idea survived for centuries until its official end in 1806 in the aftermath of Napoleon's defeat of Prussia.

The German stake in a Holy Roman Empire of the German nation always seems to have been high. Long before the repetitive waves of German assaults finally succeeded in crumbling the actual Roman empire, Germans already had penetrated the daily life of that empire by serving the Romans as mercenaries and in other capacities. Against this historical background, new fantasy elaborations could be construed. Some Germans could now see themselves as the barbarians from the northeast who infused an older and higher order civilization with new blood, thus revitalizing it and thereby earning the right to carry the mantle of the new civilization. That is one reason why, after the collapse of the first Holy Roman Empire founded by Charlemagne in A.D. 800 (his successors failed to hold it together), it was revived again in the tenth century. Heer (1968, 10) pointed out that it was Saxon imperial bishops and lower-level clergy, nobly born people both ecclesiastical and lay, who built the empire afresh. Heer attributed their motivation to a desire to preserve the double aspect of the original Carolingian religious-political incorporation of the Saxons into the empire. Under this arrangement, the clergy exercised both a religious and a political authority. But this religious-political stake in holding on to existing power and economic privilege does not explain the amazing staying power of the popular idea of a Holy Roman Empire among Germans for generations. This staying power seems to have come from a shared fantasy of being the continuation of Greco-Roman civilization. This meant being the contemporary uphold-ers of the most advanced civilization (Greece) as well as being an impe-rial power with martial superiority and subjugation of inferior peoples (Rome.)

As practically every German schoolchild was familiar with the ideal of the Holy Roman Empire of the German Nation, the idea and its rever-berations became a standard staple in the common pool of German na-tional fantasies. In drawing from this pool, Hitler accentuated the racial ramifications that attached to this blend of political and cultural fantasy construction. His assorted ideas, which will now be summed up, led inexorably toward racial destiny. One of Hitler's notions was that with-out Christianity, but under Germanic (pagan) influence, the Roman em-pire would have continued to develop in the direction of world domination, while humanity would not have extinguished fifteen centu-ries of civilization at a single stroke due to Christianity. Another notion of Hitler's was that the Romans did not dislike the Germans, as attested by his assertion that blond hair was popular among the Romans. More-over, according to Hitler, many Goths (German tribes) had dark hair. What Hitler seemed to maintain was that some Romans tried to look like Germans while some Germans already looked like Romans—a situ-ation that facilitated intermingling. Hitler went on to assert that there was such a preference in Rome for fair-haired women that many Roman women dyed their hair; the result was that Germanic blood constantly regenerated Roman society (as Roman men interbred with real blond German women).

Still another ideological crotchet of Hitler's was the notion that Rome was destroyed by Christianity, which bolshevized it. What he meant by bolshevization was the annulment of the hierarchy of personality as a cardinal principle in the conduct of Roman civilization. In this connec-tion, he asserted that in its time this bolshevization was as destructive in Rome as it later proved to be in Russia. Thus, the fall of Rome was brought about not by Germans or Huns but by Christianity. A related idea of Hitler's was that Bolshevism was achieving on the materialist and technical level what Christianity had achieved on a metaphysical level. What these ideas might have meant was that Bolshevist corruption started with the body while Christian corruption began with the soul. All this accorded with Hitler's view of both Christianity and Bolshevism as Jewish inventions. Nolte (1969, 417–22, 511–13) has described how, under the influence of Dietrich Eckart, Hitler came to view Moses as the originator of Bolshevism and the Apostle Paul as its great reinforcer. By contrast, Hitler provided the racial stamp of approval to the Holy Roman Empire. He claimed that Charlemagne gathered the Germans into a well-cemented community and created an empire that was made of the best stuff of the ancient Roman Empire. It was therefore seen for centuries as a successor to the universal empire of the Caesars. That it was named "the Holy Roman Empire" had nothing to do with the church or religion (Trevor-Roper 1953, 6, 7, 64–65, 207, 310). It should be noted that in Hitler's description, Charlemagne's well-cemented community sounds similar to a *Volksgemeinschaft,* while the creation of the Holy Roman Empire out of the "best stuff" of the ancient Roman Empire alludes to blood and racial merit.

Trevor-Roper summed up Hitler's broad outlook on this subject as follows:

A barbarous millennium! Hitler would not have denied it; for barbarism, he maintained, was the first basis of all culture, the only means whereby a new civilisation could replace an old. The German conquerors of the Roman Empire had been barbarians; but they had replaced an old and rotten society by the basis of a new and vigorous civilisation. Similarly, the Nazis must be barbarians to replace with their millennium the dying culture of the west. "Yes," he had declared in 1933, "we are barbarians! We want to be barbarians! It is an honourable title. We shall rejuvenate the world. This world is near its end." By "historical necessity" barbarian forces must break up decaying civilisations and "snatch the torch of life from their dying fires." (Trevor-Roper 1953, xix)

Trevor-Roper was right in underscoring the identification with barbarians. This identification was a natural for a racially colored self-image. It was not difficult for Nazis to view the Germans as healthy barbarians whose rejuvenation of the Roman Empire was based on the infusion of new blood. Whereas the scourge of blood mixture with Jews represents the original sin of humanity, blood mixture among noble stocks such as old Greco-Roman with the new Germanic can do wonders. For a while blood, the magic stuff of life, rejuvenated a civilization that had started to decay. A glorious future of world domination could have been accomplished by this fusion of blood and empire if it were not for the metaphysical corruption by Christianity (Jewishness in disguise) that led to the fall of Rome. And nowadays Bolshevism is doing the same thing at a materialist and technical level.

This last key point of the racial fantasy propelled it from the past into the immediate future to produce dread. For one thing, in the weltanschauung of psychophysical integrity, there is no real separation of the metaphysical domain from the materialist and technical domain. Any damage to one destroys both. That is why it is not surprising that Christianity destroyed both spirit and body then, while Bolshevism was destroying body as well as spirit now. For another thing, Bolshevism represented not only yet another derivative form of decomposing Jewishness, but was also associated with Russia, i.e., with a different racial stock of the new barbarians: the Slavs. And they were fear-inspiring, as can be gleaned from Martin Bormann's conversational report to Hitler upon returning from the Ukraine: "Such prolific breeding may one day give us a knotty problem to solve, for as a race they are much hardier by nature than we are" (Trevor-Roper 1953, 477). This could have been a Roman speaking centuries ago about the Germans.

It is not difficult to surmise what existential hopes, as well as fears, reverberated throughout the new racial colorings of the old fantasy of the Holy Roman Empire of the German Nation. Once upon a time the Germanic barbarians of the northeast gobbled up Rome to become a kind of "new improved" Rome. In turn, however, the new Rome—a civilization reinvigorated by what might be called the blood, or should one say bloody, injection of Germanic tribal health—came to fear the new barbarians from the east, namely the Slavs. By now the new Germanic Rome is itself a civilization that is infected with symptoms of degeneracy. After 1918, its big hope was to regenerate from the inside and expand to the outside. Its big fear was of the new Slavic barbarians who became the tool of world Jewry. It did not wish to be rejuvenated by them the way the Roman Empire was rejuvenated by the German barbarians. Nevertheless, a terrible fear prevailed concerning the unstoppable motion of the wheel of historic justice, which turns like the repetition of a trauma. Since it could not be stopped, the new barbarians ultimately might do to the new civilization what the old barbarians had done to the old.

Such frightening perceptions about cyclical turns of justice, or yo-yo swings of fate, were facilitated by a German history of ever changing borders. The historian A.J.P. Taylor (1962) provided some daring speculations about the historical impact of indistinct and unstable borders upon Germany and its people. The Germans were living in a country without a defined natural frontier. Mostly without sharp limits of mountain ranges but with a great plain, which is intersected by four rivers creating sharp enough dividing lines to split the Germans among themselves, there were no settled frontiers to determine either German expansion or German contraction. As a result, "in the course of a thousand years, Geographic Germany has gone out and in like a concertina." Throughout that time the Germans were imitating the west, the heir to the Roman Empire, but defending civilization against the east and its new barbarians, the Slavs. Thus, from Charlemagne to Hitler, the Germans have been "converting" the Slavs from either paganism, Orthodox Christianity, or Bolshevism or from being Slavs. These conversions often involved extermination. To quote A.J.P. Taylor, "no other people has pursued extermination as a permanent policy from generation to generation for a thousand years. . . . No one can understand the Germans who does not appreciate their anxiety to learn from, and to imitate, the West; but equally no one can understand Germans who does not appreciate their determination to exterminate the East" (A.J.P. Taylor 1962, 14). All this presumably came about as a result of the pressure of being stuck between two opposite worlds. The Germans were "the people of the middle," the barbarians on the edge of a great civilization.

Geographical position has thus influenced the German national character to foster universalism, aping of foreign traditions, and ruthlessness toward the Slavs (A.J.P. Taylor 1962, 13–16). To this short list of Taylor's, one may add strong counterreactions to all three tendencies. The Germans also developed a deep suspicion of universalism, an ardent desire for specific German ways, and a grudging admiration for the barbaric vigor of the Slavs.

The impact of the internal splintering was also felt for generations. A prime example of this was, as A.J.P. Taylor (1962, 20–21) pointed out, that the Roman Catholic Emperors tried to defend Germany from foreign invasions in spite of their universalist orientation. By contrast, the Lutheran princes, who were concerned solely with their own existence, aligned themselves with foreign invaders. And there were still other inner divisions that resulted from an old inheritance of internal German borders. In discussing Germany's legacy of centuries of religious and dynastic divisions, Sigmund Neumann (1965, 21–22) emphasized that the centrifugal forces and competitive strife between brother states led to the historical dualism between Prussia and Austria. He also underscored the idea that these divisions also reflected inner frontiers that formed insurmountable dividing lines of a European consciousness. The old *Limes Germanicus* that was the boundary path that separated "the barbarians of the north" (the Germans) from the Roman empire still continue to run right through Germany. But Hans Kohn (1960, 18–19), who traced the history of Germany's growing alienation from the west, cautioned against overstressing the impact of the old historical divisions on twentieth-century German civilization. He was referring to the establishment of a western Germany as part of the Roman *orbis*. To the east of the *Limes Germanicus* lay the primitive barbaric lands of central Germany, which were incorporated into Christianity and civilization by Charlemagne around A.D. 800, and eastern Germany, the semicolonial land of barons and serfs, which the German knights conquered in the thirteenth century. Although Kohn urged caution in interpreting these historical differences, he nevertheless surmised that it was no accident that Konrad Adenauer and Theodor Heuss, the leading statesmen representing the new Germany after 1945, came from the west. By contrast, speaking on the same subject, Peter Viereck (1965, 6) elaborated the psychological consequences of this inner conflict over the Roman wall. He maintained that they included projection, fanaticism, hysteria, instability, delusions of persecution plus persecution of others, and convulsive outbursts of physical violence.

Geography and history have thus left Germany with a problematic and mixed legacy. The lack of distinct external frontiers left the door wide open for expansion mania and contraction dread. But invading as well as being invaded lost some of its traditional territorial meaning of crossing frontiers and became equated instead with people's movement. When the bulk of one people moves into the midst of another, this constitutes an invasion. The country or homeland is simply wherever the people are. From these basic notions grew the conviction that Germany is, or at least should be, wherever the Germans are. This is why for Hitler there was eventually nothing contrived or unhistorical in dreaming of a Greater Germany, which would include, for instance, the Ukraine. But far-reaching implications also stemmed from the inner dividing lines, be they rivers, principalities, religions, or Roman "Limes," which came to symbolize the malaise of Germany and to reinforce an habitual dread of the weakening impact of splitting and strife. The combined effect of all of this was that issues of borders came to represent also issues of identity. Borders came to stand not only for external geography but for internal choices of cultural orientation, religious preference, the extent of identification with neighboring German groups, and the degree of security or amount of basic dread concerning one's place in one's locale. What all this means is that all sorts of borders now reflected issues of identity and became somewhat functionally equivalent to ego boundaries. It stands to reason to assume that such psychohistorical developments strengthened the predilection to seek psychogeographical solutions, such as the expansion of the living space, to psychological problems and identity issues.

Dreams of creating or recreating utopias require, almost by definition, a major act of reparation for what would otherwise remain a highly flawed world. Frequently, however, such a cosmic repair job cannot be executed peacefully: it requires battle. It should only be expected that the forces of evil, whose presence makes the world flawed to begin with, are going to resist repairs to the bitter end or might even try to launch a preemptive attack. The impending mythical battle over the fate of the world that is embedded in Hitler's ideology is in the worst tradition of messianic acts of salvation. It deals with a flawed world that was actually a projection of a deep sense of a flawed group self. The world was flawed, first and foremost, because it was permeated with a hostile Jewish force that aspired to world domination by means of a global state without boundaries. (This was obviously a projection on the part of Hitler and other anti-Semites.) In the case of the Jews, Hitler maintained that this alleged characteristic of being territorially unlimited was a direct outcome of an abnormal alien nature. The Jewish abnormalities included formlessness, chameleonlike appearances, and even outright invisibility. Another abnormality of the Jews was the lack of a natural attachment to a landscape, which in turn dispenses with the normal need for defined territorial borders. Last but not least the Jews possessed an abnormal as well as a demonic capacity to infect others with a deathly disease that causes the decomposition of other peoples' psychophysical well-being. To make matters worse, this creeping process of gaining world domination through the subtle afflictions of slow enfeeblement and gradual death is aided by another inherent defect of the world. Its people are flawed, even those who are of good racial stock. Their gullibility, femininity, and other internal flaws, some of which are present to begin with while some others are infused or augmented by Jewish contamination, make these basically good people classical candidates for victimization.

Pure evil thus wreaks havoc upon a flawed world with defective people, and there is only one intact force of pure goodness left. This is the genius leader, the timeless man who correctly reads history's eternal truths, the one and only one who cannot be duped. He can chart for the people the right course that avoids the original sins of blood mixture, a course that ensures survival. Thus, the Jewish people of pure evil were pitted against the führer of pure goodness in a battle over the fate of the contaminated Aryans. One could paraphrase Hitler by saying that in this battle the Jews tried to keep the people as dumb masses while he tried to turn them into a brilliant folk. A successful outcome was dependent on a basic stipulation. Only if the people aligned their will with that of the supreme leader could that magic power be found that would be capable of counteracting the demonic force of decomposition. Only the imposition of the leader's will upon the compromised people of a contaminated world could cancel the existential defect and usher in a global reparation. Then the well-guided people could be smart for a change, but only because their leader's brain would be equivalent to their collective brain. Additionally they would be powerful because their leader's indomitable will would be their very own will as well. And in this state of greater clarity, power, and effectiveness, the folkish people would be masters rather than slaves and would inherit and dominate a world of clearer territorial borders and be free of the flow of invisible infections across boundaries. It would therefore also be a safer inner world where self-boundaries are more securely demarcated and less vulnerable to internal inundations that trigger identity crises. But this sort of redemption in both inner space and outer space implied all along that the mythical battle for the fate of the physical as well as psychological world would result not in Jewish victory and Aryan defeat but rather in life for the Aryans and death to the Jews. There was going to be ultimate justice such as befits cosmic solutions, i.e., there was going to be a holocaust.

The issue of how the Holocaust could happen has baffled humanity in the twentieth century. Only partial answers can be offered, and they inevitably involve the convergence of several factors. The following suggestions are therefore offered in the modest hope that they will somewhat enhance our understanding of how such incredible horrors could ever take place.

A necessary but not sufficient condition for the Holocaust was the highly virulent anti-Semitism that took hold on German soil. Two major contributions to this subject of how the Holocaust could have been carried out by Germans other than the fanatical SS troops have been published recently. John Weiss (1996) explored the special nature of German and Austrian history, which produced an ideology of death that led to a holocaust. And Daniel Jonah Goldhagen (1996) traced the evolution of German anti-Semitism from an eliminationist mind-set into an exterminationist one. These kinds of mind-sets are akin to a preexisting cultural disposition or prior mental readiness that facilitates the final leap from theory to implementation when the call to action is heralded. It stands to reason that without such a "preexisting condition" of sorts, the participation of ordinary Germans in the extermination process, which was so aptly illustrated by Goldhagen, would not have been as widespread as it actually was. At this point it behooves us to recall that in many instances the fanatically anti-Semitic Hitler was preaching to the converted. Armed with his racist weltanschauung, which enabled him among other things to endow exterminationist anti-Semitism with a respectable German nationalist stamp of approval, the relentless

Hitler did succeed in becoming the final catalyst for genocidal collective action.

Many thoughtful and highly informed people find it very difficult to accept the conclusions of Weiss and Goldhagen. But two basic reasons lead me to accept them. The first is the depth to which racism became integrated into the German self-concept. For over a century now, there were so many mystical notions concerning German superiority that race became an important component of German identity. It was supposed to be the basis for being uniquely masterful and far better than any other group. Unfortunately this turned German anti-Semitism into a key ingredient in German self-definition. For many Germans self-affirmation and the upholding of a conviction concerning the unique superiority of the German collective now required anti-Semitic expressions for validation.

The second is the internal logic of the Nazi ideology and its dynamism, which always left room for far-flung escalation of both ends and means. Just as the quest for lebensraum could lead to world domination down the road, so could the call for the "removal" of the Jews lead to killing and extermination. In discussing what Hitler meant by the "removal" of the Jews, Jäckel pointed out that Hitler's statements ranged from being ambiguous to clear advocacy of murder (Jäckel 1981, 47–66). There was no guarantee that it would all stop at forced emigrations or expulsions. In a country where the storm troopers sang "when Jewish blood spurts from the knife, things will go better still," people were not left completely in the dark about what the "removal" of the Jews might possibly mean. With the climate so saturated with virulent anti-Semitism, even people who did not necessarily agree knew full well that the potential for killing was there. By the time the genocide was happening, it had its enthusiastic supporters and its passive tagalongs. There were also those who disagreed but were afraid to voice opposition, as well as a handful of active resisters.

A related issue was the availability of the executive powers of the complex organization of a totalitarian state. It could be argued, after all, that the Germans did not have the sole copyright to eliminationist anti-Semitism and that exterminationist tendencies could be found in other places, such as Lithuania or the Ukraine. But in the absence of the proper organizational structure and power of an intact state, their dabbling in holocausts was bound to remain amateurish and largely based on collaboration with the occupiers. It was the Germans who had the necessary organization, power, and wherewithal for implementing their ideology and systematically carrying out the Holocaust.

Most important was the existence of a comprehensive ideology whose worldview concerning Germany's place in the sun amounted to a collection of dangerous shared group fantasies. Germany's glorious world mission—yet its unfair fate and its dangerous exposure to vile conspiracies emanating from everywhere—were all ingredients that were waxing and waning in strength within the zeitgeist for ages. Ever since the trauma of Versailles, there has been an increasing pressure to unleash the kind of decisive German acts that would provide ultimate relief. The relief sought was presumed to be an all-inclusive redemption rather than a repetition of trauma. But the sheer force of the compelling pressure to act quickly suggested that action as such was sought for its immediate relief value regardless of its later consequences—be it salvation or another catastrophe. Thus, the worldview of the Nazi racial ideology drove the nation to violent acts not only against Jews based on anti-Semitism, but also against other peoples and countries, as the redistribution of the world was to be accomplished by a new justice based on German power.

The importance of ideology cannot be overstated. As used throughout this work, the term ideology denotes a set of ideas that provide a prescriptive worldview of life. Therefore, when embraced by a group, an ideology supplies and defines key elements of group identity. It can also, however, serve as an ersatz personal identity for individuals whose personality is in such a shaky state that they rigidly substitute for it ideological prescriptions for what a good person should be. What the term ideology also connotes is a reflection of personal identity issues at the group level. Certain unresolved and usually also very early individual identity issues receive new expression through the collective ideology. First and foremost, however, ideologies shape the emotional climate of the whole group. In this new arena for struggling with identity issues, lots of pathological notions can be flushed out of the zeitgeist to receive not only coherence but also legitimacy. The collective sharing, the intersubjectivity so to speak, is what gives it "objectivity" and legitimacy. And the weight of history, the reverberations of old echoes from one's bona fide past, is what gives it force. Ideologies are, therefore, very important; because they are collectively shared, they "resolve" sticky identity issues, are capable of sanctioning not only reality but also fantasy, and have the power to trigger mass action.

The availability of a lethal ideology that was embraced by the masses, and its clever manipulation by a vicious but charismatic leader, was a key element in the unleashing of destructive actions. People do not gas other people, young and old, or shoot them or smash their skulls out of mere obedience to orders. People do not engage in wholesale murder out of administrative momentum, or in retail killing out of bureaucratic inertia. There always can be individual sadists who seek opportunities to act on their personal impulses. But when a whole group carries out mass murder, what sustains the willingness and even lust to annihilate is a zealous ideological conviction that these actions are right and just. By and large it was a prior ideological commitment that enabled many Germans to persist in the dutiful and even enthusiastic execution of the murderous orders. It was the ideological sanctioning of these inhumane measures as both necessary and good that made it all possible. And it could not have happened unless large segments of the German public had truly internalized that lethal ideology and allowed it to define their individual as well as their collective identities.

The importance of this last point cannot be overemphasized. As John Weiss (1996, 287) stated, "It is time to stop believing that 'without Hitler, no Holocaust.'" Throughout his well-documented book, he demonstrated how it was an "ideology of death" that led directly to the Holocaust. For various historical, political, psychological, economic, and social reasons, this racial ideology gained momentum during the nineteenth century but even more so during the twentieth. Its adoption by wide strata of German and Austrian societies is what made its implementation possible. Indeed, attributing it all to Hitler is a defensive myth. Hitler was not a foreign implant in Germanic culture that corrupted it and altered its nature. This notion amounts to still another shared group fantasy of a contaminating agent, Adolf Hitler, who infected the decent but helpless German people with the disease of exterminationist anti-Semitism. In the prevailing group fantasy until the demise of Nazism, German society was viewed as the victim of Jewish machinations. Yet with this new fantasy twist of blaming Hitler alone, German society is now seen instead as a victim of a Hitler's malfeasance.

But Hitler was not an external plague that descended from far away. He actually came from within the zeitgeist where he fleshed out the prescription order for the desired ideology and leadership notions that was left there by the public at large. After duly filling this prescription, he went back to the people to deliver the requested remedies. And he did it in a demagogic fashion, presenting his newfound cures as if they were the original product of his individual genius rather than plagiarized material that was borrowed from the masses themselves. They were the ones who clamored for the old/new remedies with increasing frequency. It is therefore conceivable that without Hitler a holocaust could still have taken place, although under another racist ideological leader. This, however, certainly was not inevitable. In all likelihood, a Hitler in Denmark would have gotten nowhere, not only because it was too small a country to dream on a global scale (so actually were the trauma-hungry Germans), but because that country was not receptive to such an ideology. In sum, either the tacit or enthusiastic acceptance of the Nazi ideology by wide segments of the German populace was a major factor in propelling Germany toward a second world war and genocide. As for the somewhat murky issue of how much of this development can be attributed to Hitler and how much to the Germans, a recent formulation by Ian Kershaw, a biographer of Hitler, seems like a fair statement: "The Nazi assault on the roots of civilization has been a defining feature of the twentieth century. Hitler was the epicenter of that assault. But he was its chief exponent, not its prime cause" (Kershaw 1998, xxx).

Two additional factors facilitated the ideologically driven tendency among Germans to strike out in explosive actions so as to play out the preprogrammed and largely unconscious national fantasies. The first has to do with the European concert of nations between the two world wars, which also acted out unconscious fantasies. The inexorable European dance of death assigned to Germany the hopeless role of an uncontrollable and incorrigible bête noire that was destined to launch future wars of conquest as hereditary enemies inevitably do. This deathly and mutually reinforcing development was very aptly described in great detail by the psychohistorian David R. Beisel as a process of a "suicidal embrace" using one of Neville Chamberlain's expressions. This unfortunate process resulted in rigid policies on the part of the former allies, especially France, which were supposedly designed to ensure that the past will not be repeated in the future but which actually secured its future recurrence. This unconscious trade of role assignments by the European powers was instrumental in catapulting some of the worst German shared fantasies into the forefront of the national psyche. It therefore made the outbreak of war all the more probable. And in the brewing Nazi ideology, war on Germany's enemies was going to include all the Jews wherever they were.

The second factor is more an internal German product and consists of a particular trait that was part of the German national character, inadequately understood as that concept may be (Inkeles 1997, 214–20). It was Rauschning (1946, 212) who underscored this German trait of passion for absolutes. After noting an increasing centuries-long trend toward the total conversion of the nature and values of social institutions into organized barbarism, and after highlighting in this regard the inherent connection between biological pessimism and barbarism, Rauschning diagnosed the major cause for these unfortunate long-term trends as follow: "The Germans with their everlasting passion for absolutes and extremes were so unfortunate as to draw the ultimate conclusions in the universal debunking of all values—to accept these conclusions not merely in the realms of adventurous thinking, as did Nietzsche, but in the hard, literal, brutal world of reality. The Germans first demonstrated what all nations might come to" (Rauschning 1946, 211–12).

Rauschning's diagnosis carries with it far-reaching implications. It suggests that the German passion for working with ultimate dimensions sweeps the total range of experience. Consequently, ultimates do not remain the preserve of the merely theoretical or the sole domain of the abstract dimension. To the contrary, if a concept is ultimately right in the abstract, then it is also no less correct in the concrete. Thus, what is right in the absolute continues to remain right no matter what. Since the starting point as an ultimate idea or first principle is absolutely right, its subsequent implementation and conversion to operational definitions must also be absolutely correct and must therefore be fully carried out. Its implementation must therefore proceed in an unhindered fashion to its very logical conclusion and end without any interference by extraneous thoughts that would inevitably detract from the ultimate correctness of the whole endeavor. But by so trafficking with absolutes to the point of the absurd, the flexibility so needed for pragmatic action gets thrown out the window. Whenever what is right in the abstract must at all costs be also correct in the concrete, then pragmatism, moral scruples, and even the commonsense logic of daily life are all sacrificed. What takes their place is a rigid moralistic stance capable of implementing with a vengeance a variety of cruelties that are nevertheless deemed to be ultimately right. Consequently, the world of absolutes is narrow, constrictive, and unidimensional. In this kind of world, whatever is ultimately not right must perforce be righted, and anything that is incorrect must be thoroughly corrected. Any tolerance that opens the door to compromises where things might be somewhat wrong is judged to be utterly wrong at all levels of experience. This passion for the absolutes is therefore not exactly a formula for an Anglo-Saxon type of pragmatism. It is rigid thinking, which insists on drawing unbridgeable boundaries between right and wrong even in complicated and overlapping situations. Because of this, even that which does not look all that bad in the here and now and might even do some good is immediately ruled out because it is presumed to be ultimately bad. Conversely, no matter how terrible something might look in the here and now, even a horrible holocaust, no moral brakes will be applied to veto it. This is because the ultimate good commands staying the course and also because absolute moral imperatives must always be obeyed. Hitler's insistence on unconditional obedience may have benefited from some confusion in the public's mind between ultimate orders and absolute moral imperatives. It is this passion for absolutes and habitual dealing with ultimate dimensions that rigidly and preemptively prejudges all situations and events.

Clearly all this reverts back to primitive needs to set up well-defined psychological borders that shore up ego boundaries and definitions of self. It leads to rigidity among playing toddlers, who think that it is absolutely right not to share one's own toy for the reason that it is one's very own. It also leads to the notoriously rigid moralism that is characteristic of adolescents who apply black-and-white thinking to moral dilemmas, a type of thinking in which a legalistic letter-of-the-law approach wins hands down over the spirit of the law. Finally, a relic of this drift down toward primitivism appears in many academic exercises in situation ethics, where plenty of common sense and even compassionate concrete solutions are rejected by being linked to an absolutistic principle that would ultimately be violated by the concrete solution. The result of this Platonic-like insistence on patterning the fleeting world of the senses as much as possible after the eternal models of the world of the ideas is a catastrophic loss of psychological maturity. Plenty of concrete and reasonable options in the mundane world are negated and effectively ruled out by their compulsive linkage to absolutes whose standards they violate. But these academic scenarios do not even come close to actually sanctioning inhuman and barbarous acts as moral because of their supposed linkage to an ultimate aim equated with an absolute good. With this kind of mind-set applied without any brakes, one could even rationalize and withstand unspeakable horrors because, in the final analysis, what is right is right.

Two comments need to be made at this point. The first is that the Germans demonstrated what the rest of humanity is potentially capable of under certain conditions where a destructive ideology, demagogic leadership, uncontrolled emotions, and historical traumas coalesce into an explosive combination. Indeed, what is doubly and triply frightening about the German example is that it illustrates the dangers of a murderous drive that is embedded in the human psyche and that under certain circumstances can be triggered in more than one country. It would be comfortable to believe that only Germans could ever be capable of something like this, but this is not true, and such a belief reflects a defensive flight from self-knowledge.

The second comment cautions us not to regard national character and specific national traits as something immutable, which seals a people's psychological fate by locking them in the grip of a cultural vise from which there is no escape. I do not believe that, as the twentieth century draws to a close, contemporary Germans are as rigid about the process of concrete implementation of what is ultimately right as their forefathers were. It rather seems that their conception of historical justice has mellowed considerably. Consequently, as German reunification (October 3, 1990) and further European integration came about, the Germans did not let historical grievances go to their heads and did not allow ghosts of the past, such as the post–World War II Polish border issue or the expulsion of the Sudetenland Germans from Czechoslovakia, torpedo pragmatism in the name of lack of "justice." It is thus heartening to observe that today's Germany, with all its flaws, is a far cry from what Nazi Germany was.

But we need to get back to the predominant view of the particular nature of the world as depicted in Nazi ideology. It was a most precarious world. The universe was Manichean so that it split the world into good and evil forces. Appearances were deceptive to the point of masking true reality. The ongoing obfuscation included external borders as well as inner boundaries, so much so that what were clear and solid demarcations at one moment proved fuzzy and permeable at the next. Thus the whole uncertain world came to reflect the inner precarious self. When things were not as they appeared to be, good might hide evil, safety might harbor danger, innocence sheltered conspiracies. When what looks benign is quite malignant, and the outside can turn into the inside, then the world can turn into self and vice versa. In such a chronic state of confusion and fear, it is not beyond the realm of possibility that even the enemy will prove to be a mirror image of no less than the self. No wonder that in defensive maneuvers the enemy is repeatedly projected outside as much as possible. And through paranoid and phobic outlooks the hitherto baffled self disperses confusion, imposes clear demarcations, and escapes impotence by attacking the newly exposed enemies, both within and without. But this restoration of omnipotence proves fleeting indeed because underneath its deceptive appearance lurks once more a reality of impotence in the face of a mortal threat. Somehow the elusive and highly mobile enemy is never fully vanquished, and for some mysterious reason it stays alive as long as the self persists.

Under the compelling psychological rules of this kind of a Manichean universe, identity is highly rigid, but also extremely volatile, and can always revert to its flip side. It becomes somewhat like a sock that can be presented in its normal exterior side but can be instantaneously turned inside out and presented that way. Psychologically speaking, therefore, the split Manichean world of deceptive appearances and treacherous boundaries, which induces paranoid and phobic fears, is an uncanny universe. It is uncanny because there is always something about it that is both recognizable and not recognizable, namely the old self. While this archaic self can shrivel in terror to become infinitesimal, it can also expand into primordial omnipotence to encapsulate the whole world, yet fail to recognize this world even though it looks strangely and eerily familiar. Thus, in a psychohistorical irony of fate, the geographically wandering Jews have been superseded by the psychologically no-madic Germans, who stumbled everywhere upon uncanny encounters with their own, unrecognizable but eerily familiar, group self.

The cardinal role of blood in Hitler's ideology also serves to expose the vulnerability of a universe that is characterized by permeability. Blood, which is the magical substance par excellence, has a free-flowing and border-crossing quality on multiple levels. It is a concrete biological concept that also transcends into the mystical dimension. As such it could propel Nazis from biological pessimism (the impact of pollution) to barbarism (annihilating polluters) as indicated by Rauschning. It is body but also spirit, thus uniting what would otherwise be the great psychophysical divide. It resides inside, yet can be spilled onto the outside. It giveth life but also decrees death. Most alarming is its predilection to cross racial lines—that kind of border crossing that represents the original sin of humanity according to Hitler. Left unregulated, it can float back and forth from Aryans to Jews and lose its magical qualities. This forfeiture of magic is indeed an unpardonable sin, which is punished by sickness, decline, and death. But when it is strictly regulated by the power of the will, it regenerates and imparts its magic to its protectors. The fantasy of the pure blood of old—its unfortunate contamination but also its future purification—is a story of magic lost and won as racial destiny moved across symbolic borders passing from the phases of past utopia and post-utopian disaster into the coming phase of a new utopia. Time and again the multisymbolism of blood, as well as its inherent predilection to flow across both concrete and imaginary boundaries, pointed toward the pitfall of mortal dangers but also toward the glorious opportunity of scooping up the magic stuff and miraculous powers of this world. No longer did godly powers belong to God in heaven. They were now on earth at the disposal of that gifted man who had the vision to see them and the will to use them. Under his divine, i.e., racially inspired, regulation the German folk became the organic body within which its blood evolved into spirit that remained protected by a constant war against all enemies Jewish, Slavic, and otherwise. Thus, the magic of a utopian enclave within the faulty and highly permeable world yielded permanent barbarism. Chances are that utopian barbarism is the worst kind there is because it legitimizes inhumanity as an act of reparation and because it is carried out with the fanaticism of wounded and narcissistically injured groups who believe in the healing powers of revenge.

The biomystical concept of blood served also as the ideological basis for imposing totalitarian control upon society and state. The correlate of the underlying level of blood quality was personality worth, and it dictated the ordering of society in accordance with the stratification of this inherent merit across individuals. All this gives new meaning to the standard notion that "everything is in order." It now means that everything without exception should be regulated, that the imposition of this regulation should be compulsory and done by force when need be, and that the wide-scale assignment of roles to everybody should not cross forbidden boundaries. What the latter means is that the assignments should conform to the limits of the personal merits of each individual and should not transgress racial rules of blood quality. Seemingly everything must always be in order in Germany; otherwise the resultant crossing of symbolic borders spells peril to the self. Hence magic comes with an inordinate amount of regulation, which means that it comes at a very high cost. And if the cost is at the expense of reality, then it is indeed too high.

The mythology of blood served also to justify Hitler, the gifted genius and supreme leader, in his total control over the multitudes of brilliant dummies. It was the great chasm in force of personality between him and them by which nature ordained him to exercise the power of his will over them. And he did it in a style that made him a spellbinding dominator, a forceful seducer, and a masculine charmer of the receptive audiences. And while he became identified as the collective talisman of his nation, he even acquired a sort of "ego quality" that enabled all individuals to partake in his magic. The result was a widespread magical feeling of a benevolent transformation basically from impotence to omnipotence. This kind of radical transformation is just one more illustration of the ease with which an identity may revert to its flip side. Under the impact of such a ravishing seduction, which triggered an orgasmic switch from inferiority to superiority, almost the whole nation felt ready and destined for racial glory even as it was in actuality thoroughly regimented by Hitler. As the legend went, it was by virtue of his force of personality that he evolved into the mightiest protector of blood purity of all time, and he was chosen for this role by destiny, which meant by the underlying quality of his own blood. Now the entire nation was expected to catapult itself by this kind of a tautological magic, where the people guard the blood, which in turn invigorates them, in an ever escalating folkish prowess of a master race ready to dominate the world.

Yet this appetite for taking on the whole world was a dressed-up version of the archaic oral urge to take in the whole world. The illusion of omnipotence that sustains such limitless drives is based on a fundamental condition of the primordial psychic environment where most things are still largely merged with each other. This merged condition, which places everything within easy reach, is what enabled the rudimentary self to devour everything. It is therefore the very condition of being merged that serves as an illusionary source of surpassing power. In consequence, if a given group is overly concerned with historical divisions and is obsessed with fears of powerlessness, the urge to merge can reassert itself in future times in an attempt to revive the old kind of magical power, which would once again make possible the great oral engulfment of everything. It is therefore no coincidence that the Nazi ambition to rule Europe and to dominate the world was conditioned on the merging of people and leader to produce a single omnipotent will. The condition of *ein Volk, ein Reich, ein Führer* was a merged state of being that psychologically recreated in the modern and complex totalitarian state the much less differentiated condition of an infant who thrusts at the blurry world with all his oral might. And with the emergence of the unified political will, there was also the reemergence of the archaic oral will, the old devouring and omnipotent will, that kind of will that magically transforms "wanting" into "having." Nothing, therefore, could stand in the way of such an indomitable will (Hitler's favorite concept). Should reality have the temerity to stand in the way between wish and wish-fulfillment, the magical will would unceremoniously brush it aside.

One way of looking at Hitler's ideology is that it designated a specific racial group, the Aryans, as "chosen people" of sorts. They were chosen by nature to be the carriers of better blood. This made them superior, in fantasy, in a fully integrated psychophysical sense. And it entitled them, again in fantasy, by virtue of their blood to a special justice that would grant them the extra allotment that, it was believed, providentially superior people deserve. The underlying assumptions that go into such a sweeping perception are powerful and carry a psychological allure. Hence the unfortunate attraction-power of some racist notions. First and foremost there is the health notion of psychophysical integrity with its imposition of a monistic fate upon the old dualism of body and soul. It meant that everything, both material and spiritual, had to be manipulated in tandem. This had to be done because without such uniform control any damage to psychophysical health could spread and bring about decline and death in conformity to the rules of monistic fate. Thus, the ideological requirement of the monistic health notion was the practice of that kind of complete control that amounted to totalitarianism. In turn, totalitarianism involved the wholesale and rigid implementation of the hierarchical leadership principle that served as a magic power formula. The implementation of the leadership principle was expected to result in the preservation of psychophysical integrity throughout the national organism, thus fulfilling a prerequisite of an ideal unity of mind and body where the power of the will prevails. And the resultant magic that was ultimately derived from blood was going to be used to secure the blood entitlement—the special justice for the chosen people. For blood entitlement was thus far not rewarded with the proper extra allotment of worldly fortunes because of the machinations of other evil powers. This criminal discrepancy between original entitlement and actual allotment was against nature and was in and by itself an irrefutable proof of injustice. Being shortchanged—in spite of providential entitlement—was the core meaning of injustice. Even the famous injustice of Versailles was but the outer symbol for this underlying ontological conception of injustice. Versailles, however, provided Hitler with the smoking gun, proof positive of the crime of injustice against Germany, which he was going to rectify with blazing guns.

In his study of the Nazi doctors and the psychology of genocide, Robert Jay Lifton put forward the principle of doubling as a psychological mechanism for handling conflicts of identity. Doubling is the division of the self into two separate functioning wholes so that each part-self could act as an entire self (Lifton 1986, 418). He also suggested that although a certain amount of doubling is a pervasive phenomenon, a destructive version of it, which he named "victimizer's doubling" and which is less prevalent, was in operation in Nazi Germany. Resorting to this mechanism enabled the Germans to tap in a more extensive way the underlying and general human potential for mobilizing evil (Lifton 1986, 464). While Lifton's suggestion concerning doubling and the Nazi doctors seems plausible, its extension in the form of victimizer's doubling to cover most German Nazis is problematic. The Nazi doctors encountered a clash of two ideologies. Their Hippocratic oath mandated healing, not killing. But the Nazi ideology promoted killing for the sake of healing the collective. To overcome the healing versus killing contradiction, which Lifton depicted so well, doubling was a handy psychological maneuver since it provided two separate selves for two separate tasks. But this was not the case for the population at large. Those who became committed Nazis did not view Nazi ideology as something that contradicted their previous beliefs. There was no clash there. The new ideology reaffirmed long-held convictions but provided new ways of living up to them. The ideology of death to the Jews but life to the Germans did not put the German self in conflict with its past beliefs. Consequently no doubling of the self for the sake of handling a conflict was necessary. By contrast, total psychological repression of any awareness of the possibility that the mythical Jew is a projection of the German self was very necessary. For with such an awareness creeping into consciousness, death to the Jews would have also meant death to the Germans. In that case the barbarism of killing would have lost its utopian quality of healing. Such a stupendous loss would require giving up such precious psychic commodities as the possession of magic, self-righteous cruelty, claims to superiority, and mighty dreams for eternal victory. In sum, rather than creating contradictions, which could stress the self, the ideology of death, which relied on massive repressions, tied everything neatly together into the psychological package deal of an harmonious single self.

The fusion of contradictory images that went into the portrayal of the ideal national organism is of great psychological significance. As we may recall, in practice the folkish state represented the triumph of mechanism. This led Franz Neumann (1966, 439) to speak about the destruction of spontaneity, the incorporation of the population into a super-machine, and the cardinal role of magic in Nazi culture. In a somewhat similar fashion, Mumford regarded the coercive political organization of human beings into megamachines as an inherently destructive force, which kills people and which suppresses the spontaneity, individuality, and creativity of the living. Nazism also fell into this pattern but with a certain distinction. Mumford described the work of the Nazi megamachine in concentration camps as "far more thrifty in carefully conserving the by-products—the human wastes, the gold from the teeth, the fat, the bone meal for fertilizers—even the skin for lamp-shades" (Mumford 1970, 278–79). What Mumford seemed to have implied here was that the thrifty, possibly anal, Germans cared more than others to put the physical remains of the destructive work of the megamachine into material production. They therefore excelled in the conversion of living humans into inanimate material goods.

There also are important psychocultural implications to Neumann's pairing of a super-machine with what amounts to the infantile magic of old. The blurring of boundaries among members of the folkish community and the attempted reduction of their collective existence to the undifferentiated level that characterizes infants were both utopian and totalitarian. In reality there are no such creatures as psychologically borderless adults except for instances of very severe psychopathology, and this fact could not be obliterated by the promise of an orgasmic redemption through fusion with the collective national being. The whole venture was unrealistic to begin with since such an infantilization could not be fully implemented and permanently sustained with adults, in spite of the regressive tendencies that groups can foster and in spite of the totalitarian coercion by the folkish state.

But as the myth went, this undifferentiated, i.e., infantile, national organism was supposed to continue functioning at the level of technologically capable adults able to wage the most modern of warfares. What this meant was that the folk comrades should technically fight like adults, but psychologically function like infants, or fight like machines but die like humans. Indeed, in spite of its "organic" label, the folkish state was a war machine whose infantilized inhabitants were imbued with the spirit of the sacrifice. And this hallowed national organism, this undifferentiated collectivity that was a "crossbreed" between infant and machine, was programmed for the two interlocking tasks of incorporation and expulsion. With its limitless dynamism, it was going to engage in permanently gobbling up new living spaces while at the same time expelling poison, decay, and rot. In other words, it was going to eat territories and shit Jews. It was going to roll over the entire world, take it all in, decompose the decomposers, and expel the decay into oblivion. This was the universal Nazi juggernaut, an infantile perpetuum mobile machine for cleansing the earth. And as usual, the endeavor to set up a perpetual motion device represented magic rather than science. In the best Nazi traditions of "movement" and "energy," the mechanical human organism was set up to accomplish its task by incorporating more and more chunks of the earth into the ever extended German self while spewing out all its disease agents. And there was no chance that it was ever going to stop. It was meant to last for a thousand years, meaning forever, and it was never meant to come to a halt in some static state of summum bonum (highest good). Energy and life mean constant dynamism and ceaseless action. Only death means eternal rest. And there had never been a destiny of eternal rest set up for the collective national organism, which was going to live forever. The infantile machine was therefore destined to keep on rolling, finding new sacrificial humans to waste wherever it could. After disposing of all Jews, it would have done away with all corrupted others, all Judaized non-Jews who represent the new ferment of decomposition, which would eventually include everybody. Even Germans were no longer safe from it. It was therefore necessary for the world to stop the infantile living machine, and it was time for the Germans to grow up.

In the present context "to grow up" implies some form of character change. Our exploration of what Weiss (1996, 317) called the twin "final solutions" of lebensraum and genocide exposed underlying psychological drives for incorporation and expulsion, which pattern themselves after biology. It is not surprising that themes that float in the public domain and affect popular imagination and the life of the collective can have personality implications. One need not, however, go through a lengthy detour of studying psychology, ideology, history, and shared fantasies in order to "discover" that people can be oral and anal. The pertinent issue here is not that people have basic drives, but rather how these drives are woven into a symbolic expression of the conflict between their hopes and dreams on the one hand and their terrors and fears on the other. Whatever "resolution" this conflict receives, it ends up shaping character, including national character.

In popular parlance, the Germans have a reputation for being overwhelmingly on the side of what can be stereotypically labeled as anally retentive in character. Who has not heard that Germans are pedantic, meticulous, sticklers for details, compulsive about cleanliness, obsessive about executing work with precision, and extremely punctual with just about anything ranging from train schedules to social engagements. Under the impact of such stereotypes, one could easily forget that the Germans are also hopelessly romantic and even capable of the kind of upheavals and explosions that demonic romanticism generates. One could even acknowledge that the Germans are fairly oral and seem to love to eat good food and drink beer. But in spite of the prevalence of pot bellies among Germans, they do not let it get out of hand, and they distinguish between eating like a human being (*essen*) and gobbling like an animal (*fressen*). Thus, in spite of some observable oral characteristics, the overall reputation of the German character is predominantly anal.

But I do not think that this popular verdict is correct, and in order to help settle the issue we need to identify the psychological ramifications of orality and anality. Orality as a character trait goes way beyond the love of food. The old mode of oral incorporation comes to symbolize the desired satisfaction of any nice or nasty wish taken from a huge wish list of wants. The oral mode signifies a fixation on that kind of stance toward life that repeatedly proclaims, "I want, I want, I want. . . ." Not only can the "wants" be limitless in number, but they each can be unlimited in quality. One wants to be the best, to have the most, to dominate others, to be worshiped, to receive the sweet tasting food of recognition, and so on and on and on. Another way of putting it would be to say that one wants nothing less than all the material and spiritual assets of this world. And incorporation, both actual and symbolic, stands for the actual fulfillment of each specific desire. It reaffirms that what was wanted has been taken, even taken in, has become part of the self. The character trait of orality is therefore in the business of incorporating the unlimited. It is a trait that betrays vestiges of infantile magic, harking back to a time when fulfilling limitless wishes was still "possible" because the world did not yet include a sufficient amount of borders, boundaries, or for that matter, limits.

By contrast, the anal mode is supposed to have evolved out of the social pressure to learn to control retention and elimination. It therefore puts a premium on rules and regulations, on propriety and impropriety, on delay and on timing, and, on the whole, on maintaining control over the entire process. Consequently, the anal mode becomes an expression of preference for setting limits and boundaries on a wide array of human endeavors that go way beyond the regulation of bodily functions.

We are in a better position now to understand the role of the reputed anality of the German national character. It is a reaction to as well as setting limits upon an insatiable oral greed. With its unyielding demand for magical wish fulfillment, oral greed could easily burst out of control. There is a good chance that the historical impetus for settling upon the oral mode came from a deeply felt sense of injustice that justified the taking of exceptional measures in line with oral excess. Kohn (1960, 97) described this feeling as follows: "Situated in the center of Europe, open to influences and incursions from all sides, deprived by historical fate and enemy envy of their national unity and world-historical rank, the Germans felt that they had been ill-treated by history. Therefore they had a right—and even a moral obligation—to take recourse to exceptional measures in order to remedy this intolerable situation."

One possible implication of all this is that the constant need to reverse the existential status quo out of a sense of victimization reinforced the predilection to adopt the sweeping style of the oral mode. It signaled readiness to challenge history and represented the protest of the victimized. This implied that with a German self-image changing away from victimization, the vigor of the oral mode could lessen. It should be remembered, though, that the fixation at the level of the limitless oral avarice came at the price of fuzzy boundaries. This made limits impossible and the fulfillment of limitless wishes possible. But such a borderless state of affairs carried with it not only the glory of wish fulfillment but also the terror of being invaded, diffused, sucked dry, and annihilated. Therefore limit-setting in the anal mode must have been welcomed grudgingly, as some magic had to be forsaken, but also with relief, as some of the internal terror was kept at bay. Together the two modes reflected an orientation toward life that aspired for the mental luxury of the simultaneous utilization of discipline combined with uncontrollability. The combination of the two modes kept the German character in a psychological blend that can best be termed meticulously emotional.

History has shown by now that the reinstitution of psychological boundaries and limits through anal compulsiveness is a poor substitute for reality. So long as the reaching out continues to be primarily oral in nature and is anchored in limitless magic, many endeavors are fated to remain programs for failure. Ultimately the character flaw is biting off more than one can chew. And the end result of this flaw in the German national character has been repetition of trauma. In order to break this vicious cycle, one needs to undergo character changes. Growing up means realizing that one is special because one is unique, not because one is providentially superior. The rewards of setting out to achieve realistic endeavors outstrip illusionary oral magic as well the oppressing constraints of anality. My impression, for whatever it is worth, is that the majority of Germans nowadays have their feet anchored in reality.

But there is no question that the horrors that were visited upon humanity during the Nazi era point toward the flawed nature of human beings, which allows them to commit atrocities when under the influence of ideologies of death. The underlying problem, and not specifically with regard to Germany, merits a few metapsychological speculations, which are offered here as metaphors, perhaps useful ones. In terms of the psychological birth of the human being, it seems that in the beginning there was the primordial split between self and world, which slowly arose out of a state that until then was characterized by total diffusion and nondifferentiation. Therefore, the first available model of a sense of being was already a split model. In consequence, when a sense of self crystallized a bit more it also settled into a split model after which it was initially patterned. Thus, there may always be traces of a breach within the individual as well as group self, which reflect the fuzzy primordial split of self and world. This newer breach within the self has been frequently handled or surmounted by endowing one part with a "bad" ego quality and projecting it outside to others. Through this maneuver the "bad" element is transformed from being part of one's conscious self into an external alien. This early development receives further elaborations in individuals and in collective life by externalization to other groups. The developmental sequence may therefore be as follows. Out of total followed by near-total diffusion arises a barely differentiated being that revolves around a split between self and world. The primordial split develops into a breached self that utilizes projections. These projections create a collective division of "us" and "them," which the group members maintain by means of externalizations. The mechanism that facilitates this practice of dividing the world into enemies and allies

lies in the postverbal development of specific and suitable targets of externalization, as amply illustrated by Volkan (1988).

So in the psychological beginning there was the split after which all later developments have been patterned. But what happens if at some future time, for traumatic, ideological, or other reasons, the externalization of "bad" parts as a "remedy" proves insufficient for retaining a sense of inner wholeness and goodness. At such times, for the sake of "healing" the breach, externalization may be compelled to proceed further into annihilation of the split-off part of the self, i.e., killing in war, or even extermination in a holocaust. The breached being of human beings may every so often erupt into cosmic rage as the narcissistic injury of "injustice" propels a dynamism of limitless revenge against the bad side of the split. Be it tiny terrorist groups or small as well as large nations, the capacity for mass murder during surging rage is there because of the mounting psychic pressure to do away with the existential condition of being split, by exterminating the bad part of the split self. With traumatic histories and under the influence of ideological worldviews, which make the tolerance of "badness" narcissistically impossible, a shared fantasy of healing through killing can take over and usher in a new venture of utopian barbarism. Due to different psychohistorical developments, different human groups are not alike in being so predisposed. But the genocidal potential of humanity is unfortunately always there. It bodes ill for the future.

It would be easy to succumb to a pessimistic mood and to a judgmental conclusion that says that Germans will always be Germans and that, if they did it once, they could do it again. But try as I may to anticipate future trends, I keep coming up with a more optimistic conclusion. In essence it seems to me that the cycle of trauma repetition has been broken. My impressions, which are based only on observations from afar, pertain to the more general and dominant trends. They are not meant to ignore the disturbing phenomenon of Holocaust deniers or to underestimate vestiges of the past among some Germans of the older generation and the existence and activities of neo-Nazi groups that include young people. I can only paint the following picture in broad strokes.

To begin with, the post–World War II history of Germany did not seem at all to consist of a psychohistorical replay of the Weimar Republic, where a shaky democratic government was under constant violent attacks from both the extreme political right and the extreme political left. This time the democratic center patterned itself more after the British model of the party in power facing a loyal opposition. The reasons for this break with the past may go back to the two world wars. Fritz Stern (1965) conducted a penetrating analysis of a particular type of cultural despair that drove Germans toward a leap from despair to utopia across all existing reality. And he maintained that this mood, which originated in the second half of the nineteenth century, seized both the German right and the Nazis. He thus concluded that in many respects Nazi ideology resembled this earlier Germanic ideology. It was because of this particular historical legacy of cultural despair that certain consequences followed. Peace in 1919 signified only the continuation of war by other means, it ushered in a period of unprecedented violence, and in fact a second Thirty Years' War had begun (F. Stern 1975, 120). To elaborate, within the German psyche the First World War did not really end in 1918, so that eventually the Second World War unfolded as a psychohistorical replay of the first.

But this time there has been no replay of the original defeat scenario. It was as if the politics of cultural despair lost their potency for one reason or another. Germany was indeed defeated. Yet the "almost factor" in German history did not repeat itself. It did not seem that by cruel machinations, which require conspiratorial explanations, defeat was snatched at the last moment from the jaws of a tantalizing "almost" victory. No surprise this time. Some Germans had already figured it out when Germany proved incapable of invading England. Others had an inkling of what was to come when the *Wehrmacht* was pushed away from the gates of Moscow. But most Germans knew after Stalingrad that only defeat lay ahead. The increasingly extensive bombing of German cities as the war progressed also alerted the population to the prospect of an impending defeat. There was therefore no last-minute and shocking surprise to leave the seemingly victorious Germans highly baffled over the sudden turn of events. In other words, this second Thirty Years' War, in which World War II was but a continuation of World War I, finally ended. It ended in a definite verdict of defeat. This time there would be no lost victories to retrieve and no defeats to reverse during future psychohistorical replays of the past. An exhausted Germany accepted defeat.

Defeat brought with it the division of Germany. In past times such a condition of cutting into the national body could easily foster dreams of power and revenge. But it seems that the majority of people in both Germanies felt, quite realistically, like midgets among giants. It was a reality that was hard to ignore. Rather than clinging to illusions concerning the redressing of injustice by German might, most Germans seemed to have felt the way the Poles traditionally did, i.e., like a small power stuck between two superpowers.

Fortunately the aftermath of defeat did not seem to resemble the history that followed the Versailles peace treaty. In East Germany total subservience to the Soviet Union was the order of the day, as it was in the rest of Eastern Europe. It was not pleasant but it represented the consequences of superpower rivalry, which was not reserved for Germans only by virtue of being Germans. This fact defused any fantasies concerning Germans' being singled out unfairly. In West Germany, America was viewed as a benefactor ever since the final days of the war, when German soldiers were trying to surrender in droves to the Americans. And the allies were conscious of the post-Versailles history in which to the Germans "the terms of the armistice, of the interim demands for deliveries from current German production, and the peace treaty and the interpretation that France put upon its fulfillment became one of the most monumental pieces of hypocrisy of all time" (Davidson 1977, 114). Therefore, all three allies were this time determined to avoid economic suffocation (the Marshall Plan included Germany) and a repetition of political measures that would make Germans feel like pariahs and cause them to seek revenge. They succeeded. Most Germans did not sink into a bitter obsession over maltreatment by the victorious powers. So once again a replay has been avoided—this time a replay of the psychic trauma of the *Diktat* of Versailles.

More recently still another replay failed to materialize when the reunification of east and west Germany took place. There was jubilation, of course, which was tempered by pocketbook concerns that Chancellor Kohl tried to minimize. This was not exactly a picture of running amuck with heady nationalism. After some initial hesitation, Kohl accepted the need to leave the issue of the Polish border as is, and not open up a hornets' nest. Pragmatism prevailed as Germans living abroad were welcomed back from Silesia, Volga, etc. Reunification so far does not seem to have revived the old dreams of a German Middle Europe that would serve as a springboard toward world domination.

The latest evidence for positive changes in German identity and character is the passage on May 21, 1999, by the Reichstag of a new immigration law that makes it easier for residents of foreign origin to acquire German citizenship. Beforehand, the conception of German nationality and the resultant eligibility for German citizenship rested on the notion of ethnic German blood lines, which disqualified many immigrants. It was not easy for the German public to reach this point, and it took a lot of political bickering and heated public debates to finally get there. The painful controversy and subsequent success of the new immigration law were of great psychological significance. They signaled the collective process of a gradual redefinition of German identity by moving away from the historically lethal notion of the sacred status of blood. This latest evidence of flexibility and change within the culture is heartening.

All in all, the second half of the twentieth century does not show a German history that is significantly saturated with psychohistorical replays. Such a saturation is the basic criterion for passing or failing "the sense of foreboding" test. Contemporary Germany gets a definite pass, and the situation is most likely going to improve even more as the younger generation takes over. As a matter of fact, most young Germans feel very friendly toward the French and vice versa; neither of them represents the hereditary enemy any longer. To these young Germans "replay" dreams of marching in a victory parade in the *Champs-Elysées* would truly seem like madness. Psychohistorical replays just don't seem to be the order of the day, but historical reexamination is. The great popularity, albeit not among the establishment of the historical profession, of Goldhagen's book (1996) on the participation of many ordinary Germans in the Holocaust is another sign that contemporary Germans seek new understandings rather than old/new replays. There is a good chance that the seeking of such knowledge is going to serve as a major antidote to racism. At the end of this journey it may no longer be necessary for large numbers of Germans to project disowned parts of the self into demonic others, such as Turks, or to carry a split self-image of brilliant dummies. It all signals a growing willingness on the part of Germans to acknowledge responsibility for the past and to secure a realistic future that is neither utopian nor barbaric.

Bibliography

Allen, William Sheridan. *The Nazi Seizure of Power: The Experience of a Single German Town 1930–1935.* Chicago: Quadrangle Books, 1965.

Anderson, Flavia. *The Ancient Secret: Fire from the Sun.* Orpington, Kent, England: B. & J. Hargreaves, 1987.

Bailey, George. *Germans: Biography of an Obsession.* New York: Avon Books, 1974.

Baynes, Norman H., ed. *The Speeches of Adolf Hitler, April 1922–August 1939.* 2 vols. New York: Oxford Univ. Press, 1942.

Beisel, David R. *Suicidal Embrace.* Forthcoming.

Bessel, Richard. *Germany after the First World War.* New York: Oxford Univ. Press, 1993.

Binion, Rudolph. *Hitler among the Germans.* 2d corrected printing. New York: Elsevier, 1979.

———. "Hitler Looks East." *Soundings: Psychohistorical and Psycholiterary,* 97–115. New York: Psychohistory Press, 1981.

———. "'Der Jude ist weg': Machtpolitische Auswirkungen des Hitlerschen Rassengedankens." In *Die Deutsche Frage im 19. und 20. Jahrhundert,* ed. Joseph Becker and Andreas Hilgruber. Munich: Ernst Vögel, 1983, 347–72.

———. "Corrigenda." *Psychohistory Review* 5, no. 1 (1986): 69–79.

Bleuel, Hans Peter. *Sex and Society in Nazi Germany.* Ed. Heinrich Fraenkel. Trans. J. Maxwell Brownjohn. New York: Bantam, 1974.

Bracher, Karl Dietrich. *The German Dictatorship: The Origins, Structure, and Effects of National Socialism.* Trans. Jean Steinberg. New York: Praeger, 1970.

Caplan, Jane. "Bureaucracy, Politics and the National Socialist State." In *The Shaping of the Nazi State,* ed. Peter D. Stachura, 234–56. London: Croom Helm, 1978.

Cohn, Norman. *Warrant for Genocide: The Myth of the Jewish World-*

Conspiracy and the Protocols of the Elders of Zion. Harmonds-worth, Middlesex, England: Pelican, 1970.

Craig, Gordon A. *The Germans.* New York and Scarborough, Ontario: New American Library, 1982.

Davidson, Eugene. *The Making of Adolf Hitler.* New York: Macmillan, 1977.

de Roussy de Sales, Raoul, ed. *Adolf Hitler: My New Order.* New York: Reynal & Hitchcock, 1941.

Dimont, Max I. *Jews, God and History.* New York: Signet, 1962.

Domarus, Max. *Hitler: Speeches and Proclamations 1932–1945.* Vol. 1. Wauconda, Ill.: Bolchazy-Carducci, 1990.

———. *Hitler: Speeches and Proclamations 1932–1945.* Vol. 2. Wauconda, Ill.: Bolchazy-Carducci, 1992.

Eckart, Dietrich. "Jewishness in and around Us: Fundamental Reflec-tions." In Miller Lane, Barbara, and Leila J. Rupp, intro. and trans. *Nazi Ideology before 1933: A Documentation.* Austin: Univ. of Texas Press, 1978.

Erikson, Erik H. *Young Man Luther: A Study in Psychoanalysis and History.* New York: W.W. Norton, 1962.

———. *Identity: Youth and Crisis.* New York: W.W. Norton, 1968.

Falk, Avner. "Border Symbolism." *Psychoanalytic Quarterly* 43, no. 4 (1974): 650–60.

———. "Border Symbolism Revisited." *International Review of Psycho-Analysis* 10 (1983): 215–20.

Fenichel, Otto. *The Psychoanalytic Theory of Neurosis.* New York: W.W. Norton, 1945.

———. "Elements of a Psychoanalytic Theory of Anti-Semitism." In *The Collected Papers of Otto Fenichel, Second Series,* 335–48. New York: W.W. Norton, 1954a.

———. "Trophy and Triumph." In *The Collected Papers of Otto Fenichel, Second Series,* 141–62. New York: W.W. Norton, 1954b.

Fest, Joachim C. *Hitler.* Trans. Richard Winston and Clara Winston. New York: Harcourt Brace Jovanovich, 1974.

Freud, Anna. "Comments on Trauma." *Psychic Trauma,* ed. Sidney S. Furst, 235–45. New York: Basic Books, 1967.

Freud, Sigmund. "The 'Uncanny.'" In *The Standard Edition of the Com-plete Psychological Works of Sigmund Freud,* ed. James Strachy, 17:219–52. London: Hogarth Press, 1955a.

———. "Beyond the Pleasure Principle." In *The Standard Edition of the Complete Psychological Works of Sigmund Freud,* ed. James Strachy, 18:7–64. London: Hogarth Press, 1955b.

———. "Group Psychology and the Analysis of the Ego." In *The Standard Edition of the Complete Psychological Works of Sigmund Freud,* ed. James Strachy, 18:69–143. London: Hogarth Press, 1955c.

Friedländer, Saul. *Reflections of Nazism: An Essay on Kitsch and Death.* Trans. Thomas Weyr. New York: Harper & Row, 1984.

———. *Nazi Germany and the Jews.* Vol. 1, *The Years of Persecution, 1933–1939.* New York: Harper Collins, 1997.

Fromm, Erich. *The Anatomy of Human Destructiveness.* New York: Holt, Rinehart & Winston, 1973.

Germany Speaks: By 21 Leading Members of Party and State, 233. With a Preface by Joachim von Ribbentrop. London: Thornton Butterworth, 1938.

Gilbert, Martin. *The Second World War: A Complete History.* Rev. ed. New York: Henry Holt, 1989.

Goldhagen, Daniel Jonah. *Hitler's Willing Executioners: Ordinary Germans and the Holocaust.* New York, Alfred A. Knopf, 1996.

Gonen, Jay Y. *A Psychohistory of Zionism.* New York: Mason/Charter, 1975.

———. "The Israeli Illusion of Omnipotence following the Six Day War." *Journal of Psychohistory* 6, no. 2 (1978): 241–71.

Gregor, A. James. *The Ideology of Fascism: The Rationale of Totalitarianism.* New York: Free Press, 1969.

Grunberger, Richard. *The 12-Year Reich: A Social History of Nazi Germany 1933–1945.* New York: Ballantine Books, 1972.

Grunfeld, Frederic V. *The Hitler File: A Social History of Germany and the Nazis 1918–45,* 165. New York: Random House, 1974.

Gutman, Robert W. *Richard Wagner: The Man, His Mind, and His Music.* New York: Harcourt, Brace & World, 1968.

Hamilton, Charles. *The Hitler Diaries: Fakes That Fooled the World.* Lexington: Univ. Press of Kentucky, 1991.

Hanson, John H. "Nazi Aesthetics." *Psychohistory Review* 9, no. 4 (1981): 251–81.

Heer, Friedrich. *The Holy Roman Empire.* Trans. Janet Sondheimer. New York: Frederick A. Praeger, 1968.

Heiden, Konrad. *Der Fuehrer: Hitler's Rise to Power.* Trans. Ralph Manheim. Boston: Houghton Mifflin, 1944.

Hitler, Adolf. *Mein Kampf,* 651. Trans. Ralph Manheim. Boston: Houghton Mifflin, 1943.

Inkeles, Alex. *National Character: A Psycho-Social Perspective.* New Brunswick, N.J.: Transaction, 1997.

Jäckel, Eberhard. *Hitler's World View: A Blueprint for Power.* Trans. Herbert Arnold. Cambridge: Harvard Univ. Press, 1981.

Kershaw, Ian. *Hitler, 1889–1936: Hubris.* New York: W.W. Norton, 1998.

Koenigsberg, Richard A. *Hitler's Ideology: A Study in Psychoanalytic Sociology.* New York: Library of Social Science, 1975.

Kohn, Hans. *The Mind of Germany: The Education of a Nation.* New York: Charles Scribner's Sons, 1960.

Le Bon, Gustave. *The Crowd: A Study of the Popular Mind.* London: T. Fisher Unwin, 1897.

Leschnitzer, Adolf. *The Magic Background of Modern Anti-Semitism: An Analysis of the German-Jewish Relationship.* New York: International Universities Press, 1969.

Lifton, Robert Jay. *The Nazi Doctors: Medical Killing and the Psychology of Genocide.* New York: Basic Books, 1986.

Loewenberg, Peter. "The Psychohistorical Origins of the Nazi Youth Cohort." *Decoding the Past,* 240–83. New York: Alfred A. Knopf, 1983.

Mannheim, Karl. *Ideology and Utopia: An Introduction to the Sociology of Knowledge,* 39, 207, 248. Trans. Louis Wirth and Edward Shils. New York: Harcourt, Brace & World, 1936.

Marsden, Victor E., trans. *The Protocols of the Meetings of the Learned Elders of Zion with Preface and Explanatory Notes.* N.p., 1934.

Maser, Werner, ed. *Hitler's Letters and Notes.* Trans. Arnold Pomerans. New York: Bantam, 1976.

Mosse, George L. *The Nationalization of the Masses: Political Symbolism and Mass Movements in Germany from the Napoleonic Wars through the Third Reich.* New York: New American Library, 1977.

———. "Beauty without Sensuality: The Exhibition *Entertete Kunst.*" In *"Degenerate Art": The Fate of the Avant-Garde in Nazi Germany,* ed. Stephanie Barron, 25–31. New York: Harry N. Abrams, 1991.

———. *The Fascist Revolution: Toward a General Theory of Fascism.* New York: Howard Fertig, 1999.

Mumford, Lewis. *The Myth of the Machine: The Pentagon of Power.* New York: Harcourt Brace Jovanovich, 1970.

Neumann, Franz. *Behemoth: The Structure and Practice of National Socialism 1933–1944.* New York: Harper & Row, 1966.

Neumann, Sigmund. *Permanent Revolution: Totalitarianism in the Age of International Civil War.* 2d ed. New York: Frederick A. Praeger, 1965.

Noakes, J., and Pridham G., eds. *Nazism 1919–1945: A History in Documents and Eyewitness Accounts.* Vol. 1, *The Nazi Party, State and Society 1919–1939.* New York: Schocken Books, 1990.

———. *Nazism 1919–1945: A History in Documents and Eyewitness Accounts.* Vol. 2, *Foreign Policy, War and Racial Extermination.* New York: Schocken Books, 1990.

Nolte, Ernst. *Three Faces of Fascism: Action Française, Italian Fascism, National Socialism.* Trans. Leila Vennewitz. New York: New American Library, 1969.

Ranke, Kurt, ed. *Folktales of Germany.* Trans. Lotte Baumann. Chicago: Univ. of Chicago Press, 1966.

Rauschning, Hermann. *The Revolution of Nihilism: Warning to the West.* New York: Alliance Book Corporation, 1939.

———. *Time of Delirium.* Trans. Richard Winston and Clara Winston. New York: D. Appleton-Century, 1946.

Reinhardt, Kurt F. *Germany: 2000 Years.* Vol. 1, *The Rise and Fall of the "Holy Empire."* New York: Frederick Ungar, 1961.

Rhodes, James M. *The Hitler Movement: A Modern Millenarian Revolution.* Stanford, Calif.: Hoover Institution Press, 1980.

Schoenbaum, David. *Hitler's Social Revolution: Class and Status in Nazi Germany 1933–1939.* Garden City, N.Y.: Doubleday, 1966.

Schuman, Frederick L. *The Nazi Dictatorship: A Study in Social Psychology and the Politics of Fascism.* New York: Alfred A. Knopf, 1935.

Shirer, William L. *The Rise and Fall of the Third Reich: A History of Nazi Germany.* Greenwich, Conn.: Fawcett, 1968.

———. *The Nightmare Years: 1930–1940.* New York: Bantam Books, 1985.

Stern, J.P. *Hitler: The Führer and the People.* Berkeley and Los Angeles: Univ. of California Press, 1975.

Stern, Fritz. *The Politics of Cultural Despair: A Study in the Rise of the Germanic Ideology.* Garden City, N.Y.: Doubleday, 1965.

———. *The Failure of Illiberalism: Essays on the Political Culture of Modern Germany.* Chicago: Univ. of Chicago Press, 1975.

Sternhell, Zeev. *The Birth of Fascist Ideology: From Cultural Rebellion to Political Revolution.* Trans. David Maisel. Princeton: Princeton Univ. Press, 1994.

Stierlin, Helm. *Adolf Hitler: A Family Perspective.* New York: Psychohistory Press, 1976.

Summers, Montague, trans. *The Malleus Maleficarum of Heinrich Kramer and James Sprenger.* New York: Dover, 1971.

Taylor, A.J.P. *The Course of German History: A Survey of the Development of Germany since 1815.* New York: Capricorn Books, 1962.

Taylor, Fred, trans. and ed. *The Goebbels Diaries 1939–1941.* New York: Penguin Books, 1984.

Taylor, Telford. *Hitler's Secret Book.* Trans. Salvator Attanasio. New York: Grove Press, 1983.

Trevor-Roper, H.R., ed. *Hitler's Secret Conversations 1941–1944,* 77, 269, 574. Trans. Norman Cameron and R.H. Stevens. New York: Farrar, Straus & Young, 1953.

Vermeil, Edmond. *Germany in the Twentieth Century: A Political and Cultural History of the Weimar Republic and the Third Reich.* New York: Frederick A. Praeger, 1956.

Viereck, Peter. *Metapolitics: The Roots of the Nazi Mind.* New York: Capricorn Books, 1965.

Volkan, Vamik D. *The Need to Have Enemies and Allies: From Clinical Practice to International Relationships.* Northvale, N.J.: Jason Aronson, 1988.

Waite, Robert G.L. *The Psychopathic God: Adolf Hitler.* New York: Basic Books, 1977.

Weininger, Otto. *Sex and Character.* Authorized trans. from the 6th German ed. London: William Heinemann, 1906.

Weiss, John. *Ideology of Death: Why the Holocaust Happened in Germany.* Chicago: Ivan R. Dee, 1996.

Index